# OLD DEMONS, NEW DEBATES

Anti-Semitism in the West

# OLD DEMONS, NEW DEBATES

## Anti-Semitism in the West

Edited by
## David I. Kertzer

*Published in cooperation with the YIVO Institute for Jewish Research*

Holmes & Meier Publishers, Inc.

Published in 2005 by

Holmes & Meier Publishers, Inc.
P.O. B. 943
Teaneck, NJ 07666
www.holmesandmeier.com

Library of Congress Cataloging-in-Publication Data

Old demons, new debates : anti-semitism in the West /
edited by David I. Kertzer.
p. cm.
Proceedings of a conference sponsored by Yivo Institute for Jewish
Research, May 11-14, 2003, plus an essay by Omer Bartov.
Includes bibliographical references and index.
ISBN 0-8419-1439-7 paperback
ISBN 0-8419-1443-5 hardcover
1. Antisemitism—Congresses. I. Kertzer, David I.
II. Yivo Institute for Jewish Research.
DS145.O37    305.892'4'009051—dc22    2005009947

Cover design by Lisa Barfield

The paper in this book meets the guidelines for permanence and durability
of the Committee on Production Guidelines for Book Longevity
of the Council of Library Resources.

PRINTED IN THE UNITED STATES OF AMERICA

# Contents

# Preface

Until recently, many Jews—and not only Jews—were confident that following the mass murder of European Jewry in the mid-twentieth century, the Western world had become inoculated against the toxin of anti-Semitism. Surely, they thought, anti-Semitism—now so closely identified with the ravings of Hitler and the slaughter that was the Shoah—could not easily rise again, at least as other than a crackpot movement identified with the mentally unstable. And if there was a time in the not too distant past when all too many Europeans seemed fixated on the Jews as the occult source of their problems, surely, most of us thought, such dismal days were behind us for good.

And yet, in many parts of Europe today, Jews feel newly vulnerable. Not only have we been receiving a disturbing series of reports of fire-bombings of synagogues, desecrations of Jewish cemeteries, and verbal and physical assaults on Jews because they are Jews, but the blaming of Jews for the world's problems has again begun to gain currency. And all this comes in a setting where the memory of the Shoah remains very much alive, etched in the very buildings that people walk by every day.

Of course, this new feeling of vulnerability comes in the context of the continuing Israeli-Palestinian conflict. But while events in the Middle East certainly help explain this vulnerability, they have also introduced an element that has made the Jews feel even more isolated. The vilification of the Jews now has political cover, at least on the left, that it did not have before. Crowds of French or Italian or British demonstrations for this or that cause are now commonly dotted with placards equating the Israelis with the Nazis.

Let me offer what I find a particularly chilling, although in its way absolutely typical, example: In 2002, the scholar Ruggero Taradel was asked to speak at one of Rome's most prestigious public high schools, known for training the Italian elite. The occasion was Holocaust Remembrance Day. He brought with him a local survivor, and after Professor Taradel had given a historical overview of what had happened to Italy's Jews during the war, the survivor spoke about her own experiences. Hundreds of students and their teachers were packed into the auditorium. When the time came for questions, a hand shot up from among the students. "I don't see why we should be spending our time here talking about the Holocaust when the Jews are doing to the Palestinians the same things that the Nazis did to them." The assembled students greeted the remark with enthusiastic, prolonged applause, joined by their teachers. Professor Taradel and the Holocaust survivor began to try to respond in as reasonable a way as they could, but they were interrupted by angry shouts, and so the teacher in charge had to get up precipitously, thank them for coming, and call the assembly to a close. The two were rushed out of the hall to avoid further unpleasantness and were ushered into the principal's office. Making no mention of the scene that had just transpired, much less offering any apologies, the principal instead presented them with a volume recounting the school's history. Thereafter, the school abandoned the idea of marking Holocaust Remembrance Day.

In order to take stock of this situation and to try to trace its contours and measure its magnitude and path, the YIVO Institute for Jewish Research sponsored an international conference in May 2003. The ambitious event took place over four days, the hundreds of people coming to hear each session spilling out into an adjacent hall for remote viewing. They were not disappointed, as the thirty-five speakers included leading intellectuals from both Europe and the United States, and their talks—grim as their subject matter was—sparkled with new insight.

It was the strong feeling of those who attended the conference that the subject's timeliness and the importance of what was said there made it desirable to prepare a book that could make these insights available to a much wider audience. I approached those among the thirty-five speakers whose remarks I thought most lent themselves to a publication of this sort and asked if they would be willing to transform what were in some cases intended only as relatively brief oral remarks into a fuller form. I also asked that the developments in the year following the conference be taken into account in the chapters they prepared for this book.

The result is what you have in your hands. Of these fifteen chapters, fourteen grew out of the presentations given at the YIVO conference. In February 2004, an essay on anti-Semitism by noted historian Omer Bartov appeared in the *New Republic*. It raised excellent and stimulating points not otherwise fully covered in our chapters; I was very pleased that Professor Bartov agreed to prepare a revised version of this piece for this volume. Bartov is thus the only author in this book who was not a speaker at the 2003 conference.

Some of these chapters take a broad view, focusing on such subjects as the ambiguous role of European intellectuals in the rise of anti-Semitism, the role of Israel and anti-Zionism in fueling anti-Semitism, and the thorny problem of distinguishing between legitimate criticism of Israeli government policy and the use of widespread European antipathy toward Israeli settlement policy as a cover for the spread of anti-Semitism. Some of our authors remain quite optimistic—most notably Nathan Glazer in his essay on why he believes U.S. "exceptionalism" extends to the inhospitality of U.S. soil to the growth of anti-Semitism, but also Konstanty Gebert, who argues that the Poles have not been given sufficient credit for the strides they have made in overcoming a history of anti-Semitism. Others, many others, strike a more pessimistic note. The book opens with Leon Wieseltier's lament that anti-Semitism should still be with us after all these years. Omer Bartov expresses his distress at the failure of intellectuals to take anti-Semites at their word and at the reluctance of European and American journalists to call attention to anti-Semitic motivations behind various violent acts, especially when these come from Muslims, a point also made by Robert S. Wistrich and others. Mark Lilla sees the Jews as caught in a no-win situation: Previously they were mocked, he tells us, for being a people who lacked their own nation-state; now they are mocked for having one and wanting to hold on to it. Fiamma Nirenstein, whose anger at the wave of anti-Semitism seeps clearly through her chapter, argues that "Europe has always been ready to be anti-Semitic and anti-American but not to admit it." Pierre Birnbaum's account of Jewish anguish in France today is chilling, telling us that French Jews feel they have recently embarked on an unwanted journey into a "fearful heart of darkness." Indeed, increasing numbers of French Jews believe that France is no longer a comfortable place for Jews to live. Konstanty Gebert begins his chapter by telling of his own experience wearing a Jewish skullcap in Paris, where onlookers stood by while he was attacked for the "crime" of being a Jew. Nor does his experience appear to be unusual: France's chief rabbi recently recommended that men avoid wearing their skullcaps in public, replacing them with more anonymous caps. Once again, it is dangerous to be identifiable as a Jew on the streets in parts of Europe.

I will resist the temptation to steal the thunder from the authors of the chapters that follow, for each tells a compelling story. Together, they paint an unsettling picture. For an understanding of the nature of anti-Semitism in Europe today and of just how serious it is, I don't think the reader can do better than to read them.

David I. Kertzer

March 2005

# Old Demons, New Debates

*Leon Wieseltier*

It is outrageous that we are still discussing the foul subject of anti-Semitism, that it has not yet passed into oblivion in the way of many illusions and lunacies, that the historical consequences of the superstitions about the Jews have not sufficed to retire it forever—all this is outrageous, but it is not surprising. Jews, and students of Jewish history, long ago developed what Rebecca West once called "an unsurprisable mind." I do not believe that Jewish experience leaves one only with grounds for dourness and despair, but it certainly does not make one think well of the world or of the prospects for strangers within it. In recent years, it has become increasingly acceptable, in our politics and in our philosophy, to proclaim the end of the Enlightenment, or to dream of it. The spectacle of contemporary anti-Semitism, the extraordinary durability of the antipathy toward the Jews, should embarrass this idea, even if the Enlightenment was itself shot through with the intolerance that it brilliantly denounced. If there is still any question that the human world, including the Western parts of it, does not yet suffer from a surfeit of reason and decency, the re-symbolization of the Jew in our time should answer it. "Very few phenomena of human history have a history of approximately two thousand years," Victor Tcherikover once remarked. "Anti-Semitism is one of them."

And so we now have a whole array of Judeophobias to consider. The taxonomy of present-day anti-Semitism is ominously large. There are religious varieties and secular varieties; theological varieties and ideological varieties; political varieties and cultural varieties; old varieties and new varieties. There is the anti-Semitism of Christians, which comes in many forms, and the anti-Semitism of Muslims, which comes in many forms. There is the anti-Semitism of the Right, in Europe and in the United States, still stubbornly blaming the Jews for modernity (I must say that I have always found that particular allegation to be rather a compliment); and there is the anti-Semitism of the Left, most recently seeking shelter (and finding it) in the antiglobalization movement, which has presided over a revival of the New Left's dogmas about capitalism and liberalism and Americanism. And there is the anti-Semitism that manifests itself as anti-Zionism. This is, I think, the most dangerous anti-Semitism of them all. It is not the case, of course, that every criticism of the Jewish state is an instance of anti-Semitism, but it is certainly the case that every instance of anti-Semitism is a criticism of the Jewish state, a fundamental criticism, since it denies the legitimacy of the ideal of a normal life for Jews, who are consigned by anti-Semites of one kind or another to an endless abnormality of one kind or another. If Israel cannot be above criticism, neither can Israel's critics be above criticism, and the anxiety that many critics of Israeli policy are at bottom critics of Israeli reality, that the opposition to Israeli actions in Jenin or Gaza is sometimes motivated by a prior historical or religious dogma, is not an outlandish anxiety. A prejudice is not a criticism. Those of us who are not reluctant to criticize Israeli policies must be particularly careful not to be fooled.

When I say that it is outrageous that we are still discussing this subject, I mean also that this is not actually *our* subject—that is, it is not a Jewish subject. It is, strictly speaking—and who would not wish to speak with strictness here?—a non-Jewish subject. Anti-Semitism should be the occasion for an international conference at a center for *non*-Jewish history. Let me explain. The hatred of the Jews is a matter of urgent concern to Jews because of the injury they may suffer as a result of it. The Jewish investigation of anti-Semitism is plainly a requirement of self-interest, and it is also a requirement of dignity, because defending oneself against one's enemy is an ethical duty of the most elementary sort. The search for security has a foundation in morality. Still, the solution to the problem of anti-Semitism is not to be sought in the Jewish struggle against it. It is indecent to ask the victims to make themselves responsible for an end to their victimization. After all, they are not doing this to themselves. This is being done to them. If anti-Semitism ever vanishes from the earth, it will be the consequence of a transformation not in the mentality of Jews but in the mentality of non-Jews.

In this sense, anti-Semitism is not a Jewish problem at all. More concretely, I have two reasons for insisting upon such a paradoxical formulation. The first has to do with the nature of prejudice. The second has to do with the course of modern Jewish history.

Perhaps the most significant fact for the proper comprehension of prejudice is that its object is not its cause. If you wish to understand racism, study whites, not blacks. If you wish to understand misogyny, study men, not women. If you wish to understand anti-Semitism, study non-Jews, not Jews. Indeed, the view that the explanation of prejudice is to be sought in its object is itself an expression of prejudice. It justifies prejudice, insofar as it attributes to prejudice a basis in reality. For it is the distinguishing mark of prejudice that it leaves the actual behind, so as to arrive at a generalization about a group, a generalization that cannot be affected by anything that a member of the group might say or do. There is no evidence against such a generalization, because the evidence for it seems to be everywhere, and where evidence is everywhere, evidence is nowhere. Prejudice is not a mistake; it is a fiction. Mistakes can be corrected, but prejudice can only be fought. Anti-Semitic beliefs about the Jews are not merely false; they are also, for those who believe them, unfalsifiable. For the anti-Semite, everything a Jew thinks or does is regarded as a Jewish thought or a Jewish deed. Such a generalization is most accurately described as a fantasy. Anti-Semitism is a tradition of fantasy that non-Jews have of Jews.

A few days ago I came upon a fine example of this abandonment of the empirical in favor of the stereotypical, of this common process of hostile abstraction. It is not at all, by the standards of anti-Semitic literature, an extreme example, but its conventionality makes it all the more interesting:

One wonders how Mrs. Loeb became a rich woman. It seems an accident; she might be behind a counter. They had a great gas fire, burning in a florid drawing room. She is a fat Jewess, aged 56 (she tells her age to ingratiate herself) coarsely skinned, with drooping, and tumbled hair. She fawned upon us, flattered us and wheedled us, in a voice that rubbed away the edges of all her words and had a falling cadence. It seemed as though she wished to ingratiate herself with her guests and expected to be kicked by them. Thus at dinner she pressed everyone to eat, and feared, when she saw an empty plate, that the guest was criticising her. Her food, of course, swam in oil and was nasty.

She adjusted her flattery, to suit me, whom she took to be severe and intellectual, and Miss Timothy whom she thought lively and flirtatious. To me she talked of her joy in the open air (she drives regularly in her own carriage), of the "companionship of books for a lonely woman" (and yet she only dines alone once a week) of her white bedroom, with its bare walls and open windows. She rallied Miss T. (a chocolate box young woman, a business woman, used to protecting herself) upon the attentions of the hundred men of the orchestra; upon her fat arms; upon the attentions of Syd, her son. What was the truth of the matter, I wonder? I imagine her to be a shrewd woman of business, in the daytime, moving in a circle of city people; "young people" tickle her coarse palate; she wishes to be popular, and is, perhaps, kind, in her vulgar way, ostentatiously kind to poor relations. The one end she aims at for them, is the society of men and marriage. It seemed very elementary, very little disguised, and very unpleasant.[1]

This text was written on November 3, 1909, in a notebook that unexpectedly came to light recently and was published for the first time in 2003. Its author was Virginia Woolf. What is so striking, and so ugly, about this entry in this diary is the title, the single word, that Woolf wrote at the top of the page. She called her little portrait "Jews." Not "Mrs. Loeb", or "An Unpleasant Woman", but "Jews". When Woolf gave her disagreeable sketch that title, she raised it—or rather, she lowered it—from observation into hallucination, from a hateful picture of a person into a hateful picture of a people.

The view that prejudice is a fiction is not as obvious as it might seem. For it seems just as obvious that there would have been no anti-Semitism if there had been no Jews. Never mind that in many places and in many times the presence of Jews has not been required for the presence of anti-Semitism. (Japanese anti-Semitism is an almost comic illustration of this point.) In the books about anti-Semitism, one reads again and again that anti-Semitism is "as old as Judaism" or "as old as the Jews." We must be careful with such language. When it is not a historical banality, it is an essentialist error. So it is important that we understand correctly the proposition that the hatred of the Jews has no basis in the reality of the Jews. For there was something about the Jews that made the hatred of them plausible and popular, particularly in Europe.

I refer, of course, to their apartness. The classical anti-Semitic allegation against the Jews was lucidly stated by Haman in his cunning speech to the weak-minded king of Persia: "There is a certain people that is scattered abroad and dispersed among the people in all the provinces of thy kingdom; and their laws are diverse from all peoples; neither keep they the king's laws; therefore it is not for the king's profit to suffer them." [Esther 3: 8] The otherness of the Jews was their offense. They would not mix, they would not dissolve, and they would not vanish. They did not attack, but they did not surrender. This view of the Jews as fundamentally unassimilable is common to Jew-hatreds that share almost no other characteristics. The *amixia* and *misanthropia* and *diversitate* for which Jews were vilified by Greek and Roman writers, the spiritual incorrigibility for which they were impugned and oppressed in the supersessionist theology of the medieval Church, the corporatism for which Jewish communities were resented in the modern period, when Jews were attacked as a "state within a state" (an innuendo that was invented by an obscure German writer in the 1780s and introduced into the political culture of modern Europe by Fichte—these were all condemnations of difference. "They have separated themselves from other nations to such a degree as to incur the hatred of all," Baruch Spinoza wrote vituperatively, drawing directly upon Tacitus. And even when Jews did assimilate to a significant degree—unwillingly, in the coerced conversions in the Iberian peninsula in the fifteenth century, or willingly, in the uncoerced conversions in Western Europe and elsewhere in the nineteenth and twentieth centuries—new definitions of otherness were devised, racial and biological ones, so that the phobic mythologization of Jewishness, the terrifying rumor of Jewish nonconformity, might live.

Jewish difference certainly was real. The anti-Semites who dwelled upon the alterity of the Jews were not imagining it. The institution of the ghetto did not begin its infamous career as an instrument of anti-Jewish persecution; it was an arrangement that was welcomed and even demanded by certain medieval Jewish communities for the security and insularity that it would provide. And yet all this does not imply that the object of this prejudice was its cause. The intolerance of the majority must not be confused with or excused by the exclusiveness of the minority. And what was sinister, or conspiratorial, about the exclusiveness of the minority? The Jews conspired at nothing except their own continuance, their perseverance as themselves. The minority impertinently declared to the majority: I am not the other, I am merely myself. I am not outside your form of life, I am inside my form of life. For you, of course, I am outside, I am the other; but I do not live first and foremost in relation to you. I have a universe of my own to cultivate. And from this point of regard, I am the center, and you are the periphery. I am powerless, but I am autonomous.

Perhaps that was the Jewish insult: the essential indifference that is the mark of genuine difference; the natural independence of an authentic identity. There are many explanations of Jewish apartness—religious, philosophical, cultural, sociological—but finally it comes down to a sensation of honor so deep and so magnificent that it was immune to the influence of kings and popes and armies and mobs. Writing in 1880 in praise of the Jews, Friedrich Nietzsche remarked upon their "heroism *spernere se sperni*": They despise that they are despised. So it may indeed be said, then, that anti-Semitism has a historical basis in the otherness of the Jews, but it is more precise to say that it has a historical basis in the spectacular failure of the non-Jews to accept that otherness, to experience it as anything but a provocation, an impediment to their pretensions to universality. *This* was the cause of which the Jews became the object. There was nothing the Jews could do to mitigate or to eliminate this cause except to disappear. And so it came to pass that the refusal to disappear was maliciously interpreted as an attitude of defiance.

For this reason, then, I am suggesting that anti-Semitism is not a Jewish problem. The Jews can do nothing about the hatred of the Jews except defend themselves against it. But I have another reason for making this suggestion, which I am quite confident will be misunderstood as an argument for Jewish complacence in the matter of anti-Semitism. The other reason is this: The conditions for a successful Jewish defense against the hatred of the Jews have never been better. A brief look at the course of modern Jewish history shows why.

It is obscene to talk of a positive consequence for the Jews of World War II, and yet it is important to observe, with some satisfaction, that the conclusion of that war also marked the conclusion of the European age in Jewish history. There are still Jews in the European countries, of course; but the destiny of the Jewish people has at last left Europe. It has escaped the savage Continental (and somewhat less savage English) incompetence about inclusion. The fate of the Jews (and the fate of Judaism) will be determined elsewhere, in Israel and in the United States. This period in our history is characterized by a friendly competition for the Jewish future between the Israeli dispensation, under which the Jews enjoy the protections and the privileges of sovereignty, and the American dispensation, under which the Jews enjoy the protections and the privileges of pluralist democracy. Both of these dispensations regard the old European melodrama about rights—which, since they are given, may be taken away—as inadequate and obsolete. In Israel and in the United States, the rights of the Jews are axiomatic. No erasure is required for their purchase. By the standards of Jewish history, this contest between the Jewish attainment in Israel and the Jewish attainment in the United States is truly an embarrassment of riches. We must not permit the collective memory of our people to inhibit us from the imagination of happiness. We—I refer to most of world Jewry—may finally be living in the sun.

It will be clear that I do not hold a Zionist analysis of American Jewish circumstances. I do not believe that the United States is just another address for Jews on the run, just a safer haven. I believe, rather, that the United States represents a revolution in Jewish history, a country that is—in its philosophical foundations and in its political practices—structurally hospitable to us. We cannot be pilloried as a state within a state in a state that is made up of states within a state. We cannot be excoriated for difference in a society in which difference is the substance of sameness. To use the Zionist terms, I would define the American innovation in Jewish history as the establishment of a diaspora that is not an exile, a *t'futzah* that is not a *golah*. I do not mean to contend that there is no anti-Semitism in the United States. Not at all. But the story of Jew-hatred in the United States differs profoundly from the story of Jew-hatred in Europe. It is a scandal to be refused admission to a school or a hotel or a club; but it is not an expulsion or a pogrom. And it is not only the virulence of anti-Semitism that has been diminished in the United States. Its legitimacy, too, has been diminished. In fact, its legitimacy has been altogether repudiated. The remarkable fact about the Jewish campaign against anti-Semitism in the United States is that, like the African American campaign there against racism, it is made in the name of American principles. It is the bigotry against the Jews that is the anomaly here, not the Jews.

A scholar of anti-Semitism recently observed about the Jewish situation in the United States that "ultimately the important issue is not anti-Semitism; it is Jewish security." Surely this is the first era in Jewish history when the discussion of anti-Semitism and the discussion of Jewish security is not always the same discussion. Something really has changed. We must bless the discontinuity. The change is not entirely an affair of luck: Jews brought about this alteration in their fortunes, in Israel and in the United States, by kindling to the prospect of their own historical agency and by seizing upon the opportunities for self-reliance and self-realization that were presented by the advent of liberal nationalism and pluralist democracy. Furthermore, the change is not perfect: Many of our brothers and our sisters are still trapped in the old terms—in Argentina, perhaps also in Russia, and in certain precincts of Europe. (Though we must immediately remind ourselves that no anti-Semitic atrocity that was committed in Europe in recent years can responsibly be compared to the murder of a quarter of a million Muslims in the Balkans a decade ago: Europe has moved on to another other.) So the need for Jewish vigilance is by no means gone. Our solidarity will still be tested. And yet we have earned the pleasure of pronouncing, vigilantly, vigilantly, a *she'hekheyanu*.

It is not enough to acknowledge the existence of a threat. One must also take its measure. Every danger is not equally dire. Every foe is not equally strong. We must think empirically about the nonempirical thinking of our anti-Semitic enemies. There will be various assessments of the vulnerability of various Jewries. The authors gathered here in this book allow all these assessments to collide. My own view, obviously, is that the village is not burning. I am regularly frightened by the indefatigable attempts of jihadist, Jew-hating maniacs to acquire weapons of mass destruction, but I am also regularly struck by the really awesome magnitude of Israeli power, and one already hears about the possibility of an Israeli strike against the nuclear installations of Iran. *Haba le'horgekha hashkem l'horgo*: If somebody is coming to kill you, be early to kill him. That is the ancient rabbinic doctrine of strategic preemption, and Israel possesses the means both to be early and to make the kill. But as I say, we are not all alike in our fears.

The analysis of anti-Semitism must take place somewhere between indifference and hysteria. The most loyal Jew is not the most hysterical Jew. Love sometimes speaks calmly. The cult of victimization is no more attractive and no less coarsening when it is the cult of *our* victimization. It was never true that adversity was what held the Jews together, that anti-Semitism was what kept the Jews Jewish, though this fallacy has a long and distinguished provenance. In all their tormented history, the Jews did not install their torments at the heart of their identity. They suffered, but they would not be reduced to their suffering. They never seized upon their ill-treatment as an alibi for a relaxation of their principles. They never succumbed to anger, which is strikingly rare in Jewish literature. They never conceived of life as an eternal war. The morbidity of the Jews always met its match in the vitality of the Jews. Even in the midst of a resurgence of anti-Semitism, it is worth remembering that anti-anti-Semitism is not all, or even most, of what is asked of us.

# 2

# The New Anti-Semitism

## Genealogy and Implications

*Omer Bartov*

### I

If we wish to gain insight into contemporary anti-Semitism and to contemplate its future potential, we must look at its past and consider its pedigree. Chronic diseases like anti-Semitism cannot be understood by a spot check at a given moment in time. They linger, become endemic, and occasionally, when circumstances allow, blossom into a full-blown illness. The illness contains within itself its own history. And this history is a warning that we would be well advised to heed. Such chronic diseases cannot be cured. But if the symptoms are not treated as soon as they appear, they will rapidly transform themselves from an indication of abnormality to a normal, all-pervasive condition.

It is worth reflecting in this context on Adolf Hitler's so-called second book, the most sustained policy statement written by a man who carried the ideology of anti-Semitism to its logical conclusion of outright genocide. The book was written hastily in late June and early July 1928. It was not published in the author's lifetime, initially because it would have competed with *Mein Kampf*, which was selling very badly, and after Hitler's appointment as chancellor because it disclosed his foreign policy plans too explicitly. The second book was locked away and remained virtually unknown until Gerhard Weinberg discovered it in 1958.[1]

But this book should have been read in its time, and it should be read now. It was an unequivocal warning to the world of what could be expected from

This is a revised version of "He Meant What He Said: Did Hitlerism Die with Hitler?" *New Republic,* February 2, 2004, 25–33.

the future Führer of the Third Reich. When Hitler wrote it, no one could tell whether his plans and fantasies, also expressed in numerous other publications and speeches, would ever be transformed into policy. It was generally thought that once in power, Hitler would be constrained by the realities of diplomacy, the limits of Germany's power, the national interests of the Reich, and the military, economic, and political partners with whom he had to cooperate.

Today we know that this was a fatal misunderstanding, rooted more in wishful thinking than in the kind of realism on which contemporary observers prided themselves and which they expected would eventually keep Hitler, too, in his place. Today we know that Hitler said precisely what he meant to say. We can also note, with the benefit of hindsight, that Hitler was neither insane nor irrational nor a fool. In the second book, Hitler discusses with disarming frankness both his future policy and its underlying motivations. His rhetoric here is no more empty-headed than that of many of his contemporaries; his use of clichés hardly exceeds what one encountered in the newspapers; his knowledge of history, his psychological insights, and his criticism of political rivals are in many respects typical of his place and time.

But of course Hitler was also a pathological mass murderer who caused the death of millions and the destruction of Europe. Because of this, it is important to know that he did precisely what he had promised to do. For we still do not seem to have learned the simple crucial lesson that Hitler taught us more definitively than anyone else in history: some people, some regimes, some ideologies, some political programs, and yes, some religious groups must be taken at their word. Some people mean what they say, and say what they will do, and do what they say they will.

Most liberal-minded, optimistic, well-meaning people are loath to believe this. They would rather think that fanaticism is merely an "epiphenomenal" façade for politics, that opinions can be changed, that everyone can be corrected and improved. In many cases, this is true—but not in all cases, and not in the most dangerous ones. There are those who practice what they preach and are proud of it. They view those who act otherwise, who compromise and pull back from ultimate conclusions, as opportunists, as weaklings, or as targets to be easily conquered and subdued by their own greater determination, hardness, and ruthlessness. When they say they will kill you, they will kill you—if you do not kill them first.

In today's violent reality, Hitler's second book should serve as an instructive introduction to journalists, political observers, and all concerned people who have the stomach to recognize evil when they confront it. For one of the most frightening aspects of Hitler's book is not that he said what he said at the time but that much of what he said can be found today in innumerable places: Internet sites, propaganda brochures, political speeches, protest placards, academic publications, religious sermons, you name it. As long as it does not have Hitler's name attached to it, this deranged discourse is ignored or allowed to pass. The voices that express these opinions do not belong to a single political or ideological current, and they are much harder to distinguish than they were in the 1930s. They belong to the Right and the Left, to the religious and the secular, to the West and the East, to the rabble and the leaders, to terrorists and intellectuals, students and peasants, pacifists and militants, expansionists and antiglobalization activists. The diplomacy advocated by Hitler is no longer relevant, but his reason for it, his legitimization of his worldview, is alive and kicking, and it may still kick us.

## II

Hitler never had a particularly complicated ideology, and in the present context I will merely highlight those aspects of it that remain relevant today. Hitler painted a clear picture of the world, distinguishing between the bad and the good, the sinful and the righteous, the guilty and the innocent, the dirty and the clean, the inferior and the superior. Significantly, Hitler did not recognize any distinction between his "analysis" of world history and his plans for Germany's future. "Politics," he wrote, "is not just the struggle of a people for its survival as such; rather . . . it is the art of the implementation of this struggle." Indeed, "the two concepts of a peace policy or a war policy thus immediately become meaningless. Because the stake that is struggled for through politics is always life."[2]

Hitler's main policy goals were to establish domestic racial unity and freedom from polluting elements and to conquer a vast and undefined "living space" in the east. Germany's main foreign enemies were France, which had become "negroized," and the United States, whose healthy Aryan stock had turned its back on the Fatherland. The Slavs, and especially the Poles and Russians, were to be taken over because they were incapable of ruling themselves and because they owed anything of value in their lands to German colonizers and rulers.

Hitler saw no limits to the Reich's expansion. As he noted, "Wherever our success ends, that will always be the starting point of a new battle."[3] Strenuously opposed to a mere revision of the Versailles Treaty, Hitler stressed that "the national conception will . . . be determined . . . by ethnic and racial conceptions" whereas the "German borders of 1914 . . . represented something just as unfinished as peoples' borders always are." Indeed, he believed that the "division of territory on the earth is always the momentary result of a struggle and an evolution that is in no way finished."[4]

Consequently, appeasement had no room in Hitler's mind. As early as 1928, he had advocated the ethnic cleansing and colonization of Poland with which he charged Heinrich Himmler eleven years later.[5] But this was hardly enough, for the "only area in Europe that could be considered" as Germany's future "living space" was Russia.[6] The instrument of conquest would be a vast new and modern military machine. By 1935, Hitler was well on his way to creating the Wehrmacht. Having ruthlessly purged his own Sturm Abteilung (SA), which threatened to become an alternative revolutionary army, Hitler declared universal conscription in complete defiance of the Versailles Treaty.[7] But even this was not enough. For once Europe was in German hands, the Reich—being "the only state . . . that has understood how . . . to raise the racial value of its people"— would have "to stand up to North America" as well.[8] Consequently, plans were made for the production of aircraft and ships that would facilitate effective military action against the United States.[9]

Even as he planned the establishment of a Nazi-ruled world empire, however, Hitler denounced "internationalism" as a Jewish conspiracy to take over the world. In fact, Germany's most mortal enemies were not foreign countries and armies but the Jews, who, he held, ruled the Soviet Union and were behind all the Marxist parties in Europe and at the same time were also the bosses and the manipulators of international capitalism. The Jews ruled the world through a global conspiracy, and it was Germany's duty to destroy them before they subjugated humanity forever. These agents of globalization, he charged, sought to "kill the others through peaceful industry," depriving the Germans of the *Lebensraum* they need for healthy development and condemning them to urban centers that are "hotbeds of blood-mixing and bastardization . . . ensuring the degeneration of the race and resulting in that purulent herd in which the maggots of the international Jewish community flourish and cause the ultimate decay of the people." As the infected people lose their soul, they "descend into the confusion of international perceptions and the cultural chaos that springs from them. Then the Jew can move in, and not rest until he has completely uprooted and thereby corrupted such a people."[10]

Hitler clearly associated the emergence of a "global economy" and a pan-European movement with the "Jewish instigated systematic . . . bastardization and niggerization of civilized humanity" that enabled the Jews to become "masters of the world."[11] The Jews were behind every tragedy that befell the Germans. It was they and their Marxist allies who had stabbed Germany in the back in 1918. Unlike Germany's foreign enemies, the Jews deserved no mercy. Hitler declared "the most relentless fight against the intolerable defilers of German honor. . . . I could reconcile myself with every one of those old [foreign] enemies, but," Hitler admitted frankly, "my hate for the traitors in our own ranks is unforgiving and will remain."[12]

Hitler's entire political career was guided by his obsession with "the Jew." The concluding comments to the second book—his policy agenda—are remarkably similar to the closing pronouncements of his political testament, dictated briefly before his suicide in 1945 sealed his career.[13] For Hitler, there was no doubt what had always been at the root of all evil and misfortune in the world. To be sure, much of what he said merely repeated the anti-Semitic verbiage of the previous decades. But his position gave his words an entirely different weight and meaning. The Jews, according to Hitler, were "a people with certain essential particularities that distinguish it from all other peoples living on earth." The most important "essence of the Jewish people" is that they lack "the productive forces to build and sustain a territorial state." Therefore, the Jews must lead "a parasitic existence within the life of other peoples," and their "ultimate goal" was "the enslavement of productively active peoples."[14]

This goal is sought by fighting "for equality and then for superiority" in domestic policies, whereas in foreign policy the Jews "hurl [other peoples] into wars with one another, and thus gradually—with the help of the power of money and propaganda—become their masters." The Jews sought "the denationalization and chaotic bastardization of the other peoples . . . and domination over this racial mush through the eradication of these peoples' intelligentsias and their replacement with the members of [their] own race." Having accomplished the "economic conquest of Europe," the Jews began "with securing it politically . . . in the form of revolutions" and by "systematically agitating for world war." The victims of Jewish "inhuman torture and barbarity" in Russia "totaled twenty-eight million dead," even as the Jews "tore away all the ties of orderliness, morality, custom . . . and proclaimed . . . universal licentiousness" with the assistance of such pernicious allies as "Freemasonry . . . the press . . . [and] Marxism." And yet "Jewish domination always ends with the decline of all culture and ultimately the insanity of the Jew himself. Because he is a parasite on the peoples, and his victory means his own end just as much as the death of his victim." But finally, declares Hitler, an end will be put to all this, for "the National Socialist movement . . . has taken up the fight against this execrable crime against humanity."[15]

It is truly astonishing to see how every sin that Hitler ascribed to "the Jew" became part of his own policies as he himself outlined them in his second book and later implemented them: the destruction of entire nations by elimination of their elites, mass deportation of the population, and in the case of the Jews, their outright genocide. And it is just as mind-boggling to note that the endless depravity attributed by Hitler to the Jews became the reality of German conduct under his rule, which deprived the Reich of every remnant of moral restraint and finally drove it into an insane storm of self-destruction. What Hitler said would be done to Germany, he did unto others, and he and his people became victims of the nemesis that he prophesied for his enemies. When Hitler wrote his second book, he was staring into a mirror.

# III

But those who have followed the current wave of anti-Semitism emanating from the most disparate sources in the last few years may sense that they, too, are staring into a mirror, a distorted mirror of a resurrected past, a mutilated, transplanted, transformed, contorted, monstrous specter whose allegedly exhausted powers seem to be increasing day by day.

Hitler is dead, as Leon Wieseltier rightly proclaimed a couple of years ago on the pages of the *New Republic*.[16] What alarmed Wieseltier was the common predilection to view every threat as the ultimate threat, every anti-Semitic harangue as the gateway to another Final Solution. Clearly we are not facing the danger of a second Auschwitz. The hysterics need to remember that Hitler and the Third Reich are history. Germany apologized and paid generous restitution. The Nazis were tried or they hid or they metamorphosed into good democrats. The State of Israel was established. The Jews have never been more prosperous and more successful and more safe than they are in the United States. (The same could even be said about the nervous Jews of Western Europe.) The last remnants of Communist anti-Semitism vanished with the fall of that "evil empire." Jews in our day have reason to feel much more secure than their ancestors.

But all is not well, not by a long shot. Criticism of Israeli policies against the Palestinians has long been attached to anti-Americanism, and in World War II, the Nazis were already saying that the United States was dominated by the Jews. Criticism of U.S. imperialism is often associated with its support for

Israel, allegedly a colonial outpost populated by Jews in the heart of Arab and Islamic civilization. Of course, one should never confuse the legitimate criticism of Israeli policies with what all reasonable people agree is the despicable ideology of anti-Semitism. The policies of the current Israeli government in the territories are indeed contrary to the strategic and moral interests of the Jewish state. So there is every reason in the world to reject attempts to justify objectionable Israeli policies by reference to the Holocaust.

But this does not mean that we should refuse to see the writing on the wall when anti-Israeli sentiments are transformed into blatant and virulent anti-Semitism. This was precisely the argument made in the report on anti-Semitism in the European Union submitted by the Center for Research on Anti-Semitism in Berlin to the European Monitoring Centre on Racism and Xenophobia, which had originally commissioned it.[17] The Monitoring Centre tried to suppress its own report because it examined anti-Semitic violence by Muslims in Europe and because its definition of anti-Semitism included the activities of those who call for the destruction of Israel. And these grim truths were politically incorrect. The Israeli occupation of the West Bank and the Gaza Strip is stupid and destructive, and it should be ended through the creation of a Palestinian state, but those who preach the destruction of the Jewish state should not be allowed to hide behind Ariel Sharon's unfortunate policies. It is one thing to support the cause of Palestinian nationhood, and quite another to deny the Jews the right to live in their own state.

What we are witnessing today is a broad front of opinion of people spanning the entire spectrum of the political and religious scene whose criticism of U.S. and Israeli policies and whose fears and phobias about present conditions, utopian dreams of a better future, and nostalgic fantasies of a mythical past all converge in a bizarre and increasingly frightening way on a single figure, a single cause: "the Jew." I have long believed that it is pointless and dishonorable to debate anti-Semites. Such an exchange of "ideas" only confers legitimacy upon them. But there are times when absurdities become political facts and cannot be ignored. Anti-Semites must, instead, be directly challenged—not by explaining away their violent ideas and feelings, but by putting limits to those ideas, feelings, and the actions that result from them, through all available means, political, judicial, and if necessary, by the use of legitimate force. For these are people who mean what they say. If you do not destroy them, they will destroy you. There are precedents for this.

Consider again what Hitler wrote in 1928. Yes, it is insane; but take out the word "race" and replace it, for example, with "Zionism" or "U.S. imperialism" and replace the references to the Soviet Union with references to the United States, and suddenly the discourse is not only crazy but also quite common. The "soft core" of this poisonous rhetoric is to be found among some sectors of European and U.S. intellectuals and academics. It tends to identify Israelis as culprits and Jews as potential Israelis. It is obsessed with the influence of Jews on culture, politics, and economics around the world. The partially successful boycott of Israeli academics in recent years is a case in point, not least because it tends to affect precisely those who number among the most determined and articulate opponents of the current Israeli government's policies. The divestment campaign, calling on U.S. and European universities to desist from any investments in Israel, is another example; this campaign provides cover, and even immunity, for all the regimes around the world that have never recognized academic freedom. The sympathetic understanding expressed in academic settings and in liberal and left-wing publications for suicide bombers who blow up innocent civilians in Israel creates a climate of tolerance for murder that is cleverly couched in the righteous language of liberation and justice.[18]

Some allegations of an apparent takeover by Jews or by Jewish themes of this or that cultural sphere seem to have nothing to do with Israel. In October 2001, the *Chronicle of Higher Education* published an article by Mark Anderson, a professor of Germanic languages at Columbia University. Anderson expressed fears about "the way in which American scholars have distorted the study of German culture" by reducing "the canon of German literature to a tiny handful of teachable authors who often have a Jewish background." This "excessive focus on German-Jewish authors," he argued, "relied on the subtext of Jewish suffering." This "has undermined intellectual freedom in American universities" and is "testimony to an ongoing intellectual paralysis that could and should be relieved."[19]

It is not clear from Anderson's argument who is to blame, apart from an ill-defined "pressure from American culture to focus on minority issues, as well as our fascination with Hitler and the Holocaust." It is also somewhat ironic that Anderson himself edited a volume on exiles of the Nazi regime in the United States, which testifies to his own fascination with this topic, if not to his recognition of its importance.[20] Still, one cannot help but detect here a clear connection between the alleged overemphasis on Jewish authors and Jewish themes "identified" by Anderson and its distorting effects both on the study of German literature and on U.S. intellectual freedom. Somehow the focus on Jewish victims seems to have that effect.

Sometimes this sort of intellectual-academic-journalistic obsession with Jews becomes intimately linked with anti-Americanism. Several best-selling books published in France and Germany by academics, politicians, and journalists have "confirmed" the already widespread belief (held by 19 percent of the German population according to a recent poll, and apparently by a majority in many Arab and Islamic countries) that the September 11, 2001, attacks on the United States were orchestrated by the CIA and the Mossad and that the latter warned Jews working in the World Trade Center not to come to work that day.[21] Indeed, the United States, attacked by Europeans for its support of Israel, has been repeatedly depicted as controlled by the Jews, whose lobbies, financial and electoral levers of power, and key figures in the White House and Pentagon are said to be manipulating both the U.S. public and world politics.[22]

At the same time, Israel has been portrayed as the perpetrator of Nazi-like crimes even as these very portrayals carry echoes of the Nazis' representation of Jews. Thus, the European media, especially its more highbrow representatives, were as keen to portray the Israeli operation in Jenin in the spring of 2002 as a war crime and a massacre as they were reluctant to admit that they had been fooled by Palestinian propaganda and in turn had misinformed their publics about the nature of the operation, greatly inflating the number of Palestinian civilians killed in order to justify its description as a massacre.[23] The Israeli prime minister was depicted in a cartoon published in the *Independent* in London on January 27, 2003, as a bloody ogre devouring Palestinian children, his features eerily reminiscent of those popularized by the Nazi magazine *Der Stürmer*.[24]

Anyone who has access to racist, anti-Semitic, and neo-Nazi publications in the United States and elsewhere (that is, anyone on the Internet) will find almost precisely the same opinions and depictions. These hateful representations are normally not much remarked upon. But there are some important exceptions. Most striking was the speech made by Martin Hohmann, a parliamentary representative of the Christian Democratic Union (CDU) in the German Bundestag, to an audience of 130 people on October 3, 2003. Hohmann argued that one had no right to speak of the Germans as a "people of perpetrators" (*Tätervolk*) because the Jews—presumably those making that argument—were themselves a "people of perpetrators," considering their high representation among the murderous Bolsheviks.[25] This was the first time since the end of Nazism that a member of the Bundestag made an anti-Semitic argument based on the very logic of Hitler's rationalization for war against the

Soviet Union. And an elite Bundeswehr general expressed agreement with Hohmann's speech. Under much public pressure, Hohmann was eventually ejected from the parliamentary representation of the CDU—but 20 percent of his colleagues opposed his removal.[26] And Hohmann knew, as did so many fascists before him, that he had said what many others were thinking. In a poll whose results were issued by the University of Bielefeld on December 11, 2003, it was found that 70 percent of Germans resent being blamed for the Holocaust, and 25 percent believe that the Jews are trying to make political capital out of their own genocide (and another 30 percent say that there is a measure of truth in this assertion), and three-quarters believe that there are too many foreigners in Germany.[27]

Much more publicity has been given to anti-Israel protests on U.S. campuses, and these have demonstrated a troubling trend. A group calling itself New Jersey Solidarity (NJS): Activists for the Liberation of Palestine called for a "Divestment Conference" to be held on the campus of Rutgers University, New Brunswick, in October 2003. The group's Web site declares itself "opposed to the existence of the apartheid colonial settler state of Israel, as it is based on the racist ideology of Zionism and is an expression of colonialism and imperialism."[28] The Rutgers Association for Middle East Justice, a student group closely associated with NJS, displayed a banner at various university student centers with the slogan "From the River to the Sea Palestine Will Be Free."[29]

Richard McCormick, the president of Rutgers University and a former member of its History Department, where I also taught during the 1990s, issued an open letter on the planned meeting. He stated that he found "abhorrent some elements of NJ Solidarity's mission." But he went on to say that "intrinsic to Rutgers' own mission is the free exchange of ideas and discourse on a variety of issues, including those that are controversial. This university must remain a model of debate, dialogue and education. . . . We encourage our students to express their beliefs and analyze the difficult issues of the day."[30] So some may think that destroying Israel is legitimate and some may think otherwise. Some may think that Israel is an apartheid colonial settler state based on a racist ideology, and some may have a different opinion. There are two sides to the question. Through such a "free exchange of ideas" we will all prosper intellectually. This brings to mind Hannah Arendt's observation when she visited Germany in 1950 for the first time since she had fled the Nazis, that the Germans viewed the extermination of the Jews as a matter of opinion: Some said it happened, some said it had not happened. Who could tell? The "average German," she wrote, "honestly believes this free-for-all, this nihilistic relativity about facts, to be the essence of democracy."[31]

On campuses throughout the United States, students associated with Arab and Islamic organizations, Christian groups, and the Left carried flags, banners, and posters that were mostly focused on one theme: the equation of Zionism, or Israel, with Nazism. Banners portrayed a swastika joined by an equal sign to a Star of David and an Israeli flag featuring a swastika instead of a Star of David. Placards issued the call to "End the Holocaust" and proclaimed that "Zionism = racism = ethnic cleansing," that "Zionism Is Ethnic Cleansing," and that "Sharon = Hitler." A particularly ingenious sign asserted: "1943: Warsaw" followed by "2002: Jenin." While some summarized their views with the slogan "Zionazis," others warned, "First Jesus Now Arafat."[32]

What makes this virulent anti-Semitism respectable is that it presents itself as anti-Nazism. To accomplish this sinister exculpatory purpose, it needs only to declare that Zionism equals Nazism, just as the old canard of a Jewish conspiracy to take over the world is legitimized by its association with U.S. imperialism, capitalism, and globalization. That the vocabulary of this rhetoric is taken directly (whether consciously or not) from Nazi texts is so clear that one wonders why there is such a reluctance to recognize it. In part, this is attributable to ignorance, which is as rampant today in journalism and political commentary as it always has been. In part, it is attributable to the fact that those who would most readily identify the provenance of these words and ideas are largely liberals, some of whom also happen to be Jewish, and thus are likely to be most harmed, both personally and ideologically, by making this identification. By exposing the anti-Semitic underbelly of this phenomenon, they would expose themselves as Jews and friends of Jews and would open themselves to the argument that their opposition to this phenomenon is precisely the best proof of Jewish domination in the world.

# IV

That, incidentally, is precisely the claim Prime Minister Mahathir Mohamad of Malaysia made following Western protests against his warmly received pronouncement to the Organization of the Islamic Conference that the Jews control the world: "The reaction of the world shows that they [the Jews] control the world."[33] Mahathir's speech, delivered on October 16, 2003, at the opening of the tenth session of the Islamic summit conference in Malaysia, was genuinely astonishing. For the first time since World War II, a major head of state made a speech—to no fewer than fifty-seven other heads of state and well over two thousand journalists—whose fundamental argument was that the Jews are to blame for all the ills that have beset Islamic civilization. And not a single person left the room in protest.[34]

For Paul Krugman, writing in the *New York Times*, Mahathir's anti-Semitic remarks were both "inexcusable" and "calculated," made by a "cagey politician, who is neither ignorant nor foolish." Krugman did not elaborate on why such remarks are "inexcusable." Instead, he preferred to see them as reflecting "how badly things are going for U.S. foreign policy." Mahathir may be "guilty of serious abuses of power," but he is also, said Krugman, "as forward-looking a Muslim leader as we're likely to find." Hence, he should be encouraged, not denounced. His anti-Semitism is merely "part of Mr. Mahathir's domestic balancing act."[35]

Progressive modernizer that he is, in other words, Mahathir cannot possibly be stupid enough to believe what he spouts, and because he does not believe it and uses it merely as a tool for the good cause of modernizing Malaysia and combating the Muslim clerics who oppose the acquisition of knowledge, his anti-Semitism is in some way understandable. This is reminiscent of what many said about Hitler's anti-Semitism in the 1930s: It was inexcusable but calculated, and thus it was ultimately both excusable and in the service of a good cause, the modernization of Germany and its reintegration into the community of nations.

For Krugman, Mahathir's "hateful words" serve only to "cover his domestic flank." They do not say anything about his own thinking, but they indicate "more accurately than any poll, just how strong the rising tide of anti-Americanism and anti-Semitism among Muslims in Southeast Asia has become." And what is the cause of this tide? It is the U.S. "war in Iraq and its unconditional support for Ariel Sharon." Just as Mahathir is not anti-Semitic but merely a good reader of his people's collective mind, so, too, his people are not anti-Semitic but merely outraged by the same things that outrage Krugman: Ariel Sharon and George W. Bush.

The Malaysian prime minister's speech was both more offensive and more interesting than most commentators (including Krugman) have observed.[36] In many ways it was a restatement of the urge to modernize, the Nietzschean will to power, and the fantasies of destruction that characterize fascism. Mahathir proposed to "disprove the perception of Islam as a religion of backwardness and terror." He wanted to "restore the honor of Islam and of the Muslims" and "to free their brothers and sisters from the oppression and humiliation from which they suffer today." What sort of action does Mahathir propose? In part, as Krugman pointed out, he was indeed critical of the intellectual and political decline of Islam. He thus insisted that, although according to Islam "we are enjoined . . . to acquire knowledge," it was due to "intellectual regression" that "the great Muslim civilization began to falter and wither," causing it to miss entirely the Industrial Revolution. Yet other influences from the West have actually subverted Islam, among which he counted "the Western democratic system" that "divided us." Moreover, it was thanks to this democratically induced division that the Europeans "could excise Muslim land to create the state of Israel to solve their Jewish problem." Thus, the West both denied the Muslims the means to defend themselves through modern technology and industry and divided them by the introduction of democracy, all with the goal of solving a European "Jewish problem" at the expense of Islamic lands.[37]

This "Jewish problem" is not at all peripheral to Mahathir's argument; it is not just a sort of tithe to the masses and the clerics in order to push his program of modernization. It is central to his thinking. Modernization is justified, in his account, by the necessity of destroying the entity that has penetrated the Muslim world and polluted its soul. For, as he said, "We are all oppressed. We are all being humiliated." And thus the numerical and economic strength of Muslims must be complemented by military prowess: "We are now 1.3 billion strong. We have the biggest oil reserve in the world. We have great wealth. . . . We control 57 out of 180 countries in world. Our votes can make or break international organizations. . . . [But] we need guns and rockets, bombs and warplanes, tanks and warships for our defense." Hitler used to mock those who were obsessed with obscure Germanic traditions, who were filled with rage at the defeat of 1918 and who dreamed up all sorts of harebrained conspiracies in marginal militant fraternities. He wanted to build a powerful modern military. He was, in this way, a modernizer.

Mahathir, for his part, notes that

today we, the whole Muslim ummah are treated with contempt and dishonor. . . . Our only reaction is to become more and more angry. Angry people cannot think properly. And so we find people reacting irrationally. They launch their own attacks, killing just about anybody . . . to vent their anger and frustration. . . . But the attacks solve nothing. The Muslims simply get more oppressed. . . . The Muslims will forever be oppressed and dominated by the Europeans and the Jews. . . . Is there no other way than to ask our young people to blow themselves up and kill people and invite the massacre of more of our own people?

This is the voice of the rational politician. This is not an Arab preaching an endless cycle of revenge but an Asian Muslim calling for patience and calculation. Suicide bombers will never win the war. There must be another way. After all, "1.3 billion Muslims cannot be defeated by a few million Jews." Hence, he says, Muslims need "to think, to assess [their] weaknesses and [their] strength, to plan, to strategize and then to counter attack . . . [to] devise a plan, a strategy that can win [them] final victory. . . . It is winning the struggle that is important, not angry retaliation, not revenge." Is this merely a subtle way of calling on Muslims to focus on their own societies rather than wasting their energies on the struggle with Israel? Perhaps. But it is just as possible that Mahathir, like so many before him, means what he says. And Mahathir paints the Jewish enemy in colors taken directly from Hitler's diabolical palette:

> The enemy will probably welcome these proposals and we will conclude that the promoters are working for the enemy. But think. We are up against a people who think. They survived 2000 years of pogroms not by hitting back, but by thinking. They invented and successfully promoted Socialism, Communism, human rights and democracy so that persecuting them would appear to be wrong, so they may enjoy equal rights with others. With these they have now gained control of the most powerful countries and they, this tiny community, have become a world power. We cannot fight them through brawn alone. We must use our brains also.

The Islamists need none of the fancy extenuations offered by certain European and U.S. intellectuals, for they have a direct link with anti-Semitism going back to the Nazis. Mahathir's anti-Semitic pronouncement was not simply triggered by frustration with the lack of development in Islamic countries or by rage at U.S. and Israeli policies or by some deep-seated traditional Muslim anti-Semitism. Rather, the analysis that he presented reflects the continuing impact of a relatively new and pernicious phenomenon whose roots can be traced back to the foundation of the Muslim Brotherhood in Egypt in 1928 and its success in launching Islamism as a mass movement. As the German political scientist Matthias Küntzel has recently shown, Islamism quickly became a primarily anti-Zionist and anti-Semitic movement that was greatly influenced by European anti-Semitism and directly influenced by Nazism. Indeed, as anti-Semitism lost its impetus as a revolutionary political movement in Europe in the wake of World War II, it was transplanted to the Middle East and from there to other parts of the Muslim world.[38]

This development was responsible for the slaughter of Daniel Pearl in Pakistan in 2003, which was explicitly anti-Semitic in its motivation. The reluctance of the Western media to concede that Pearl was murdered not as an

American, a journalist, a "spy," or someone who might have uncovered connections between the Pakistani secret service and al Qaeda but first and foremost as a Jew—in what was after all a highly ritualized act of killing recorded on videotape—merely manifests the embarrassment that European and U.S. observers feel upon discovering that one of the dirtiest "secrets" of Christian civilization has been so seamlessly transplanted into the Islamic world.[39] After all, it is more difficult to empathize with the plight of those who are still largely victims of Western economic exploitation if they turn out to be led by murderous bigots flaunting slogans that recall Europe's own genocidal past.

But the most explicit and frightening link between Hitler's anti-Semitism and the contemporary wave of violence, hatred, paranoia, and conspiracy theories can be found, first, in the testimony given by the perpetrators of the September 11 terrorist attacks, and, second, in the official charter of the Palestinian Hamas movement. As Küntzel wrote, citing Reuters reporter Christian Eggers, during the trial of Mounir el Motassadeq, a core member of the Al Qaeda cell in Hamburg that planned the attacks of September 11, the motivation of the perpetrators was amply documented, but the media have not reported much of what was said at the trial, which took place in Hamburg, Germany, between October 2002 and February 2003. The witness Shahid Nickels, a member of Mohammed Atta's core group, insisted that "Atta's worldview was based on a National Socialist way of thinking. He was convinced that 'the Jews' are determined to achieve world domination. He considered New York City to be the center of world Jewry, which was, in his opinion, Enemy Number One." Nickels said that Atta's group was "convinced that Jews control the American government as well as the media and the economy of the United States . . . that a worldwide conspiracy of Jews exists . . . [that] America wants to dominate the world so that Jews can pile up capital." Similarly, the witness Ahmed Maglad, who participated in the group's meetings, testified that "for us, Israel didn't have any right to exist as a state. . . . We believed . . . the USA . . . to be the mother of Israel." And Ralf Götsche, who shared the student dormitory with Motassadeq, testified that the accused had said, "What Hitler did to the Jews was not at all bad," and he commented that "Motassadeq's attitude was blatantly antisemitic."[40]

There is a history to such statements, which connects the anti-Semitism of Al Qaeda members planning mass murder in Hamburg in the 1990s to the anti-Semitism of Hitler fantasizing about mass murder in Munich in the 1920s. It is not difficult to find. The charter of the Hamas movement, issued in 1988 as the fundamental document of this Palestinian branch of the Muslim

Brotherhood, must be read to be believed. It contains, among its fundamentalist Islamic preachings, the most blatant anti-Semitic statements made in a publicly available document since Hitler's own pronouncements. Citing an array of Islamic sources, Hamas promises that "Israel will rise and will remain erect until Islam eliminates it as it had eliminated its predecessors." The Islamic Resistance Movement has "raised the banner of Jihad in the face of the oppressors in order to extricate the country and the people from the [oppressors'] desecration, filth and evil." The Prophet, we are reminded, said that "the time will not come until Muslims will fight the Jews (and kill them); until the Jews hide behind rocks and trees, which will cry: O Muslim! There is a Jew hiding behind me, come on and kill him!" Here there is no talk of compromise or reconciliation. The document states plainly that "the so-called peaceful solutions, and the international conferences to resolve the Palestinian problem, are all contrary to the beliefs of the Islamic Resistance Movement. For renouncing any part of Palestine means renouncing part of the religion. . . . The initiatives, proposals, and International Conferences are but a waste of time, an exercise in futility."[41]

The opposition expressed by Hamas to any compromise over Palestine is also intimately linked with its view of the Jewish-Zionist enemy. These enemies, according to the charter,

> have been scheming for a long time. . . . They accumulated a huge and influential material wealth . . . [which] permitted them to take over control of the world media such as news agencies, the press, publication houses, broadcasting and the like. [They also used this] wealth to stir revolutions in various parts of the globe, in order to fulfill their interests and pick the fruits. They stood behind the French and the Communist Revolutions and behind most of the revolutions we hear about here and there. They also used the money to establish clandestine organizations which are spreading around the world, in order to destroy societies and carry out Zionist interests. Such organizations are: the Freemasons, Rotary Clubs, Lions Clubs, B'nai B'rith and the like. All of them are destructive spying organizations. They also used the money to take over control of the Imperialist states and made them colonize many countries in order to exploit the wealth of those countries and spread their corruption therein. . . . they stood behind World War I. . . . and took control of many sources of wealth. They obtained the Balfour Declaration and established the League of Nations in order to rule the world. . . . They also stood behind World War II, where they collected immense benefits from trading with war materials and prepared for the establishment of their state. They inspired the United Nations and the Security Council . . . in order to rule the world. . . . There was no war that broke out anywhere without their fingerprints on it. . . . The forces of Imperialism in both the Capitalist West and the Communist East support the enemy with all their might, in material and human terms.

This international Jewish conspiracy to take over the world has also a moral goal. For, as this document goes on to say, the "secret organizations" working for Zionism "strive to demolish societies, to destroy values, to wreck answerableness, to totter virtues and to wipe out Islam." Zionism "stands behind the diffusion of drugs and toxics of all kinds in order to facilitate its control and expansion." To be sure, Hamas has its own expansionist goals, for it plans to control the entire region of the Middle East, promising in turn "safety and security . . . for the members of the three religions" as long as they agree to live "under the shadow of Islam." But Hamas "is only hostile to those who are hostile towards it, or stand in its way in order to disturb its moves or to frustrate its efforts" to dominate the region. Meanwhile "Zionist scheming has no end, and after Palestine they will covet expansion from the Nile to the Euphrates. . . . Their scheme has been laid out in the Protocols of the Elders of Zion, and their present [conduct] is the best proof of what is said there." Hitler could not have put it better.

So Hitler is dead, but there is a Hitlerite quality to the new anti-Semitism, which now legitimizes not only opposition to Zionism but also the resurrection of the myth of Jewish world domination. This means not that Islamic fundamentalism and Nazism are synonymous—they obviously are not—but that Islamism has internalized a very European, Nazi-like, genocidal anti-Semitism. I also do not mean that any of this should immunize Israel from criticism; rather, I mean that attributing Nazi qualities to Zionism is both false and ends up legitimizing mass murder of Jews in the name of fighting Nazism, a peculiarly ironic outcome considering the history of the last century.[42] Those who foolishly think that doing away with Israel, not least in a "one-state solution," would remove anti-Semitism had better look more closely at the language of these enemies. For those enemies insist that the Jews are everywhere, and so they must be uprooted everywhere. Their outpost may be Israel, but their "power center" is in the United States, and their synagogues and intellectuals are in Germany and France, and their academics are in Russia and Britain. Since they are the cause of all evil and misfortune, the world will be a happier place without them, whether it is dominated by the Aryan Master Race or by the ideological soldiers of the Muslim Brotherhood.

Hitler taught humanity an important lesson. It is that when you see a Nazi, a fascist, a bigot, or an anti-Semite, say what you see. If you want to justify it or excuse it, describe accurately what it is that you are trying to excuse. If a British newspaper publishes an anti-Semitic cartoon, call it anti-Semitic. If the attacks on the World Trade Center were animated by anti-Semitic arguments, say so. If a Malaysian prime minister expresses anti-Semitic views, do not try to excuse the inexcusable. If a self-proclaimed liberation organization calls for the extermination of the Jewish state, do not pretend that it is calling for anything else. The absence of clarity is the beginning of complicity.

# 3

# The End of Politics

*Mark Lilla*

Somewhere in his writings Leo Strauss remarks that the Jewish problem is the political problem *in nuce*. This pregnant remark was meant to invite two sorts of reflections. One, the most obvious, concerns the historical fate of world Jewry, from the biblical age down through the Diaspora and the establishment of the state of Israel. The other, less obvious, concerns the light that Judaism as a social fact sheds on our understanding of politics more generally. Here Strauss had in mind what he called the "theological-political problem," which he saw as the unavoidable tension between political authority and divine revelation. But the Jewish problem is significant in a third sense, too. For how nations or civilizations cope with the existence of the Jews can, at certain historical junctures, reveal political pathologies whose causes have little or nothing to do with Judaism as such. There are periods when the acuteness of the Jewish problem is a symptom of a deeper malaise in political life and political ideas.

There is little doubt that contemporary Europe is passing through such a moment. It is not the first. Throughout Europe's history there have been periods in which a crisis in political ideas had important consequences for Jews in their relations with other Europeans. The anti-Semitic persecutions of the Middle Ages, which had many sources, also coincided with a disturbance in European thinking about the relation between ecclesiastical power and secular power, between the City of God and the City of Man. The emancipation of the Jews in the eighteenth and nineteenth centuries coincided with the epochal shift from absolutism to theories of republicanism and democracy. And the rejection of those Enlightenment political concepts in the late nineteenth and early twentieth centuries in the name of nationalist, racialist, and anti-modern ideals portended events that will shape Jewish consciousness for all time.

Today Europeans find themselves living in what historians call a "saddle period." One distinct age has passed, that of the Cold War, and an obscure new one has begun. Looking back on the era just ended, one fact is especially striking about the intellectual life of Western Europe, or "old Europe": the omnipresence of political ideologies and passions, and the relative absence of serious political thought, understood as disciplined and impartial reflection about distinctly political experience. There were exceptions to this intellectual collapse, and they are widely recognized and revered today: Isaiah Berlin and Michael Oakeshott in Britain, Raymond Aron in France, Norberto Bobbio in Italy, and perhaps a few others. But due to the overwhelming attraction of Marxism and structuralism in all their variants, the influence of these thinkers on wider intellectual discussions was actually quite limited in this period. What was paradoxical about those schools was that they encouraged political engagement while at the same time absorbing all thinking about political experience into amorphous discussions of larger historical, economic, or linguistic forces. The result was that political action intensified as political thought atrophied.

Viewed in retrospect, the intellectual flight from political thought in Europe now appears as a reaction to, and a means of coping with, the unique conditions of the Cold War. After the disasters of the first half of the twentieth century, Western European politics were put on ice—or at least some of the essential questions were. Economies were reorganized, constitutions rewritten, parliaments and parties reconstituted, social mores revised. But the most fundamental issue for all modern nation-states—the issue of sovereignty—could not be addressed, because neither the European community as a whole nor Western European countries individually were fully sovereign. The concept of "sovereignty" has been given many, even incompatible, meanings over the centuries, but at its core is the notion of autonomy, which in political terms means the capacity to defend oneself and, when necessary, to decide to wage war. In this respect European nations were not sovereign during the Cold War. There were good reasons why that was so, and why for decades Western European thinkers were relieved not to have to think about such matters, and the United States and NATO were relieved to do their thinking for them. It was a prudent arrangement, but in the end it had unhealthy intellectual consequences.

Those consequences have been on public display in two related spheres since 1989. The most important is Continental thinking about the European Union. In the early postwar decades, there was some inspiring talk about a "United States of Europe," but as the decades wore on, the concept of "Europe" came to have little meaning beyond economic cooperation. Over the past decade, though, we have witnessed an extremely uncritical embrace of the idea of Europe among Western European intellectuals generally, and its invocation as a kind of charm against the most difficult political questions facing the Continent today. There are many reasons for this, and they differ country by country. In formerly fascist countries—Germany, Italy, Spain—the idea of the nation-state remains in ill repute, while the blissfully undefined notion of "Europe" inspires pacific, post-political hopes. In France, the idea of Europe is generally seen not as a substitute for the nation but as a tool for constraining German might on the Continent and American influence from across the Atlantic. And for intellectuals in the smaller countries, belonging to "Europe" means the hope of escaping cultural obscurity.

What Europe means as a distinctly political entity remains a mystery to all involved. The wisest European commentators worry about this. They are concerned about what is called the "democratic deficit" in the European institutions of Brussels and Strasbourg. They also wonder how widely the community can be extended, not only in economic terms but, as in the case of Turkey, also in cultural ones. Yet serious reflection about the nature of European sovereignty and its relation to national sovereignty is rare these days, except among academic specialists. And so natural concerns about the future of the nation, and the public debate about it, have been left to xenophobes and chauvinists, of whom there are more than a few in every European country.

It is nothing less than extraordinary that the idea of the nation-state as the locus of political action and political reflection fell so quickly and so silently into oblivion among Western European thinkers in our time. The great exception that proves the rule is France, where passionate appeals to the Gaullist tradition of national autonomy have run up against equally passionate appeals to European and international cooperation, leading to the kind of diplomatic incoherence that was recently put on display at the United Nations. There are some understandable reasons for this development, too. After all, one of the important lessons that Europeans have drawn from their twentieth-century history is that nationalism is always a danger, and that it can infect and eventually destroy liberal democracy.

But what are the serious alternatives to the nation-state as a form of political life? Historically speaking, we know what they are: tribe and empire, neither of which Europeans wish to restore as their preferred form of political association. Between those extremes there have been short-lived experiments with small, defenseless republics and weak, ephemeral leagues or alliances. But for more than two centuries the fate of decent and humane politics in Europe has been tied to that of the nation-state as the dominant form of European political life. And we can see why. If a moderately sized political entity is to attract the loyalty and the commitment of its citizens, it must find a way to bind them together; and among the ties it finds ready to hand are those of language, religion, and culture, broadly understood. Yes, those ties are artifacts of history, subject to manipulation and "invention"; they are not brute facts. But they are, politically speaking, extremely useful inventions, given that only the rarest of states could generate those ties by civic means alone. (Not even the United States or Switzerland manages to do so.) One of the long-standing puzzles of politics is how to wed political attachment (which is particular) to political decency (which knows no borders). The nation-state has been the best modern means discovered so far of squaring the circle, opening a political space for both reasonable reflection and effective action.

It may be that the European Union will turn out to be something new, and beneficent, on the European political landscape. I am skeptical, but it is possible. What is certainly clear, though, is that European institutions have not yet reached that stage, nor do they have the kind of public legitimacy that would permit them to be the focus of political life in terms of action or attachment, let alone reflection. So what is the focus of intellectual reflection on European politics today? The nation is still there, but it must lurk in the background, unacknowledged. To paraphrase the wicked Joseph de Maistre, I have never yet met a "European" intellectual: I have met French intellectuals, Italian intellectuals, and German intellectuals, and I have heard it rumored that there are English intellectuals; but there are no "European" intellectuals. Writers and thinkers still use their national languages, they still absorb themselves in parochial national debates, and they still take rather characteristic national stands on certain issues. Yet all these realities notwithstanding, the idea of the nation-state as a distinct form of political life is simply not an important theme for Western European thinkers at this time. They have, thankfully, stopped trying to answer the question of whether a nation has an "essence"—Renan's famous question, *qu'est-ce qu'une nation?* (What is a nation?) But they have also, more disturbingly, ceased to think seriously about the political function of nation-states—*à quoi sert la nation?* (What purpose does the nation serve?)

The debacle of the Balkans in the late 1990s, and Western Europe's painfully slow response to the threats of political collapse and even genocide there, had something to do with this intellectual paralysis. For the first time in fifty years, European thinkers faced a military crisis to which they could have responded, and probably should have responded, without American assistance. But who exactly was supposed to respond? The nation-states of Europe, acting alone or in concert? Or "Europe," the European community, conceived as a coherent political entity? Many European intellectuals were opposed to any intervention, on different grounds, and sometimes on purely pacifist ones, as in Germany. A number of quite prominent thinkers, especially in France, called for intervention on humanitarian grounds, though without much caring what sort of political entity handled the job. As German Foreign Minister Joschka Fischer, one of the earliest and most vigorous supporters of intervention, remarked in a recent interview, pan-European institutions simply are not yet capable of handling these sorts of crises. And so the catastrophe in the Balkans proceeded for a long time unimpeded. Europeans no longer think of the nation-state as the sole place where foreign policy should be determined and military means chosen, but they are not yet able to treat the European Union as that place. As a result, they have generally ceased to think seriously and responsibly about such matters.

It will be said by some intellectuals that that is because Europeans, given their recent history, have discovered the need to regulate such matters through international law and organizations. But this simply removes the problem to a higher and far less stable plane. If the sovereignty and the political legitimacy of the European Union is a complicated business, the moral and political authority of the United Nations or a World Criminal Court or nongovernmental organizations is infinitely more so. It is simply a fantasy to think that the perennial problems of politics can be dissolved through progressive juridification or humanitarian aid, which is what some very serious European thinkers, notably Jürgen Habermas, clearly have in mind. The danger is not that thinking so might make it true; it is that no amount of thinking ever will. Wars that involve European nations will happen, sovereignty will be exercised, and European thinkers will simply be less prepared to understand both of those inevitabilities if the fantasy of escaping them retains its grip on the European mind.

It is against the backdrop of this intellectual crisis of sovereignty that we must see the contemporary "Jewish question" in Europe. For centuries that question was, broadly speaking, one of inclusion: What sorts of people could be citizens and under what conditions, whether religion mattered, whether differences could be tolerated. This form of the problem still exists in Europe, though today Muslims are more likely to be the object of prejudice and violence than Jews are. The battle for toleration as an idea has largely been won; the challenges now are to put tolerance into practice and to understand its limits within each national context.

It is not the idea of tolerance that is in crisis in Europe today; it is the idea of the nation-state and the related concepts of sovereignty and the use of force. And these ideas have also affected European intellectual attitudes toward world Jewry, and specifically toward Israel. Here there is an extraordinary paradox that deserves to be savored. For centuries Jews were the stateless people and suffered at the hands of Europeans who were deeply rooted in their own nations. The early Zionists, from Hess to Herzl, drew a very simple lesson from this experience: that Jews could not live safely or decently until they had their own state. Those who claim today that the state of Israel is the brainchild of nineteenth-century European thought are not wrong; this is hardly a secret. But the point is often made with sinister intent, as if to suggest that Israel and the Zionist enterprise more generally represent some kind of political atavism that enlightened Europeans should spurn. Once upon a time, the Jews were mocked for not having a nation-state. Now they are criticized for having one.

And not just any nation-state, but one whose founding is still fresh in living memory. All political foundings, without exception, are morally ambiguous enterprises, and Israel has not escaped these ambiguities. Two kinds of fools and bigots refuse to see this: those who deny or explain away the Palestinian suffering caused by Israel's founding, and those who treat that suffering as the unprecedented consequence of a uniquely sinister ideology. The moral balance-sheet of Israel's founding, which is still being composed, must be compared to those of other nations at their conception, not to the behavior of other nations after their existence was secured. And it is no secret that Israel must still defend itself against nations and peoples who have not reconciled themselves to its existence—an old, but now forgotten, European practice. Many Western European intellectuals, including those whose toleration and even affection for Jews cannot be questioned, find all this incomprehensible. The reason is not anti-Semitism nor even anti-Zionism in the usual sense. It is that Israel is, and is proud to be, a nationstate—the nation-state of the Jews. And that is profoundly embarrassing to post-national Europe.

Consider the issue from the perspective of a young European who might have grown up in the postwar world. From his first day of school he would have been taught the following lesson about twentieth-century history: that all its disasters can be traced to nationalism, militarism, and racism. He might even have learned that Jews were the main victims of these political pathologies, and would have developed a certain sympathy for their plight. But as he grew up he would have begun to learn about contemporary Israel, mainly in light of the conflict with the Palestinians, and his views would probably have begun to change. From his own history he would have concluded that nations are suspect entities, that the distinction they make between insider and outsider is immoral, and that military force is to be forsworn. He would then have likely concluded that contemporary Israel violates all these maxims: it is proudly independent, it distinguishes between Jew and non-Jew, it defends itself without apology. The charges that Zionism is racism, or that Israel is behaving like the Nazis in the occupied territories, undoubtedly have roots in anti-Semitism; but frustration with the very existence of Israel and the way it handles its challenges has a more proximate cause in European intellectual life. That cause is the crisis in the European idea of a nation-state.

Anyone who pays close attention to how the Israeli-Palestinian conflict is handled in the European press, and even in intellectual journals, will see this frustration expressed on a regular basis. I do not think this can be ascribed solely to European pro-Arabism, just as American press coverage cannot be attributed entirely to the feelings of Jewish Americans for Israel. I am convinced that at a deeper level the differences have something to do with the way Americans and Europeans think about political life more generally today, differences that Robert Kagan has highlighted in his powerful little book *Of Paradise and Power*. While it may not be true that Americans are uniformly Martian (Woodrow Wilson was not Belgian, after all), Kagan is correct that the European consensus today, from left to right, is thoroughly Venutian in spirit. This causes occasional friction with the United States, but it is a source of fundamental disaccord with the Zionist project. For Zionists today are indeed from Mars, *par la force des choses*.

Even European sympathy for the Palestinian people, which is understandable and honorable, has an oddly apolitical quality to it. One would think that those concerned about the future of the Palestinians, and not simply about their present suffering, would be thinking chiefly about how to remove them from tutelage to terrorist and fundamentalist organizations, and how to establish a legitimate, law-abiding, and liberal political authority that could negotiate in good faith with Israel and manage Palestinian domestic affairs in a transparent manner. But there is almost no intellectual awareness in Europe of the political obstacles to peace that exist among the Palestinians, nor has there been much encouragement of political reform. To judge by what is written, the European fantasy of the future Middle East is not of decent, liberal nation-states living side by side in peace, but of some sort of post-national, post-political order growing up under permanent international supervision. Not Menachem Begin and Anwar Sadat shaking hands, but Hans Blix zipping around Palestine in his little truck.

Anyone schooled in the history of the nineteenth and twentieth centuries is well aware of the political pathologies of the nation-state and the idolatry that it invites. The legitimacy of the nation-state should not be confused with the idolatry of the nation-state. But for many in Western Europe today, learning the grim lesson of modern history has also brought with it a forgetting of all the long-standing problems that the nation-state, as a modern form of political life, managed to solve. The Zionist tradition knows what those problems were. It remembers what it was to be stateless, and the indignities of tribalism and imperialism. It remembers the wisdom of borders and the need for collective autonomy to establish self-respect and to demand respect from others. It recognizes that there is a cost, a moral cost, to defending a nation-state and exercising sovereignty; but it also recognizes that the cost is worth paying, given the alternatives. Eventually Western Europeans will have to re-learn these lessons, which are, after all, the lessons of their own pre-modern history. Until they do, the mutual incomprehension regarding Israel between Europeans and Jews committed to Zionism will remain deep. There is indeed a new Jewish problem in Europe, because there is a new political problem in Europe.

4

# Zionism and Anti-Semitism

*Hillel Halkin*

Who would have thought, but a few years ago, that we would today feel the need to examine anti-Semitism, considered not as a historical phenomenon or as a lingering social or geographical aberration of our times but as—once again—a clear and present danger to the Jewish people? One has the awful feeling of awakening to what the still half-sleeping mind, in the seconds it takes, to organize, struggles in vain to believe is but a recurrent bad dream.

When we ask, therefore, whether the modern prejudice against the Jews is just a secularized version of the medieval prejudice against the Jews, this is not simply a matter of theory. If we are faced with an epidemic of a disease that had been thought, at least in the democratic world, to be under control since the end of World War II, it would seem important to know whether its agent is a new mutation and whether the disease itself has one or multiple causes. The medical analogy seems apt, not because anti-Semitism is necessarily a disease in anything but a metaphorical sense but because in medicine one sometimes encounters similar questions, as, for example, in tracing the etiology of cancer.

And yet compared to the classification of cancers, the classification of anti-Semitisms is simple. Historically, we can point to half a dozen major varieties. There is the pre-Christian anti-Semitism of the ancient Graeco-Roman world. There is the Christian anti-Semitism of antiquity and the Middle Ages, extending into modern times. There is traditional Moslem anti-Semitism. There is the political, social, and economic anti-Semitism of Enlightenment and post-Enlightenment Europe. There is the racial anti-Semitism that culminated in

Nazism. And there is the contemporary anti-Semitism that confronts us today: the anti-Semitism of Israelophobia or hatred of the State of Israel.

These six types are, I think, fairly inclusive. One can argue that only the first of them has ever been found in a pure form uninfluenced by any of the others, but it would be difficult to imagine a seventh that is more than a recombination of some or all of the first six. And so, to widen the question beyond the binary opposition of medieval versus modern, what we really seem to be asking ourselves is whether the various types of anti-Semitism known to us from history are essentially different from one another or are all variations on a single theme.

Nonetheless, since two of anything are easier to deal with than six, let us conduct a simplifying thought experiment. Let us imagine that a panel was convened to examine the nature of anti-Semitism not in the twenty-first century but in the fourth, when type 2 anti-Semitism, the Christian type, was first becoming a serious problem for Jews. Here we are, then, assembled in a Roman villa to ask, "Is Christian prejudice against the Jews just a theologized version of pagan prejudice against the Jews? Or has the rise of Christianity permanently changed the context for an analysis of anti-Semitism?" How would we respond?

I suppose one of us might observe, quite sensibly, that Christian anti-Semitism is not just pre-Christian anti-Semitism in a religious guise. What is the connection, he would ask, between disliking Jews because they are arrogant, superstitious, lazy, clannish, and antisocial—the typical charges made against them in pagan antiquity—and because they have murdered and disowned a fellow Jew, the son of God who, incarnated as one of them, was sent to bring salvation to mankind? Indeed, Christian anti-Semitism is based on acceptance of precisely the Jewish claim that pre-Christian anti-Semites found most repellent, namely, that the Jews were God's chosen people. Clearly, Christian anti-Semitism is something radically new.

"Not so fast," a second panelist might object. "You're looking at rationalizations for hating Jews rather than at the hatred of them. The fact is that no other people beside the Jews has been widely despised by others not because it ruled them, warred with them, or did them any harm, but simply because of who it is. And yet you are proposing that when both pagans and Christians hate Jews in this unprecedented way, the two phenomena are unrelated. Surely that would be an unlikely coincidence! We are not, then, looking at two different things, but at two forms of the same thing."

Fortunately, in those days too, conference panels had three members, the third of whom regularly demonstrated that the first two were mistaken.

"Gentlemen!" our tertium quid now exclaims. "This argument is foolish. You are both wrong—but only because you are both right. Of course Christian anti-Semitism is something new, and of course it is a continuation of something old. In fact, it would never have come into being had not pre-Christian anti-Semitism preceded it. Had we Jews been considered just another people when Christianity came along, would the Christians, even if they had reason to hate us, have bothered or been able to turn this hatred to public advantage? Who would have cared or listened to them? The paradox is that it is only because the pagans reviled us for claiming to be God's chosen people that the Christians now revile us for no longer being it."

I suspect that with the advantage of hindsight, we would agree that our third panelist has a point. And we would also agree, I think, that this point applies even more to the subsequent history of anti-Semitism. The post-Christian anti-Semitism of eighteenth- and nineteenth-century Europe was, intellectually, a new development; yet without a millennium and a half of Christian anti-Semitism at its back, what eighteenth- or nineteenth-century secular European intellectual would have conceived of blaming the Jews for the world's ills, much less have found a responsive audience for the accusation? And the same can be said of the racial anti-Semitism of the Nazis and the anti-Semitism of contemporary Israelophobia. While no one would question the novelty of demonizing a Jewish state, would this have happened had the people of this state never before aroused the antipathy of humankind? Although historically, then, we can distinguish between different types of anti-Semitism, each type has had as its necessary condition at least some of the types that preceded it. And so, just as two oncologists might find fruitless the question of whether a skin cancer that has metastasized to the lungs is or is not the same illness, it is a quibble to debate whether or not we are dealing with the same anti-Semitism. We are and we aren't.

And yet something about the question remains unanswered and continues to trouble us.

This something can be expressed in different ways. One might say, for instance: "All this is stating the obvious. Now tell us, however: Is Israel being demonized because previous anti-Semitism has made this possible, or has previous anti-Semitism undergone a resurgence because Israel has made this possible?"

Or one might say: "Granted that type 6 anti-Semitism would not have emerged without the previous types. But given the previous types, did it *have* to emerge? Had, for example, the 1967 war, with its Israeli occupation of Palestinian territories, never taken place, would type 6 have emerged anyway?"

Or one might ask: "If a political solution to the Israeli-Arab conflict causes type 6 to disappear, will there be a type 7?"

Or simply: "Will anti-Semitism ever cease?"

And yet deep in our hearts we know there is yet another question that lurks behind this question, and that is *the* question we usually refrain from asking in polite company. It is: when we ask ourselves whether anti-Semitism is essentially one thing or many, just as when we ask ourselves whether or how it will cease—when we ask, in other words, what must change to make it cease—are we not in fact asking whether the real cause of anti-Semitism is to be found in the Jews or in the world?

Before anyone protests that even to raise the possibility that the Jews are the cause of anti-Semitism is capitulating to the anti-Semites, I would remind you that the belief that they *are* the cause of it has been traditionally shared by anti-Semites *with* Jews. Why are the Jews like the fruit of the olive tree, ask the rabbis in the Midrash? "Because," they answer, "as all liquids mix with each other, but the oil of the olive does not, so Israel does not mix with the Gentiles. . . . And as the olive does not yield its oil unless it is crushed, so Israel does not follow the right path unless it is crushed by affliction."[1] Being chosen and set apart, according to Jewish tradition, exacts a double price. It makes an envious and indignant world persecute the Jews, and it makes a pedagogical God encourage this to happen. My own great-grandfather, Rabbi Naftali Tsvi Yehuda Berlin, the head of the great Lithuanian yeshiva of Volozhin, wrote a book about anti-Semitism called *She'erit Yisra'el* (The Remnant of Israel), in which he maintained that "persecution by our enemies arises from rejection of Torah study by Israel."[2] Anti-Semitism is built into the Jewish role in the scheme of things, and the less Jews accept this role, the worse it will get. Historically, this is the normative Jewish point of view.

Classical Zionism, too, viewed the Jews as the cause of anti-Semitism. Here is Leo Pinsker's *Auto-Emancipation,* published fourteen years before Theodor Herzl's *The Jewish State:*

> Among the living nations of the earth the Jews occupy the position of a nation long since dead. . . . If the fear of ghosts is something inborn, and has a certain justification in the psychic life of humanity, is it any wonder that it asserted itself powerfully at the sight of this dead and yet living nation? . . . The misfortunes of the Jews are due, above all, to their lack of desire for national independence.

Zionism understood the Jews' misfortunes differently from the way rabbinic Judaism did, which is why it was more optimistic about overcoming them.

And yet there is in all self-blame a peculiar sort of optimism that helps to explain why, starting with the biblical prophets, there has been so much of it among Jews; for if one is the root cause of one's suffering, one has the ability to rectify it, as one does not if the cause is elsewhere. Imagine that, in its early years, Zionism had declared proudly and defiantly: "Do not blame the Jews! It is not their fault that they have become the scapegoats of a sick humanity, which has projected onto them, and will continue to project onto them, all its fears, hatreds, and phobias." Such a Zionism would also have had to say: "Because people will always have fears, hatred, and phobias, there will always be anti-Semitism, which no Jewish state can put an end to. On the contrary: Such a state will simply become anti-Semitism's new focus." How many followers would a Herzl who said this have attracted?

If anti-Semitism has a single cause—the Jews—it is a dragon that can be slain. If it has many causes—as many as the world has fears, hatreds, and phobias—it is a hydra: Cut off one head, and it will grow another. What we are then asking when we ask whether the new anti-Semitism is the old one all over again is: Are we are fighting a dragon or a hydra?

I have two friends who have thought more passionately about anti-Semitism than anyone else I know, although they could hardly disagree more about it. They are the scholar and critic of Jewish literature Ruth Wisse and the Israeli novelist A.B. Yehoshua.

Ruth Wisse rejects the notion that the Jews have caused anti-Semitism, except insofar, perhaps, as they have not been militant enough in combating it. Jewish self-blame, she thinks, is a habitual introjection of anti-Semitic attitudes that turns the anger of Jews inward rather than outward at their enemies. Anti-Semitism is hydra-headed, and she argues in a book she now is writing that its latest form, hatred of Israel, should be viewed not primarily as another round of "discrimination against Jews or even persecution of Jews" but as "a political instrument to oppose liberal democracy by harnessing ancient prejudice to brand-new fears." The battle for democracy—the one form of government under which Jews have always prospered—and the battle against Israelophobia are one and the same, since Israel is "democracy's fighting front line."[4]

A.B.Yehoshua is writing a book too. In it, he maintains that the Jews themselves are the ultimate reason for anti-Semitism. Although this does not excuse or justify prejudice against them, throughout their history, Yehoshua believes, the Jews have baffled and exasperated the world. They have done this by taking two ideas that were their contribution to civilization and by which civilization subsequently organized itself—the idea of monotheistic universalism and the idea of national particularism—and fusing them in a way that has subverted both, thus ironically making themselves the symbolic enemy of both humanity and the nation alike. It is this fusion, or confusion, Yehoshua argues, that has enabled the Arab states to turn a political and territorial conflict with Israel into a successful anti-Semitic campaign, since Israel's failure to distinguish clearly between religion and nationality—that is, between Jewish and Israeli identity—makes it an anomaly among democracies and exposes it to charges of racism and discrimination.

I do not wish to comment here on the intrinsic merits of either of these positions, each of which draws on a broad hinterland of thought. I would merely point out that if we ask, "Has the sovereignty of Jews in the state of Israel and the flourishing of Jews in the United States permanently changed the context for the analysis of anti-Semitism," Wisse says yes and Yehoshua, no, whereas if we ask, "Do the Jews have the power to put an end to anti-Semitism," Wisse says no and Yehoshua, yes.

Yehoshua's yes is based on the conviction that if Israel and Diaspora Jewry would pursue the Zionist revolution to its logical end, they would finally disentangle the Jewish confusion of religion and nationality that has rankled humankind for over two thousand years, leaving us with two discrete identities—a Jewish religious one and an Israeli national one. Since such a Judaism could no longer be suspected of supranational allegiances and such an Israel could no longer be accused of undemocratic practices, type 6 anti-Semitism would fade, and—in the absence of a cause for type 7—anti-Semitism would pass at last from the world.

Wisse would object to this strongly. She would counter that Judaism without Jewish nationhood would not be Judaism, just as a non-Jewish Israel would not be Israel, and that Yehoshua is simply demonstrating the illusion of thinking that, short of disappearing themselves, the Jews can make anti-Semitism disappear.

We have, then, two opposed analyses. Yet curiously, they converge on a single belief, which is that a vigorously democratic Israel in an alliance of values and interests with democratic forces around the world is the best way of combating contemporary anti-Semitism. And while I have no doubt that if they were brought together to debate these issues, Wisse, who is on the political right, and Yehoshua, who is on the political left, would be fighting tooth and nail over what such an Israel and such a Jewish politics entail, they would agree on the need for defending and promoting them with all the means at our disposal.

One might ask, of course, what the practical utility of such agreement is if it does not translate into concrete policies. For example, if I believe that the defense of democratic values in Israel calls for abolishing the Law of Return and you don't, or if you hold that U.S. Jews should back President George W. Bush because he is fighting to democratize the Arab world and I say this is a sham, what have we gained from subscribing to an apparently not very meaningful generalization about combating anti-Semitism?

Perhaps not much of immediate consequence. And yet we have established common ground that is not inconsequential either. It includes the beliefs that anti-Semitism must be fought politically in the broadest sense; that it cannot be treated by us simply as a Jewish or Israeli problem, in isolation from other issues; that in selecting these issues we must ask ourselves whom they ally us with and whether these allies have genuine and stable democratic commitments; that, as in all alliances, we must be ready not only to ask for support but also to provide it, and still other things. Such criteria can be useful. They may not enable us to decide whether anti-Semitism is best fought by voting Democratic or Republican or by making or not making Israel a multicultural "state of all its citizens," but they might provide some guidance as to whether an Israeli government should sell arms to a Latin American dictatorship or help the Kurds of Iraq, or as to whether there is a difference between Jews forging links with evangelical Christians in the United States and with followers of Jean-Marie Le Pen in France.

This is encouraging. It suggests that however differently we may approach the question of anti-Semitism, at least some of our operative conclusions may turn out to be similar. It is a little as if—to return to the metaphor of disease—our two oncologists, after arguing how and whether a new malignancy is related to a previous one, find themselves agreeing on the broad outlines of its treatment, if not on the specific drugs or techniques of surgery to be used. The history of medicine indeed tells us that successfully combating an illness need not always depend on identifying its root cause.

"Why the Jews?" will go on being asked, not because the question is resolvable or because we cannot act without the answers to it but because our anguish in the face of continued anti-Semitism makes us ask it. This anguish is especially great for those of us who have believed and still believe that Zionism and Israel were the most appropriate and far-sighted of all Jewish responses to modernity, a heroic effort on the part of the Jewish people to rejoin the human family. That this effort is now widely being represented, so soon after the Holocaust, as a new argument for excluding the Jews from the human family is a bitter blow. One could easily be driven to despair by it. This is why we should keep in mind that, nevertheless, we are part of a struggle that is bigger than just our own.

# 5

# Israel, Globalization, and Anti-Semitism in Europe

*Fiamma Nirenstein*

Over the years of the recent Intifada, many of us have expressed enormous surprise and disappointment at the huge phenomenon of global anti-Semitism, spreading like a bad weed, reaching out from Arab to European and, to a lesser extent, U.S. society.

Jews, always identified with Israel and Zionism, have become an object of physical attack and public contempt and the subject of large street demonstrations, not to mention outrageous exclamations ("that shitty little country!" by Daniel Bernard the former French ambassador to England; "The root of evil," from famed Greek composer Mikis Theodorakis).

Jews have become a favorite target of political blame for nongovernmental organizations (NGOs), human rights organizations, righteous intellectuals, and journalists, a matter of disgraceful polls to be kept as secret as possible.

The life of many has changed: I, as a journalist and an author who writes columns, features, and essays about the Middle East, have noticed a deep change in my friends and my interlocutors. I have not missed any of the wars since 1967, when, as a young visitor in a kibbutz, I became a traitor to the Left, where I naturally belonged as did almost every young person at that time. Since that turning point, which led to a divorce between the Left and Israel (which I have written about elsewhere), it has become more and more difficult to speak of the conflict in its true context: the ongoing Arab denial of the legitimate existence of the State of Israel, the terrorist campaign after the Palestinian refusal to any agreement in Camp David, the difficulty of combating the unconven-

A version of this chapter was presented at the International Conference on the Global Dimensions of Contemporary Anti-Semitism, Montreal, Canada, March 15, 2004.

tional army of terrorists that hides behind civilians, the incitement and the genocidal hate that have accompanied the wave of terrorism. This hatred of Israel
and everything connected to it created what Israeli minister Natan Sharansky
defined as "the three Ds": demonization, double standard, and denial of the right
to exist.

There has not been a Jew who could escape anti-Semitism. Renouncing the
devil Ariel Sharon is not enough to save anyone from anti-Semitism. Several
liberal intellectuals discovered that the culture of human rights they were part
of rejected and abandoned them for being Jewish. Suddenly, the State of Israel
understood that one of the basic theoretical purposes of its existence, putting
an end to anti-Semitism, had failed.

Here I leave aside analysis of the phenomenon of global anti-Semitism
itself. Much has already been very well said by good people, including many
in this volume. Let me mention only a few names as examples: Natan
Sharansky, Robert Wistrich, Irwin Cotler, Anne Bayevsky. I will focus only on
what seems to me to be a new aspect of the phenomenon. To summarize: Anti-
Semitism is part of the crisis of globalization. We have fought hard and have
already partially succeeded in defeating anti-Semitism. But to completely
defeat it, we must delve deeper into its contradictions and expose them.

From a state of depression, we have now moved on to the phase of fighting back. All the theoretical effort that I cited focuses on what we did not want
to believe: There is a new worldwide anti-Semitism, hypocritical and pervasive
and genocidal. We have identified it. We have produced hundreds and hundreds
of articles, tens of essays and books, tough reactions from Jewish institutions
(such as the Anti-Defamation League, which has changed to a tougher line of
straight support of Israel) and from democratic institutions in general, academic and political studies and conferences, media watches, student activities on
the campuses, mobilizations in many different ways by groups of Jews, and
most of all, a serious engagement of the State of Israel (examples include the
words of Sharon, the fight at The Hague, the energizing of the Global Forum
against anti-Semitism, the meetings of the Israeli foreign minister with the
diplomatic corps). All these efforts have made clear that the practice of wildly attacking the Jewish state with blood libels and prejudices is anti-Semitism,
and nothing else.

I would now like to emphasize a new and very important phenomenon. For
the first time in history, a Jewish state can fight anti-Semitism in the international arena, and this has already made things very different. The Jew is not
alone anymore. The Jewish state is a well-organized, democratic, and modern

influential body with a minister appointed to deal with anti-Semitism. Its voice is morally and strategically respected by U.S. presidents whatever their political color may be, as seen with Bill Clinton and George W. Bush. Israel is valued not for its influence as a cabal or a powerful political lobby (the Arabs have a larger and wealthier one) but for its moral and Jewish heritage and its unbelievable success in economics, art, and science despite its daily confrontations with terrible enemies.

Never before has anti-Semitism been a diplomatic issue dealt with on the level of governments and international forums. For the first time, it has become a serious matter affecting economic, military, and intelligence relations. The elected representative of the Jewish people can now officially point a finger assigning blame through resolutions and documents in the UN General Assembly or in the European Union. Furthermore, Israel has linked the anti-Semitic terror attacks against Israel and those against the Jews in Jerba, Istanbul, Kenya, and elsewhere to global Islamist terrorism. This is a warning to the European states: "Don't help anti-Semites, they are also terrorists!"

Having such strong backing from the State of Israel offers Jews an unprecedented innovation that gives new strength to the Diaspora. The World Jewish Congress wrote a protest to the president of the European Community, several Israeli ministers lodged protests with ambassadors and presidents, and many intellectuals traditionally belonging to the Left (such as Paul Berman, Andrè Glucksman, and Alain Finkielkraut) have declared their disgust at the anti-Semitism resurfacing from the sewers of history to join the ideology of terrorism.

Why have Israel and the international community been so surprised and confused by this new phenomenon for so long? Because the main theoretical problem was the identification of anti-Semitism as such. For a long time, we have been debating whether and to what extent the attack on Israel could be identified with anti-Semitism. We did not want to believe it, and we have come to realize it only by putting it in global perspective. The studies of Arab anti-Semitism, of the anti-Semitism of world institutions (the United Nations first of all), and of the media have been instrumental.

Both the Durban and Johannesburg UN conferences, with their wide participation by NGOs and their symbolic location in South Africa, were dramatic statements. Global demonization, since the UN conference of 1975 ("Zionism is Racism"), has been the premier arena for the new anti-Semitism, as it attributes to Israel all the faults of the modern world—ethnic cleansing, racism, war crimes, and crimes against humanity—and is disseminated through the airwaves. Durban caused many to connect the dots, and to realize that from then on, there was a new frame for hating Israel: The 1975 UN resolution was coming back in a new form. Leaflets with the text were distributed inside the convention center.

Because these supposed crimes were so enormous, the punishment had to be commensurate with that of sixty years ago, but this time it is the Jewish state, the collective Jew, that was to be eliminated. Emil Fackenheim wrote that three messages characterize anti-Semitism. The first tells Jews, "You can't live with us as Jews"; the second, "You can't live among us"; and the third, "You can't live." Amnon Rubinstein has noted that whereas in the 1930s, the streets of Berlin were filled with graffiti reading "Jews to Palestine" and "Jews out," now they have been happily unified in the slogan "Jews out of Palestine," a sort of "destination nowhere." In the name of the supreme doctrines of human rights and equality, the global message that has become fashionable is the destruction of the State of Israel, the denial of Israel's right to belong to the family of nations. The new anti-Semitism, characterized by the rejection of the rights of Israel, so well defined by Irwin Cotler, has become so popular just because it offers an element of unification, a simple, elementary bridge between cultures. Its ugly simplicity is just like a music that is based only on rhythm, with no melody, so that everybody can understand it. It is like a bad rap song. Groups of Islamist immigrants say, "The Jews are bad," and a more sophisticated culture nods, a cheap way of gaining friendship and maybe avoiding danger. For the Europeans, the culture of "never again" and the culture of diversity have been brought together, in the last three years, in Finkielkraut's image of the little Muslim boy in Paris, an icon for the liberal movements. This icon has replaced the one of the little Jewish boy being deported from the Warsaw Ghetto.

The tv-viewing and reading public has been complicit in this distortion of concepts and languages. With much help from the international UN consensus, the rejected and persecuted State of Israel—the small country subjected to an unprecedented wave of terrorist attacks—has been transformed into a colonialist Nazi persecutor.

The territorial dispute between Israelis and Palestinians, the occupation, the disputed areas, even the war itself have all become merely a pale scenario: The fantasy of killing the Jews has flown during this night of conscience, from the dream palace of the Arab to the dream palace of a deluded, frightened Europe. Europe has become obsessed by U.S. hegemony, haunted by the ancient fear of invasions and wars, dominated by the media.

This time, there has not been complete silence, as there was over half a century ago. There has been surprise, protest, and also strength: The Israeli ambassador to Sweden protested the obscene admiration for a terrorist expressed in a major art exhibit; organizations like CAMERA and Honest Reporting have gone after journalists, and professors on campuses have fought for a less biased reading of the Middle East's history. As I have mentioned, this has been instrumental in confronting one of the most important issues related to the new anti-Semitism: denial. Denial that anti-Semitism exists has continued even as synagogues were being torched and hundreds of Jews were being beaten and assaulted in the streets. This denial did not stop even as demonstrators were chanting that Hitler did not finish the job or when a caricature of a naked Sharon munching on Palestinian children won an international contest for political cartoons in 2003.

But the very same dynamics of globalization that have had such an impact on the dissemination and spreading of anti-Semitism have become helpful in understanding its destructive nature. President Jacques Chirac of France declared that whoever hurts a Jew is hurting France itself and invited the president of Israel to visit. The European Union and its branches organized various seminars on the topic. The pope has ordered bishops to be respectful of their elder brothers the Jews. Even though Mel Gibson's film *The Passion* was such a great commercial success, there is still a heated debate about its portrayal of the Jews.

The existence of anti-Semitism has been acknowledged and condemned. But how should one evaluate the response of European leaders, which manifests itself mainly in recalling the Holocaust? Does this express any concern for living Jews? Or is it simply an attempt to cling to one's self-respect as a defender of human rights?

In my opinion, even if such leaders' intentions are superficial and hesitant, we are nevertheless facing an important phenomenon. It is important because it is the beginning of the possibility of successfully combating anti-Semitism. The roots of the cancer that is growing in the heart of Europe are confined by the very limits of globalization. A few years ago, Europeans were filled with hopes and illusions of an integrated society where the poor and the weak would melt away in a democratic environment. This is proving to be part of a big delusion: This melting pot has been obstructed by overwhelming cultural and religious differences and ultimately by hate and sometimes terrorism. The clash of Islam with Western culture is the basic reason for the failure of globalization.

But big themes require big answers: European repentance at first sight still looks like an attempt at an easy fix for an unadmittable, dirty malaise. Simply declaring, in a conference or in a visit to the local Jewish community, one's disgust for the mortal illness that affected Europe not many years ago, relating this to the past more than to the present, will not cure anti-Semitism.

Anti-Semitism has become a signal, an indication, a yellow flag signaling a pestilence spreading in the very heart of the phenomenon of globalization itself, in its institutions (the UN, the NGOs, the European Union, the media). This is where the struggle must take place. Anti-Semites must be faced with the truth again and again without truce. And the focus of such confrontation has to be the maltreatment of Israel. It has to be made clear that the filth of the incredible quantity of lies and of international misunderstanding has been mixing itself with the smell of the terrorists' dynamite. This combination has given rise to the alchemy of Arab hate for the Jews and new post-Shoah anti-Semitism in Europe. In the past year, many people in different parts of the world have been assaulted and killed simply for being Jewish. Putting Israel out of the family of nations and consequently putting the Jews out of the family of humanity has mortal consequences: In Turkey, in Casablanca, in Jerba, in Kenya, just as in Israel, one can die just for being a Jew. The new anti-Semitism has genocidal features, and even though not all the victims are Jews, it would not be too daring to suggest that most of the world's terrorist attacks have been perpetrated by anti-Semites.

A new form of globalization involves the assassination of Christians by Muslims in many parts of the world, attacks on Americans wherever possible, and a dangerous expansion of terrorist cells in London, Milan, and Paris, all easily unified under the banner of anti-Semitism. Terrorism itself undermines the dream of integration. It is a culture, an environment that gives shelter to every kind of destructive action against democracy, as in the Madrid train bombings in 2004. The European fear and suspicion of the violent anti-Western feelings of the masses of immigrants are no longer capable of being overcome by the ideological desire for integration.

Note the request by two parties (the populist LPF [Lijst Pim Fortuyn] and the liberal VVD [Volkspartij voor Vrijheid en Democratic]) in Holland to ban the fundamentalist party Hizb-ut-Tahrir (HUT), claiming that it is a threat to the Dutch legal system. Germany banned that party after judges ruled that it is anti-Semitic and against the German constitution. HUT wanted to hold its congress in a football stadium but was prevented from doing so. In Holland too there is a request to ban Islamic extremist parties. In 2004, the Swiss government, usually reticent about discussing the issue, organized a forum on anti-

Semitism; Italy organized one as well, and the President of the Senate, Marcello Pero, invited Sharansky to address the Senate on the subject.

I cite these episodes to show that the phenomenon of anti-Semitism has been admitted, and we find a trace of real conscience not so much in the meetings themselves as in the admission that "the criticism of the state of Israel is connected with anti-Semitism" (Romano Prodi, then head of the European Commission);[1] or in the solidarity visits to Israel of Silvio Berlusconi and Gianfranco Fini—the Italian prime minister and the then deputy prime minister—or in the visit of President Moshe Katzav of Israel to President Jacques Chirac.

The acute and aggressive anti-Semitism among Europeans, connected to the state of Israel, has been an outcome of the global idea of integration: The West has sought to demonstrate that the world is smaller and more united, more economically integrated, more able to overcome differences. The Internet and McDonald's have become symbols of a great hope that, in Europe, has included the millions of Muslims who now live and work there. Subsequently, the rising fear of Islam came almost simultaneously with the search for an unified soul for Europe, and this new situation brought both great hopes and great delusions: A new rift emerged in the world, a rift that was not previously there. It appeared clearly that the idea of a religiously plural but united humanity is just a Western heritage, not necessarily the heritage of other cultures. Many Muslims have seen the idea of unifying ways of life and cultures as a sign of imperial hegemony. For many, their experience in the Western countries has simply fed their disgust and contempt.

Many Muslim immigrants have found new symbols for a struggle against an oppressing civilization. Homosexuality, sexuality, feminism, human rights, civil rights, the relation of law to religion—all have become obstacles to making the global dream come true. I think that today, once admitted, anti-Semitism too has become—or has the possibility of becoming—one of the conceptual differences associated with the rift. In a first phase, the West, and particularly Europe, has participated in the defamation of Israel and in an atrocious anti-Americanism and anti-Semitism that emanated from the mosques of Italy, England, and France. By calling such sentiments "criticism of the State of Israel," Europeans have channeled them into pro-Palestinian attitudes. European history has a tradition here of its own: A European Cold War vision became dominant in 1967, when Charles de Gaulle left Israel defenseless at a time when no one predicted that it would emerge successful from the Six-Day War. In 1973, U.S. aircraft bringing aid to Israel during the Yom Kippur War were refused permission to fly through European skies. This behavior heralded an era of pure cynicism in which Israel was viewed as culpable for every political hardship it endured. In the name of a cynical foreign policy of appeasement with the Soviet Union and its hidden anti-Americanism, Europe for a long time resorted to accusing Israel of monumental sins. Europe abandoned the Jews, distorted the truth, and helped Yasir Arafat even when it was clear that he was playing a big part in the choice to pursue a terrorist strategy and that his leadership was obstructing any peace initiative.

Then came the Islamist war against the West, and European anti-Israel positions became even stronger. Europe is ready to see Israel defeated, reduced, and dominated but not to admit that its attitude has to do with the fact that Israel is a Jewish state.

Europe has always been ready to be anti-Semitic and anti-American but not to admit it. Admitted anti-Semitism is a luxury that no political movement, regardless how cynical, can afford. Since the Holocaust, it creates a basic embarrassment, a delegitimization; it is not part of any dignified culture, not the grounds for a credible leadership. Even in France, it is not respectable; it does not respect the principle of *egalité et fraternité* and soils the memory of the Holocaust. A real anti-Semite, someone who thinks and says or implies in anti-Israeli discourse that the Jews are blood and power thirsty by their nature and that they must disappear—something found in Arab propaganda every day—loses European credibility; a person cannot be elected on an anti-Semitic platform, or even invited to dinner. When the war against terrorism came, the stench reached Europe's nose and the marriage between sympathy for terror and anti-Semitism became apparent in the inventions related to the role of the Mossad in the slaughter of 9/11.

What is clear now is that the generally recognized culture of globalization and the movements that pretend to interpret its spirit, the spirit of human rights, must all be changed. We must change the common sense of our time. What must be avoided is the possibility that Europe will try once again to build its virtue on the past, avoiding the present. It must become impossible for Europe to remove the figure of the Jew from Europe's responsibility toward Israel. The damage that Europe has done is enormous; the healing must be proportional. This can be achieved only through the revision of the politics of human rights and a commitment to the fight against terrorism. There are no shortcuts. The way to defeat anti-Semitsm in Europe is by deepening the contradiction of the globalized open society. This means accepting the ideas that much of the demonization of Israel is a cause for incitement, violence, and finally terrorism; that the memory of the Holocaust in itself has failed to teach the horror of anti-Semitism; that the grief for a dead Jew does not at all imply a wish to save those still alive; that the erroneous identification of victims and the undervaluation of hate and religious incitement to violence is a certain recipe for cultural misunderstanding. Anti-Semitism is a symptom of a flawed international politics, undervaluation of the terrorist attack on the West, the mindless wish for a position counter to that of the United States, and a misunderstanding of the meaning of global friendship and welcoming of the other.

# 6

# Anti-Semitism and the English Intelligentsia

*Anthony Julius*

## English Anti-Semitisms

English anti-Semitism is not quite understood. In certain respects, it is *mis*understood. Its complexity and its strength tend to be underestimated; its history tends to be disregarded; its literature is misinterpreted (or worse, *under*interpreted). English anti-Semitism was at one time both lethal and innovative; it continues to be innovative, precisely in the respects in which it is now *non*lethal. It once threatened Jewish lives; it has for some centuries past weakened Jewish morale. And it has been the principal contributor to the anti-Semitic literary canon.

There are many anti-Semitisms, and among that number there are four that are specifically English in provenance. They are

1. a radical anti-Semitism of libel, expropriation, and expulsion, that is, the anti-Semitism of medieval England, which lapsed in 1290 when there were no Jews left to torment ("radical anti-Semitism");
2. a literary anti-Semitism, a distinct discourse, continuously present in the literature, from the thirteenth century through to present times ("literary anti-Semitism");
3. a quotidian anti-Semitism of insult and partial exclusion, pervasive but superficial, that is, the everyday anti-Semitism of England from the

return of the Jews in the mid-seventeenth century through to the late twentieth century ("quotidian anti-Semitism"); and

4.  an emergent, anti-Semitic anti-Zionism, in which the Jews are taken to confirm the truth of the anti-Semitic account of them by their pursuit of the Zionist project, the establishment and support of a Jewish national home, that is, an English anti-Semitism of the early twentieth century to the present time ("anti-Semitic anti-Zionism").

These are ideal types; the reality, of course, is somewhat messier. The second, third and fourth of these anti-Semitisms are mutually shaping; all three are indebted, in one way or another, to the first anti-Semitism. Of the four, it is the second and the third, the literary and the quotidian, that are the most distinctively English and least indebted to international influences. At different but overlapping periods quotidian anti-Semitism coexisted with the immense ideological anti-Semitisms of the Continent (the Enlightenment and counter-Enlightenment anti-Semitisms of France, the theological and racial anti-Semitisms of Germany, the imperial and revolutionary anti-Semitisms of Russia). Radical anti-Semitism, by contrast, was an aggravated, advanced version of what was happening everywhere else in medieval Europe.

There are two versions, or "sides," of most anti-Semitisms: an unreflective or "popular" version and an "intellectual" version. The popular version is an aspect of the common sense of the generality of the population, a miscellany of fears and suspicions regarding Jews, expressed by reference to "what everyone knows about the Jews." It is thus incapable of being defended, but it is also invulnerable to attack, and it translates into a principle of violent, oppressive action only in times of social dislocation or at the direction of the state. It is not specific to any class in society. The intellectual version represents a set of adverse, hostile positions taken in relation to the Jews, positions capable of being articulated as propositions and therefore preparatory to policy or the justification of policy. Most intellectual versions both have a relation to their corresponding popular version and are also parasitic upon and deformations of more-general philosophical or political positions. Intellectuals who are also anti-Semites may adhere to either an intellectual or a popular version of their anti-Semitism. However, to the extent that there is an intellectual version of any particular anti-Semitism, it will only be found among intellectuals.

The relation between the two versions of any anti-Semitism is rarely an easy one, and the versions are rarely of equal strength. The popular version of radical anti-Semitism was derived from an amalgam of folk superstition, sermon theology, and the narratives of drama and ballad, and it coexisted with the opportunistic exploitation of the Jews by England's governing class. The intellectual version was at variance with the popular version, deprecating aspects of folk superstition and government policy while also providing the theoretical justification for the oppression of the Jews by reference to theological and juridical categories.[1] By contrast, literary anti-Semitism is almost entirely an affair of the intelligentsia; to the extent that there is a popular version, it is to be analyzed by reference to the reception history of individual literary works. Quotidian anti-Semitism reverses the balance. The popular version is much the stronger of the two. There is very little intellectual quotidian anti-Semitism. To the extent that members of the intelligentsia betray quotidian anti-Semitic attitudes, these attitudes are typically indistinguishable from those held by ordinary people. Anti-Semitic anti-Zionism is different again. Here, the intellectual version is in the ascendant. Although there is only modest general interest in the Israeli/Palestinian conflict (and even less general understanding of its history), the conflict is of obsessive concern to certain elements of the intelligentsia. The intellectual version of anti-Semitic anti-Zionism that those elements have generated, consists of positions on Israel that are specific to them and lack broader resonance. Popular anti-Semitic anti-Zionism is very weak.

The first English anti-Semitism encompassed dispossession, expropriation, and murder. Moreover, it established the precedents of blood libel and expulsion. The charge that Jews preyed on the bodies and blood of Gentile children was first made following a young man's accidental death in Norwich. England was the first European state to expel its Jews. Medieval English anti-Semitism was thus as original as it was violent. A predatory state, an intermittently but lethally violent populace, and an antagonistic Church combined to make Jewish lives always difficult, often intolerable, and finally impossible. What England initiated, other European nations imitated; what the Church initiated, England extended. This was a persecuting society. There were massacres, forced conversions, and a zealotry in enforcing discriminatory Church laws against the Jews unmatched in the rest of Europe. A war was being waged against the Jews, one that began in 1144 (the Norwich death) and ended just less than 150 years later, when not a Jew was left in England (the Expulsion). This first English anti-Semitism then migrated into the English literary imagination, where it mutated.

Though the Jews were ejected from England, the memory of them remained; that memory was refracted by a murderous, legend-laden, but most of all triumphant anti-Semitism. Over time, the memory took durable, material form in works of literature. Absent from England itself, Jews became a constant in the English cultural imagination. They figured and to a much diminished extent still figure in England's oral literature of ballad and song, in its quotidian drama and fiction and poetry, and last, in some major works in its literary canon. This literature is indebted to but also constrained by that early medieval Jew-hatred. It is marked by England's decisive defeat of the Jewish enemy. It also influences and is influenced by the more recent quotidian anti-Semitism and the even more recent anti-Semitic anti-Zionism.

Of what do most anti-Semitisms consist? One can make a list: execrations, apocalyptic ravings, pamphlets and treatises, exclusionary and discriminatory statutes and decrees, and all manner of instruments of persecution and oppression. But the products of English literary anti-Semitism, by contrast, are national assets. These anti-Semitic literary works explore themes in which Jews, Jewish history, and Judaism are negatively characterized. The master theme, or trope, supposes a well-intentioned Christian placed in peril by a sinister Jew. The Christian is usually a boy, but not always; sometimes he escapes death, but not always; if he escapes, it is by a miracle, and if he dies, the fact of the crime and the location of his body are revealed by a miracle; the Jew is usually apprehended and punished. This theme is recognizably a literary development of the blood libel. It is the story told by the first work of literary anti-Semitism, the ballad "Sir Hugh, or The Jew's Daughter" (late thirteenth century?),[2] and it is the theme of the three canonic works of literary anti-Semitism, Geoffrey Chaucer's "Prioress's Tale" (one of the *Canterbury Tales*), William Shakespeare's *Merchant of Venice*, and Charles Dickens's *Oliver Twist*.

English quotidian anti-Semitism has ensured its continuity by its contained, temperate nature. It accompanied the enlargement of collective Jewish civil liberties; it did not impede Jewish entrepreneurial accomplishment. It is underdescribed as "everyday" or "social" anti-Semitism. Its existence has not inhibited Jews from celebrating England as a place of opportunity and freedom. It is an anti-Semitism that remains surprised by Jews—by their return after a four-hundred-year absence, by their piety, by their cohesiveness, and by their commercial and intellectual achievements, all of which are overestimated (ludicrously so, in certain instances). It is thus often mixed with a certain wary admiration. In its most developed form, it wonders whether Jews can ever be wholehearted members of the English nation, given their membership in a Jewish nation. It is capable of accusing Jews of entertaining "dual loyalties." It is informed—as are most anti-Semitisms—by a measure of historic Christian perplexity and hurt (how *could* Jews reject Jesus's divinity?). But these suspicions and this perplexity and hurt have never put in jeopardy Jews' civil rights or their communal security. Quotidian anti-Semitism meets literary anti-Semitism in this formula: This is how Jews are to be treated, but this is how Jews are to be represented. It is a distinctive yoking of extremes: Deal with them like *this*, but characterize them like *that*. The blood libel, for example, has practically never figured in nonliterary, public discourse about the Jews.[3]

Last, there is English anti-Semitic anti-Zionism, which largely replicates an anti-Zionism typically European in character. (Not *every* anti-Zionism is anti-Semitic, even in present times.) This is the most recent kind of English anti-Semitism. It denies the Jews rights that it upholds for other, comparable peoples. It adheres to the principle of national self-determination, except in the Jews' case. It affirms international law, except in Israel's case. It is indifferent to Jewish suffering while being sensitive to the suffering of non-Jews. It denies the existence of Islamic anti-Semitism, other than as an import from the West. It overstates, on every occasion, any case that could be made against Israel's actions or policies, and *wildly* overstates the significance of the Israeli/ Palestinian conflict in the context of world affairs in general. It is an anti-Zionism that deploys anti-Semitic tropes, even the trope of ritual murder. It is hostile to the United States, which it believes is dominated by Jews and thus acts at their bidding. In its specifically English version, it is burdened by multiple imperial guilts: the Balfour Declaration, the Mandate, Suez.

Anti-Semitic anti-Zionism, both in its English and many non-English versions, puts the Jews at the center of world affairs (but not, so to speak, in a good way). Jews are toxic, and they need to be combated. Of course, not *all* Jews. But the Jews who are our enemies are enemies by virtue of their Jewish identity. It is Jewish interests that they promote. Jews who oppose them put other interests before their own tribal ones. Those Jews are to be applauded because they reject their Jewishness or speak up for an alternative "Jewishness" that is denuded of any specifically Jewish characteristics. Anti-Zionism has become a cause for English intellectuals, whereas quotidian anti-Semitism never was. They must explain, they must protest, they must lead.

These, then, are England's gifts to Jew-hatred. The anti-Semitism of no other country has this complexity of history. Other national anti-Semitisms are thinner—though rarely less deadly—affairs. They lack the cultural substance of English anti-Semitisms; they are more dependent on Christian precedent; they have not contributed to high culture. English anti-Semitisms are exemplary, whereas the anti-Semitisms of other nations are but variants of them. These English anti-Semitisms are among the trials of the Diaspora.

It follows that anti-Semitism subsists in contemporary England in a state of some complexity. (But it has no more than a meager existence—it is not *rampant*). Medieval anti-Semitism is barely remembered, though some fringe, neofascist groups insist that the 1290 expulsion remains in force. English literary anti-Semitism persists, not least because of the popularity of *The Merchant of Venice* and *Oliver Twist* but also because it continues to provide themes for writers hostile to Jews or to Jewish projects. Though quotidian anti-Semitism had appeared to be waning, in recent decades it has been supplemented by an anti-Semitic anti-Zionism that English Jews find truly frightening. Contemporary English anti-Semitism is thus a mix of three distinct kinds of anti-Semitism. It is in the combination of these anti-Semitisms that such anti-Semitism as one finds among English intellectuals—and there are no career anti-Semites among them—has to be understood.

## Quotidian Anti-Semitism

The study of anti-Semitism tends to gravitate toward extreme situations, when it is at its starkest and most murderous. Other anti-Semitisms are then interpreted by reference to this limiting case, which is by implication taken to disclose anti-Semitism in its essence. Yet it is not true to say that the anti-Semite is always "a murderer in his heart." It would be positively misleading to say this of the English anti-Semite. There have been no anti-Semitic atrocities in England since the Jews returned. They have not been terrorized. They have not had to "sit on packed suitcases," ready to flee at a moment's notice. We need a theory of anti-Semitism in *non*extreme situations, a theory of nonlethal, or "minor," anti-Semitism. The quotidian English anti-Semitism of the last 350 years or so is exemplary of this minor anti-Semitism.

It is an anti-Semitism of condescension and exclusion. However hostile the English perspective on the Jews may be, it is unintimidated. It does not mire itself in obsessiveness about Jews. The English anti-Semite believes that he has taken the measure of the Jew, and is unafraid. Jews can be faced down; they are not an ungovernable threat. Their disagreeable qualities can be noticed and then dismissed. The Jew has thus never been "the enemy within" (or so rarely and among groups so marginal to the polity as to be unrepresentative of any *national* quality). The consciousness of Jews has never been experienced as a burden to the English. Anti-Semitism has been a prejudice, not a preoccupation.[4] This is true, in the main, of all English anti-Semitisms. English anti-Semitism has rarely reached the intensity of a deliberate, persistent, active animus. "To be an anti-Semite," wrote the Nazi anti-Semite Robert Ley just before he killed himself in Allied captivity, "is to occupy oneself with the Jewish question."[5] More precisely: to be occupied by it. There have been few anti-Semites of this kind in England. There is little reason to suppose that this will change.

Quotidian anti-Semitism is often ambiguous in its expression, and when named as anti-Semitic, it may be defended as being humorous or ironic in intention. It is not Jew-hatred that one must write of here, but Jew-distrust. Even that may go too far. Perhaps it is Jew-wariness, accompanied by a certain disdain for Jews. Write it up as a history, and one records snubs and insults, deceit and self-deception. Jews will be insulted, and the insult misrepresented as a joke or even as an irony at anti-Semitism's own expense. Jews will be excluded, and the exclusion denied. It is an anti-Semitism that shrinks from being named anti-Semitic. The English anti-Semite—and here, of course, I do not refer to the pre-1290 kind—tends to regard anti-Semitism as vulgar and extravagant. It is taken to be characteristic of a certain kind of Continental sensibility—excitable, immoderate, ideological.

It is one thing to maintain one's distance from Jews, deprecating the pushier or ostentatious among them, ensuring that they keep to their place (and being ready to remind them of it, should they appear to forget). It is quite another to polemicize against them, legislate away their civil rights, confine them in ghettoes, and cause their women and children to suffer. This would be to act in a manner that every decent person must deplore. During periods when this latter, more dangerous, anti-Semitism is active, anti-Semites of the former (let us say, English) kind will often do what they can to help Jews, if only to demonstrate to themselves the utter distinctness of their own animus—but that is perhaps to be uncharitable. English anti-Semites deplore anti-Semitism. When they practice their anti-Semitism, they tend to do so half-persuaded, half-believing, that it is indeed not their intention (say) to exclude or restrict Jews but only some kinds of Jews, or not Jews at all, save for those who by mischance happen to qualify on grounds other than their religion. Jews who see through this (and most do) are insulted, both by the policy and by the amateur, easy self-deception that accompanies it.

This anti-Semitism, so minor as to be invisible much of the time, is also powerful enough to influence the very formation of an Anglo-Jewish identity. Its understanding of "the Jew" has contributed to Jewish self-understanding. It is a horizon of aspiration for Jews. And so each Jew strives to earn the reputation enjoyed by all Jews. They are taken to be clever, resourceful, commercially astute. But it is also an adverse judgment on Jews, more unambiguously hostile but easily internalized. They are taken to be uncultured, money-minded, incapable of altruism, unpatriotic, "low." And this is a judgment from which each Jew strives to prove himself exempt. The English Jew is what he is in part because of English anti-Semitism.

## Is There an Intellectual Version of Quotidian Anti-Semitism?

Quotidian anti-Semitism, which can be defeated by a private word (provided that it is the right word, spoken by the right person), thus tends to be limited in its articulation. It has rarely been given theoretical elaboration. In its verbal expression, one might say that it is the anti-Semitism of the remark rather than of the treatise. A "remark" wounds, it is adverse, it is ephemeral. It implies a perspective on Jews, for sure, but it is not preparatory to any extended, pretentious exposition of the perspective. It completes itself in a spasm of malice. The quotidian anti-Semitism among the English intelligentsia has for some time been an anti-Semitism of the "remark."

Take these examples, two among countless others:

Thomas Carlyle (1795–1881), the Victorian sage and man of letters, infuriated by a Bill to remove Jewish disabilities (that is, to allow Jews to be elected to Parliament), wrote to his friend Richard Monckton Milnes: "How can a real Jew, by possibility, try to be a senator, or even Citizen of any country, except his own wretched Palestine, whither all his steps and efforts tend?" Carlyle would later execrate Benjamin Disraeli as "a cursed old Jew not worth his weight in bacon."[6] Carlyle's dealings with the Jews were characterized by a kind of malicious, grim frivolity. His biographer, J.A. Froude, records him once remarking, as he stood outside the Rothschilds' Hyde Park Corner mansion:

> I do not mean that I want King John back again, but if you ask me which mode of treating these people to have been the nearest to the will of the Almighty about them—to build them palaces like that, or to take the pincers for them, I declare for the pincers.[7]

In *Sartor Resartus*, the most fantastical of Carlyle's works, with its cod-exposition of the "clothes philosophy" of the imaginary Dr. Teufelsdröckh, he has fun mocking the "cabalistico-sartorial" fancies of Talmudists concerning "Paradise and fig-leaves" and the "Old-Clothes Jewry" of Monmouth Street.[8]

English culture made available many insults to direct at Jews. These insults were often merely offensive, almost contentless, perhaps given point by some allusion to a Jewish religious practice (frequently circumcision) or religious prohibition (say, against the eating of pork). On occasion, they touched on an established theme of quotidian anti-Semitism, the questioning of whether Jews could be adequately loyal both to their own people and to their adopted nation. But these insults rarely went further than the expostulative, and the actual parliamentary debates on Jewish civil rights were themselves civil. The major debate on the issue, which occurred on December 16–17, 1847, was "long, intense, often learned, and on the whole unacrimonious." Furthermore, "this single, never to be repeated, full-scale public debate . . . differed from its analogues on the continent in . . . that it was almost entirely devoid of anti-Jewish animus."⁹ The English—even the intellectuals among them—tended to honor a tacit distinction between a public and a private discourse on the matter of the Jews. The former was restrained, moderate, "balanced." The latter was looser, mocking, disparaging.

And here is the philosopher Bertrand Russell, writing from jail to his one-time lover Ottoline Morrell, on August 18, 1918: "I hate being all tidy like a book in a library where no one reads—Prison is horribly like that—Imagine if you knew you were a delicious book, and some Jew millionaire bought you and bound you uniform with a lot of others and stuck you up in a shelf behind glass, where you merely illustrated the completeness of his System—and no anarchist was allowed to read you—That is what one feels like."¹⁰

There was a recognizable type, then, the "Jew millionaire." He was like other millionaires, except (so to speak) *more so*. He was the millionaire type uncomplicated by culture or religious sentiment. He was vulgar and philistine and acquisitive, and quite the wrong owner of precious, valuable things like books. He was also the kind of person who was a good butt for jokes. And so the use of such language—the making of such jokes—is compatible with deprecating the anti-Semitism of others, intervening to protest at discriminatory treatment of Jews, and so on. It is also compatible with maintaining very cordial relations with Jews (though perhaps not with friendships). Russell's remark is no more than a conceit. He does not suppose that either he or Ottoline will ever be the prisoner of a "Jew millionaire." The Jews do not have that kind of power, or anything like it.

Carlyle and Russell were intellectuals, and yet their anti-Semitism was utterly casual. There was, that is to say, a disjuncture between their intellectual projects and the prejudices that they expressed. The latter were hardly distinguishable from the quotidian insults and sneers circulating in the culture. They said no more than others said. Their anti-Semitism was not distinctively their own. It was not what made them Thomas Carlyle or Bertrand Russell. (In England, among the available kinds of anti-Semitism, it is only the literary kind that provides opportunities for creative projects—and it not surprising, therefore, that the *strongest* English anti-Semitism, since the Middle Ages, has been the literary one).[11] Carlyle's gibes were on occasion a good deal more splenetic than Russell's ever were, but as expressions of hostility they came to the same thing: contempt for Jews, or certain kinds of Jews. The remarks were ugly, sometimes worse than ugly. But they led nowhere.

There is a small history to be written both of the pamphlets and speeches against Jews composed by anti-Semitic polemicists and of the thematic anti-Semitism of over four hundred years in the works of many members of England's continuously peopled class of public moralists or intellectuals. There were those writers, that is to say, who addressed, in a hostile spirit, a specific issue concerning Jews, usually of an immediate, pressing political character (or what they believed to be pressing), and there were those other writers whose antagonistic stance toward the Jews was integral to their broader concerns and led them to something more than just the making of disobliging, frivolously anti-Semitic observations in the course of writing on other topics.

Among the polemicists of specific occasions, there was, for example, William Prynne (1600–1669), chief among the pamphleteer-adversaries of the Jews. His *Short Demurrer* (1655–56), which urged opposition to Jewish readmission to England, is a masterwork of sustained anti-Semitic invective, the first work of its kind in the literature of European anti-Semitism. Prynne was not, however, a career anti-Semite. Though it is said that he maintained his hatred of the Jews until the end of his life, he wrote nothing more about them.[12] Other, later Prynne emerged to challenge the Jews at moments of particular Anglo-Jewish visibility: the mid-eighteenth-century controversy over the naturalization of foreign-born Jews (the 1753 Jew Bill),[13] the mid-nineteenth-century controversy over the removal of civil disabilities, the late-nineteenth-century controversy over Jewish immigration from Eastern Europe (leading to the Aliens Act of 1905), certain moments of crisis—Jewish immigration, Arab riots—during the period of the British Mandate in Palestine, and so on. But the essential pattern was the same. A circumstance would prompt anti-Semites to make a huge fuss, pamphlets would be written, and protests would be organized. There would then be a resolution, with the anti-Semites either defeated or only notionally triumphant, and with Jewish life carrying on much as before. No anti-Semitic parties were launched; there was no legacy of publications warning future generations of the Jewish threat.

Among those writers in whose work anti-Semitism was more than merely marginal, there was William Cobbett (1762 or 1763–1835), in whose work it was *everywhere*. In his *Rural Rides* (1830), he execrates Jews at every turn: The Jews have supplanted many of the old gentry. A town is praised for not having any Jew-looking fellows with dandy coats, dirty shirts and half-heels to their shoes. To be a financier is to act the part of a Jew. The Jew-system has swept all the little gentry, the small farmers, and the domestic manufacturers away. A group on horseback appear, by their hooked noses and round eyes and by the long and sooty necks of the women, to be for the greater part Jews and Jewesses.[14] In *Paper against Gold* (1812), Cobbett elaborated a fantasy of Jewish economic vice, the "tricks and connivances carried on by the means of paper money," out of a report of the suicide of the Jewish financier Abraham Goldsmid, "the great Jew money-dealer." His suicide was prompted by the loss of part of his wealth, "a truly Jew-like motive for the commission of an act— at which human nature shudders."[15] In *Good Friday, or The Murder of Jesus Christ by the Jews* (London, 1830), the killing of Jesus is said to have been a "savage murder, committed after long premeditation, effected by hypocrisy and bribery and perjury," and so on.[16] Yet Cobbett's hatred, so persistent, so unrelenting in its articulation, was but one hatred out of a number of hatreds. "His principle is repulsion, his nature contradiction, he is made up of mere antipathies," wrote the essayist William Hazlitt, "an Ishmaelite indeed without a fellow."[17] Anti-Semitism itself never acquired in his work the status of a master principle.

And then, combining the two kinds of anti-Semitic writers (the Prynne kind and the Cobbett kind), there was Hilaire Belloc (1870–1953), who was utterly obsessed by Jews and would tell anyone who cared to listen what he thought of them. The Jewish question was a "pressing problem." He strained but failed to elevate the inconsequential Marconi affair (1912–13), a trivial enough matter of insider dealing by politicians (some of whom were Jewish), into a scandal of Dreyfus-like proportions. He failed in part precisely because the relevant institutions of the state did not mobilize against the Jewish accused. The then prime minister, H.H. Asquith, put the whole weight of the Liberal Party machine behind them.[18] Unsuccessful as a polemicist, Belloc also attempted a more discursive, more reflective, assault upon the Jews. He attempted, that is, a reasoned account of anti-Semitism and a program for the solution of the Jewish problem in *The Jews* (1922; 1937).[19] With an elaborate display of balance, a dedication to his Jewish secretary, "the best and most intimate of our Jewish friends," and chapters on causes of friction on "their" side and on "ours," he rejected both assimilation and Zionism and instead called for a "full recognition of separate nationality," a kind of apartheid *avant la lettre*.

When reviewing the work of these slightly desperate men, however, it is the limited effect of their antagonisms that is most striking. Spend enough time on any subject, of course, and one is liable to convince oneself that it amounts to something of great consequence. But in the case of anti-Semitism among the English intelligentsia, this conclusion would be mistaken. There was indeed a kind of indigenous, limited intellectual anti-Semitic discourse. Belloc, as we have seen, made an immense effort to do something with it. *The Jews*—an absurd, unread book, once reprinted but not taken up by anyone—represents the highest point of a theorized, discursive English anti-Semitism. There was nothing else that came close to it.

The only real contribution of an English intellectual to the racist-conspiracist anti-Semitism that emerged on the Continent toward the end of the nineteenth century was made by Houston Stewart Chamberlain (1855–1927), but he could not make that contribution in England. His *Foundations of the Nineteenth Century* (1899), one of the principal texts of German racism,[20] was written in German and published in Munich. Chamberlain hated England, not least because it had "studied politics with a Jew for a quarter century" (that is, Disraeli) and because Jewish financial interests prevailed there.[21] This sense that England was not receptive to anything other than a casual, dismissive disregard for Jews was a cause for exasperation among the few anti-Semitic intellectuals that England possessed. In *The Jews*, for example, Belloc acknowledged that the "English reader" might find what he had to say in his own work "fantastic," but he insisted that were his book to be "put into the hands of a jury chosen from the various nationalities of Europe and the United States it would be found too moderate in its estimate of the peril it postulated."[22] Curiously enough, then, Chamberlain's own work found a receptive audience among the English intelligentsia. George Bernard Shaw, for example, praised the English edition in the left-wing *Fabian News*, though he deprecated the extravagance of its anti-Semitism. There is no battle between the Teuton and Chaos, Shaw argued, and the enemy is not the Jew but the British greengrocer, with his "short round skull," his militarism, and his mediocrity.

There were few efforts (and those were paltry) after Belloc's own to give in England some theoretical expression to what was then described as the "Jewish problem." The attempts to do so stopped altogether in the 1930s. And after World War II, what might be termed discursive anti-Semitism bifurcated, becoming (on the one hand) especially trivial and inconsequential among mainstream intellectuals and (on the other hand) the hobbyhorse of fringe political activists, usually of a fascist or neofascist tendency.

It was not all plain sailing for Anglo-Jewry. Across the decades that followed emancipation (the 1858 act permitting Jews to sit in Parliament, the 1871 act permitting Jews to occupy high offices), English Jews were the repeated target of discursive assaults, principally directed at proxies: Disraeli, Russian-Jewish immigrants, South African Randlords, Liberal politicians and plutocrats, Bolsheviks, Zionists.[23] These were agitations principally about Britain's foreign or imperial policy or about the influence of foreign affairs on Britain. Why, it was demanded, was Disraeli siding with the Turks against Christian Russia? Why, twenty or so years later, was the British government fighting a war of gold against the Boers on behalf of Jewish magnates? What was the precise nature of the threat posed by the Russian Revolution, in which Jews appeared to have played the leading part? Why was Britain committing resources to the establishment of a Jewish home in Palestine? Why was Britain picking a fight with Hitler on behalf of the Jews? Why were Zionists attacking and killing British soldiers in Palestine?[24] Answers were available to all these questions; framed in anti-Semitic terms, they of course generated anti-Semitic responses.

These responses were very rarely given any elaborated, theoretical expression. The historians Goldwin Smith and E.A. Freeman attempted something of the kind in relation to the Eastern Question;[25] the economist J.A. Hobson likewise, in relation to the Boer War.[26] Belloc tried hard to make the case for the Jewish nature of Bolshevism. Fascist sympathizers tried very hard indeed to represent opposition to Hitler as nothing more than a "Jewish quarrel."[27] For a time, during the crises associated with these events, what these people had to say reflected broader opinion and thus had a certain currency.[28] But none one of them, not Smith or Freeman, not Hobson or Belloc, had the impact, of Edouard Drumont or Wilhelm Marr, Maurice Barrès or Eugen Düring (to name four Continental intellectual anti-Semites, among many others who could be named). Ideological anti-Semitisms make no real headway in England.[29] It was as if English anti-Semitism simply could not ascend to those levels of discursive generality at which (say) the French and German anti-Semites were accustomed to pitch their writing. It was also as if English anti-Semitism could not develop beyond a diffuse sentiment of mistrust and disregard into a political challenge to Jewish security. Ostensible Jewish foul play excited some English intellectuals to an almost unbearable degree,[30] but they were unable to communicate their excitement to any audience very much greater than a coterie of the already persuaded. English anti-Semitism could neither philosophize nor mobilize.

The medieval historian R.I. Moore, in his important and original work *The*

*Formation of a Persecuting Society* (1987), argued that the development of persecution in all its forms in the Middle Ages was a part of the tremendous extension of the power and influence of the literate and was therefore inseparable from their great and positive achievements.[31] Moore considers this to be as true of England as of anywhere else in Europe. But when this "persecuting society" returned, as it did in the late nineteenth century, and once again was led by intellectuals, England, and in particular its "literate," did not enroll. It is time to ask why this was so.

## Why Was England So Resistant to the Ideological Anti-Semitisms of the Continent, and Failed to Develop Even a Distinct, Intellectual Version of Quotidian Anti-Semitism?

Among a number of reasons that could be listed for this double achievement (something to celebrate—for a Jew to hold a British passport at pretty much any time in the twentieth century was an immeasurable piece of good luck), let me identify these few:

First, and most self-evidently, there was Britain's unmistakable commercial and imperial self-confidence. To the extent that its intellectuals deplored the rule of the "cash nexus," the "profit-and-loss philosophy," and so on, none of this could, even remotely be attributed to the influence of the Jews. It was too intimately a creation of England itself (I write indifferently of "Britain" and "England" because for the purposes of this essay, the distinction is not germane). What is more, across the nineteenth century and until the calamities of World War I and the triumph of the Bolsheviks in 1917, Britain and the world order for which it stood were just too successful, were just doing too well, to prompt the questions that the then dominant version of anti-Semitism was purporting to answer. The national reverses were too quickly remedied, the economic slumps were too limited in duration and, most of all, were too readily intelligible by reference to more proximate causes, to provide the conditions for the emergence of the modern, most pretentious version of anti-Semitism, the one summed up by the slogan "The Jews are our misfortune." Even the crises of the interwar years failed to precipitate any lurch to the anti-Semitic, extra-parliamentary Right.[32] Prosperity, a commanding position in the world, the dignity and might of being the preeminent imperial power, unequaled in human history—why should the Jews be feared?

It was only in the aftermath of World War II that the British, exhausted and in debt, were drawn to the contemplation of national decline. But it was at a moment that followed such disaster for the Jews that to entertain the thought that in some sense they might have had a hand in this loss of mastery was beyond even the absurdities tolerated by anti-Semitism. This was the moment in European history, more than any other moment, that illuminated the utter defenselessness, the impotence, of the Jews. The moment passed, of course, and the generality of self-deceiving anti-Semites thereupon recovered their faith in Jewish power.

For most of the modern period (say, until the mid-twentieth century), not only were the English in control of their own lives, but they were also in control of the lives of millions of other people. If as a general, minimum proposition, it is true to say of conspiracy theories that they appeal to people who believe that they are not in control of their own lives *but that someone else is*, it is easy to see how slight an appeal such theories would have in a strong, self-confident imperial culture. The question in England toward the end of the nineteenth century and then continuing into the first half of the twentieth century was not "Who is ruling us?", but rather, "For how long can we continue to rule others?"

By contrast, the conspiracist anti-Semitism, new to the nineteenth century, offered an answer to precisely that first question. This anti-Semitism, which has never yet taken hold in England, offered explanations for two puzzles: the puzzle of modernity and the puzzle of suffering. The Jews were behind it; the Jews were at fault. "I know," the anti-Semite Marr confided in his "Testament," "the *Jewish Question* is the axis around which the wheel of world history revolves."[33] The Jews, generally, were "responsible." The fabrication in which the Jews were supposed to have owned up to this responsibility, the *Protocols of the Elders of Zion*—a work that continues to thrill anti-Semites, as gullible as they are malicious—has never enjoyed more than a half-life in England. It was in the *London Times* that its utter bogusness was first exposed. Having speculated in May 1920 about the genuineness of the *Protocols* ("Are they a forgery? If so, whence comes the uncanny note of prophecy?"), in August 1921 the newspaper recanted its initial gullibility by publishing an authoritative account of the work's multiple literary origins.[34]

Second, there were very strong philo-Semitic and (equally strong, and equally important) pseudo-philo-Semitic traditions in England.[35]

The strands must be separated out. There was, of course, the whole dissenting, Protestant ferment of the seventeenth century, with its "Judaizing" tendencies and its millenarian expectations.[36] There was the academic study of Judaism, as much a staple of Tudor humanism as of nineteenth- and early twentieth-century university scholarship. (The defense of the Pharisees in the work of Travers Herford was particularly important). There was the writing of Jewish history: see, for example, the sympathetic, thorough account given by H.H. Milman in his *History of the Jews*.[37] There was the study of Christian anti-Semitism, transformed, if not altogether initiated by, the Rev. James Parkes in the first half of the twentieth century. There was early, committed support for the "restoration of Zion," the Jewish project in Palestine. There was also a pervasive, popular admiration for certain values regarded as specifically Jewish, including sobriety, enterprise, family loyalty, and philanthropy, and a notion that the Jews had suffered deeply and unfairly for their faith.

English pseudo-philo-Semitism is also important and is also made up of several strands. There is the principle of religious tolerance, emerging across the most troubled decades of the seventeenth century, which gathered up Jews among others in its embrace. There is the ready understanding of the commercial value of a policy of tolerance, a feature of the seventeenth and eighteenth centuries. There is the general indifference of the British state toward Jews. There was a kind of pity, a public compassion, displayed at the spectacle of Jewish suffering, especially in the late nineteenth century. Of course, none of this is quite enough. The development of an ideology of tolerance allows Jews to live undisturbed, but it does not welcome them into those private spaces in which members of a society lead their lives. Commercial self-interest will always be conditional. The indifference of the state toward Jews does not secure for them those recognitions that corporate Jewish existence requires. The tug of feeling for the unfortunate, the disadvantaged, is estimable, but there is a peculiar moral inadequacy to pity. It is consistent with a great deal of casual anti-Semitism—more specifically, consistent with a version of anti-Semitism that accents contempt for Jews—and it is of course humiliating to find oneself the object of pity.

Third, the English perspective on the two discursive tropes, or binarisms, through which anti-Semitism in modern times was articulated—that is to say, the Hebraic versus the Hellenic, and the Jewish versus the Aryan—was not the one-sided affair that it was on the Continent (to simplify somewhat). The critic and poet Matthew Arnold is the key figure in the articulation of the first binarism; Disraeli and Robert Knox are the key figures in relation to the second binarism. That is to say, the contribution to the Hebraic/Hellenic agon was made without any deprecation of the Jews, and the principal English contributions to the pseudoscience of Jewish racial identity were made (in one case) by a man who was convinced that the Jews would shortly become extinct and (in the other case) by a Jew who celebrated occult Jewish power.

There was, then, space enough for an anti-Semitism of the intelligentsia, but little enough space for an intellectual (which is always a pseudo-intellectual) anti-Semitism. English intellectuals were no more resistant to the casual Jew-scorn of the ambient culture. But to take that scorn and (so to speak) do something with it, to treat it as the raw material for the creation of something ambitious and reflective, something with explanatory value (however fantastical it might be)—that was altogether a different matter.

Jew-hatred represents a kind of temptation for the intellectual, an invitation to accept its nonsenses and *then* that terrible burden of thought, thought without end, investigation without conclusion, can be lifted, and the intellectual will have certainty. The anti-Semitism of the intellectual anti-Semite is expressly ideological. That is to say it is (1) pseudo-diagnostic (Jews are the problem); (2) programmatic (this is what needs to be done about the Jews); (3) articulated in self-conscious performance of the intellectual's role; (4) adversarial to the position of other intellectuals, but also connected with broader anti-Semitic movements; (5) typically expressed by reference to national considerations, that is to say, an aspect of the conceptualizing of the nation (in each case, the nation with which the intellectual identifies himself). Save for this last aspect, none of this describes the anti-Semitism of any but the most renegade, the most atypical, English intellectual. English intellectual anti-Semitism was a damp squib—or more precisely, a series of squibs. It was limited, save when stimulated by literary anti-Semitism, to the reproduction of quotidian anti-Semitism in its own register.

## The Contemporary Scene

How is one to characterize the contemporary engagement of the English intelligentsia with anti-Semitism? Perhaps as follows: not so much as an embracing of anti-Semitism as an indifference to it, that is, a willingness to take up positions without regard to their anti-Semitic resonance; a patchy knowledge of Jews, of Jewish history, of Judaism; a powerful resentment at any charge of anti-Semitism; more than anything else, an hostility to Israel and to the Zionist project. This is an engagement, then, that is never complete, always compromised. Consider the following instances.

A.N. Wilson

A.N. Wilson (b. 1950) is a biographer, historian, novelist, and newspaper columnist. He is also an artist of the "remark." He has been making remarks about Jews, about Israel, about Judaism, and about anti-Semitism for some time. He is himself a kind of protracted scandal, a performance artist of the scandalous, in relation to Jews.

His remarks about Israel are hostile, almost uniformly so. In 1984, writing about Hilaire Belloc's anti-Zionism, Wilson confided to his readers: "One never reads a newspaper account of that little strip of land which Belloc called *The Battleground* without being reminded of his audience with Benedict XV, and the Pope's murmured words, *'C'est une honte, c'est une honte.'"*[38] More recently, in a newspaper article, "The Tragic Reality of Israel," he wrote:

> The logic of supporting the Palestinians is to question the very right of Israel to exist. It is to that bitterly sad conclusion that the policy of Ariel Sharon has driven so many of us. Of course, we do not want the Israelis to be "driven into the sea" (as in the ominous phrase of 1967). But the 1948 experiment—claiming the "Israelis" had the "right" to exist as a state just because a few brave terrorists such as Menachem Begin killed some British army officers—this was lazy thinking, and it was doomed to failure. One now sees that Israel never was a state, and it can only be defended by constant war. Is that what we want?[39]

Wilson's hostility toward Israel has more recently pushed him into outlandish company. He has recommended the book *The Israeli Holocaust against the Palestinians*, written by the Holocaust-denier Michael Hoffman.[40] Hoffman's animus should have been obvious to him.[41] Wilson has also accused Israel of "poisoning [Palestinian] water supplies."[42]

By contrast, on the subject of Judaism, and especially the Judaism of the first centuries of the Common Era, Wilson is a typical, generous English philo-Semite (he has written studies of both Jesus and Paul). And yet in a recent, Easter-time newspaper article, Wilson refers to "the hate filled paranoias of Judaism and Islam."[43] Characteristic of this kind of writing is a readiness to make observations supported by no more than a combination of the writer's own authority and an appeal to "what everyone knows." So, for example: "We all know that the Jews regard themselves as a separate group within society. And yet there remains something unacceptable about Gentiles sharing the view Jews take of themselves."[44] In his biography *Milton*, Wilson identifies, among other "unattractive things about Judaism," its "cult of racial superiority."[45]

Wilson has worked hard to defend the indefensible anti-Semitism of fellow novelist, historian, and columnist Belloc. He does not care for the judgment that Belloc was an anti-Semite. He concedes that Belloc's opinions, from a post-Holocaust perspective, seem "hideously distasteful" and that his interest in Jews amounted to an obsession. But Belloc was not alone in his fondness for strong talk about Jews. Wilson insinuates that anti-Semitism is unavoidable and also understandable (though there is an ambiguity in his formulations, which slide between summary and endorsement of Belloc's opinions). Belloc "wrote in 1922 when, perhaps, the majority of his English readers would have thought it faintly embarrassing to talk of a 'Jewish problem.' Sixty years later, one's reaction cannot be the same." Wilson follows this with a reference to the Nazi persecution of the Jews:

> Perhaps [it] could not have been avoided. Belloc's was one of the few voices which dared to speak about it, and which dared to offer a solution. But that solution—the recognition of Jews as Jews, whatever their nationality—shocked the consciences of those who wished to pretend that "the Jewish problem" did not exist.

And later: "Belloc . . . prophesied what would happen to European Jewry with such eerie accuracy, as a direct consequence of liberal "double-thinking" on the subject."[46]

This is all nonsense, of course. Pernicious nonsense, really. But what does it add up to, when taken with everything else that Wilson has said and written about the Jews?

First, and particularly in his journalism, a desire to "stir things up," to run counter to a perceived consensus, and to meet the editorial pressure on every newspaper columnist to be provocative, memorable, opinionated. The columnist is required to possess a distinctive voice—the more paradoxical, contradictory, even *extreme* the voice, the better. Second, a fecklessness, one not limited to the references to Jews. The opinions he expresses about Israel, the Jews, and so on, are, one senses, thrown off. Third, a quality of the commonplace. The generous things he has to say about Judaism are received opinion among philo-Semitic biblical scholars. The hostile things he has to say are again nothing more than received opinion among anti-Semites. Not even fiction stimulates Wilson to think fresh thoughts about Jews. In his latest novel, *My Name Is Legion* (2004), his heroine is an intense, dark-haired Jewish beauty named Rachel Pearl. Wilson is not embarrassed to recycle the most tired of cultural tropes.

## Tam Dalyell

In the days prior to the launch of the second Iraq war, the English member of Parliament (M.P.) Tam Dalyell gave an interview to *Vanity Fair*. The journalist, David Margolick, wrote: "The senior member of the House of Commons, Tam Dalyell, even tells me he thinks Blair is unduly influenced by a cabal of Jewish advisers. He mentions Mandelson, Lord Levy and Jack Straw."[47]

Dalyell is a Labour M.P. and an opponent of the war in Iraq. Challenged when the interview got out, he shifted his position. To the BBC he said, "The cabal I referred to was American," and then named seven of George W. Bush's advisers, six of whom are Jewish. "It's the Jewish Institute for National Security Affairs combined with Christian fundamentalists." He also dropped Straw and Peter Mandelson from his Anglo-Jewish cabal. There is "one person about whom I am extremely concerned and I have to be blunt about it. That is Lord Levy, Mr. Blair's official representative in the Middle East." The problem had ceased to be a local cabal and instead had become a U.S. one, with Levy as a kind of overseas member of it. Prime Minister Tony Blair is "far too close to those people and Lord Levy . . . is part of this group." "They very much captured the ear of the President of the United States. I said [to *Vanity Fair*] I thought that Blair was very sympathetic to them. I cannot understand why." He anticipated the charge of anti-Semitism but rejected it. "It is an enormously sensitive issue and that's why very many of us have been extremely reticent about it, because we don't want to be seen as anti-Semitic." "I am fully aware that one is treading on cut glass on this issue and no one wants to be accused of anti-Semitism, but if it is a question of launching an assault on Syria or Iran . . . then one has to be candid."[48] However, "the idea of me being anti-Semitic is total rubbish. I have Jewish friends. I have been on holiday in Israel, and I have written endless affectionate obituaries for Jewish people."[49] And elsewhere, "I am not going to be labelled anti-Semitic. My children worked on a kibbutz. But the time has come for candour."[50] Several weeks later, after the fuss had subsided, he told the *Jewish Chronicle* that "cabal" had been "at least linguistically, a misjudgment."[51]

The Oxford English Dictionary (OED) defines a cabal as "a secret or private intrigue of a sinister character formed by a small body of persons." The word has a Jewish resonance, partly because it derives from the Hebrew term, Kabbalah, an esoteric element in Judaism, and partly because in an anti-Semitic fantasy of the mid-nineteenth century, the world was thought to be falling into the grip of "kabbalistic Jews." The OED cites and endorses Dr. Johnson's gloss on the word, "something less than a conspiracy." This gloss is relevant to Dalyell's use of the word. It was alleged that he was promoting a conspiracy theory about Jewish political influence, but what he actually said does not *quite* amount to that. What is at work here?

First, an allusion, falling slightly short of their actual deployment, to these classic anti-Semitic themes: conspiracy, the enmity of the Jew toward the Gentile, excessive Jewish influence (or influence exercised in secret), and the promoting of interests contrary to the interests both of justice and of the nation at large. ("I am worried about my country being led up the garden path on a Likudnik, Sharon agenda").[52] It is an instance of quotidian anti-Semitism in the skepticism it expresses concerning the patriotism of Blair's Jewish advisers, and it is comparable to remarks made during an earlier anti-Zionist moment in English politics, 1922 to 1924. It is Lord Levy who draws the fire now; then, it was the Jewish Sir Alfred Mond, industrialist, minister in Lloyd George's government, and friend of Chaim Weizmann. So the *Morning Post*, for example, troubled by dual loyalties, observed: "Despite the many virtues and great abilities of Sir Alfred Mond, we would like to see purely British representatives in a purely British parliament."[53]

Second, a culpable reluctance to acknowledge the offense caused, even after it has been made so clear to him that he could be in no doubt as to its genuineness or depth or breadth. Indeed, there was an irritated incomprehension at the reaction, a conviction that to speak out in the way that he did required courage, if only because it would attract smears. The implication here is that speaking out is a brave defiance of a censoring pressure from Jews and their allies. "The trouble is that anyone who dares criticise the Zionist operation," Dalyell told one newspaper, "is immediately labelled anti-Semitic."[54] And elsewhere: "Mr Dalyell said that he now expects to be victimised because he raised a 'whisper of criticism' about the influence which Jewish advisers hold on Tony Blair, the Prime Minister, and George Bush, the President of the US." This latter was a report in the *Scotsman*, where Dalyell was at his most robust: "When asked to explain his comments, Mr. Dalyell told *The Scotsman* yesterday he was not anti-Semitic but felt the need to lay out his fears that Zionist ministers may make Syria the 'next stop' after Iraq. 'A Jewish cabal have [*sic*] taken over the government of the United States and formed an unholy alliance with fundamentalist Christians,' he said."[55]

Third, remarks symptomatic of a broad, cultural amnesia about anti-Semitism. Certainly, all anti-Semitisms other than the Nazi version, with its yellow stars, its cattle-carts, its trenches, and its gas chambers, have been forgotten. But worse: The discursive aspect of Hitler's own anti-Semitism, as distinct from the technology of it, has also been forgotten. Dalyell himself, it would seem, simply does not remember that it was Hitler's own complaint that the Jews controlled the U.S. president. This does not make Dalyell Hitler, of course. It simply means that he is ready to use dangerous language without understanding its provenance.

He is not alone in this, and it would be wrong to isolate his remarks for special censure. On the cover of the January 14, 2002, issue of the leftist political journal the *New Statesman*, there is a gold Star of David above a supine Union Jack, the star's lower triangle piercing the flag like a dagger, and beneath that the question, "A kosher conspiracy?" It was said that the objections taken to the image mistook a question for a positive case. The intention was to raise an issue, not to level an accusation, so the defense went. If it is not allowed to do that, then free, open inquiry will be sacrificed to mollify an oversensitive special-interest group (such was the inference we were encouraged to draw). Yet the cover resonated with a very traditional anti-Semitic iconography and language.

"Conspiracy" talk has yet to capture the imagination of any but a fringe. It is a kind of distant music, no more, to an emergent anti-Semitic anti-Zionism, one that in England is complicated by many factors.

## Dave Brown and the "Independent"

On January 27, 2003, the *Independent*, a left-of-center national newspaper, published a cartoon by Dave Brown on its op-ed page showing Ariel Sharon, Israel's prime minister, eating a Palestinian child. Helicopter gunships, circling above newly wrecked Palestinian homes, broadcast the message "Sharon . . . Vote Sharon . . . Vote." Sharon himself, as if responding to an objection, snarls: "What's wrong . . . You never seen a politician kissing babies before?"

A complaint was made to the Press Complaints Commission (PCC) on behalf of the Israeli Embassy and Mr. Sharon himself about the cartoon. The PCC administers the voluntary system of self-regulation in the newspaper industry. I acted for the complainants. It was said that the cartoon breached Clause 13 of the PCC Code, which prohibits prejudicial or pejorative reference to a person's religion. Anti-Semitism, I argued, tainted the cartoon because it introduced the blood libel into an attack on Sharon. The intention of the cartoonist was irrelevant. One can no more suppress allusion to the blood libel in an image of a Jew consuming a Gentile child than one can suppress the echo of a voice sounding in a canyon. The cartoon was therefore a prejudicial reference to Sharon's religion. It encouraged readers to think the worse of the prime minister by identifying him not just as the author of a particular policy toward the deterrence of terror attacks but as a Jew like other Jews and thus capable of murdering children for no better reason than that to do so will appeal to his fellow Jews. (And what could be more prejudicial than to associate the Jewish leader of the Jewish state with the blood libel?) The letter of complaint pointed out that the blood libel is once again in wide circulation in the world and that it was therefore imperative that it should not be given any foothold in Britain—and certainly not in a mainstream, national newspaper.

The editor, Simon Kelner, responded to the complaint, insisting that the cartoon was only about Sharon and not about Jews in general. He said that it was "hard-hitting comment," which justified the use of an appalling and gruesome image. He also said that it was not the cartoonist's intention to allude to the blood libel. The cartoon alluded to Goya's *Saturn Devouring His Children* and only to that work. Were the PCC to uphold the complaint, it would compromise the newspaper's right to freedom of expression. In a later exchange of letters, just before the PCC met to adjudicate on the complaint, the editor added a further defense of the cartoon: The child being eaten was not Palestinian but Israeli, and represented the Israeli electorate. To this opportunistic misreading of the carton, one that was quite inconsistent with the other arguments advanced in its defense, the editor added the observation that he himself was a Jew and was therefore well-qualified to determine whether it was anti-Semitic, and in his judgment, it was not. "I am unashamed about publishing" the cartoon, he wrote to the PCC.

The PCC rejected the complaint. In its initial draft adjudication, the PCC reasoned that there was a disagreement about whether the cartoon was anti-Semitic and that thus it should not itself seek to resolve the question. In any event, it added, both editor and cartoonist denied any anti-Semitic intent. The adjudication was then redrafted to correct the impression given by the draft that the mere existence of a disagreement as to the meaning of the cartoon had led the PCC to reject the complaint. It did not, however, make any finding on the meaning of the cartoon. If the cartoon was acceptable to the editor and his colleagues on the newspaper, then it was acceptable to the PCC.

The PCC was wrong to reject the complaint, both because the form that the rejection took amounted to a failure to adjudicate and because doing so was inconsistent with its adjudications of comparable complaints.[56] A short while after the adjudication, the cartoonist was awarded a prize. The cartoon, the defense of the cartoon, the PCC adjudication, and finally the prize collectively indicate the extent to which anti-Semitism, as an available discourse about Jews, has returned to the mainstream in consequence of opposition to Israel—and the extent to which this return is a matter of general indifference.

Tom Paulin

Tom Paulin (b. 1949) is a poet and a literary critic. He teaches English literature at Oxford University. He is well known as a TV performer, and he appears on a weekly arts review program. He has been praised as that rare thing, a writer with a conscience. He has, he believes, a strong sense of history. He has a strong sense of the role of the public intellectual. He has made a number of public interventions in the Israeli/Palestinian conflict. These have exposed him to some criticism but do not appear to have harmed his career (though they did lead to the temporary withdrawal of an invitation from Harvard). His principal interventions consist of a poem and an interview. They have prompted him to make further interventions: another poem, at least one more interview, and some correspondence.

In interview he gave to the Egyptian newspaper *Al-Ahram* in April 2002, his student-interviewer reported that Paulin did "not attempt to hide his anger at what the Israelis are doing in Palestine." It is, he said, "an historical obscenity." He discourses generally on Israel. "I never believed that Israel had the right to exist at all." "You are either a Zionist or an anti-Zionist. Everyone who supports Israel is a Zionist." "In my view, the European culture carries a very heavy responsibility for the creation of Israel. . . . It is a product of both British and Stalin's anti-Semitism, but the British never faced their own complicity in its construction." Israel is "an ahistoric state." "It is a state created by the powerful nations somewhere else. It is an artificial state." And finally, the interviewer reports, "if there is one thing Paulin clearly abhors about Israel, it is the Brooklyn-born Jewish settlers." "They should be shot dead." "I think they are Nazis, racists. I feel nothing but hatred for them."[57]

Paulin's poem, "Killed in Crossfire," was published on February 18, 2001, in the *Observer*, a liberal Sunday newspaper with a substantial circulation. It is prefaced—shielded—by an epigraph from the German-Jewish diarist Victor Klemperer, in which he records his opinion that "the Zionists, who want to go back to the Jewish State of 70 AD, are just as offensive as the Nazis. With their nosing after blood, their ancient 'cultural roots,' their partly canting, partly obtuse winding back of the world, they are altogether a match for the National Socialists."[58] Paulin then writes:

> We're fed this inert
> this lying phrase
> like comfort food

as another little Palestinian boy
in trainers jeans and a white teeshirt
is gunned down by the Zionist SS
whose initials we should
—but we don't—dumb goys—
clock in the weasel word *crossfire*.

The "gunn[ing] down" of "Palestinian boy[s]" by "the Zionist SS" is deliberate and dishonestly attributed by them to "crossfire." But the middle letters of
the word, ss, exposes the lie, though "dumb goys" that "we" are, we do not realize it. The crime is exposed, by the murderers themselves but against their will,
if only we have the intelligence to see it. Yet they treat us as children, and feed
us "comfort food."

Though the poem is purportedly limited to Zionists, it implicates all Jews
by the use of the Hebrew word "goys." The word is not in Hebrew plural form;
it is not Israelis—not the Zionist SS—who would say "goys." The poem repris-
es the old anti-Semitic trope that Jews privately view Gentiles with contempt.[59]
This trope is allied with a newer one. The Jews, it is now being said, are no better than the Nazis. The Jews *are* Nazis. The poem thus diminishes the suffering of the Jews in the Holocaust and demotes them to the level of their
persecutors. Behind these two tropes, there is a third, the master one: Jews con-
spire to kill children and then conceal the evidence of their crimes.

The poem is expressly not related to any one, specific incident ("*another
little Palestinian boy*") but instead refers to a practice, perhaps even a policy.
This is what Israeli soldiers do, they kill children. They do this because they
are the Zionist version of, or no better than, the "SS," Hitler's S*chutzstaffel*, his
personal Protection Formation. The SS was set up in 1923 to be the Nazi
Party's internal police force. In April 1933, it was put in charge of Hitler's first
concentration camp for political prisoners, at Dachau. In the early years of the
war, the SS directed many of the mass killings on the Eastern Front.
Concentration camp guards formed a separate SS unit. SS business enterprises, often expropriated from Jews, made vast profits through the use of slave
labor.[60]

Paulin has insisted that what he has written is true. "Palestinian boys are
being deliberately gunned down," he has said.[61] He knows that Palestinian boys
have been shot and killed. He probably knows that militants are deploying
Palestinian children in the Intifada.[62] He probably also knows that Jewish children have also been killed in the conflict and that a number of them have indeed
been deliberately gunned down. And of course he knows about the blood libel.

This sum of knowledge has been subordinated to anti-Semitic literary fantasy. It is the anti-Semitic literary imagination that speaks in "Crossfire." In the poem's theme of the killing of Gentile children by perfidious Jews and the miraculous disclosure of these crimes (the very word used by the Jews to conceal them exposes them), the poem alludes to "Sir Hugh or the Jew's Daughter" and the "Prioress's Tale," among other works. These texts are also invoked by the word "little," as in "another *little* Palestinian boy." (Chaucer's Prioress repeatedly describes the child victim of the Jews as "little"; in several versions of "Sir Hugh," the boy is said to be "little.") In its use of the phrase "dumb goys," the poem alludes to these lines in Ezra Pound's *Pisan Cantos*, written just after World War II: "the yidd is a stimulant, and the goyim are cattle / in gt/ proportion and go to saleable slaughter / with the maximum of docility."[63] Jews prey upon Gentiles, but the poor dumb beasts do not see what is happening, until the poet arrives to explain it.

Entirely voluntarily but without any good reason whatever, Paulin has made himself a prisoner of anti-Semitic literary discourse. Acknowledging the violent death of Jewish children is inadmissible in that discourse. "Crossfire" is silent about Jewish deaths. A second poem written by Paulin, "On Being Dealt the Anti-Semitic Card," is silent about the blood libel—which is also inadmissible *as a libel* in anti-Semitic literary discourse. This poem fails to include the blood libel in its recitation of anti-Semitic atrocities ("the list is endless"). Why? Because to mention it would force him to confront the complicity of "Crossfire" in the contemporary circulation of the defamation of the Jews. "Crossfire" joins the company of anti-Semitic material in circulation on the Internet and in the Middle East. The Jews kill and then smear the person who dares to lift a voice against them. Or as Paulin put it, "their game / . . . the ones who play the a-s card— / of death threats the mail talking tough / the usual cynical Goebbels stuff."[64]

Paulin describes "Crossfire" as a "squib," which is "a short composition of a satirical and witty character" (*OED*). The squib, we might say, is the poetic equivalent of the "remark." It is specific to its context; limited to the expression of a particular emotion; to be taken seriously, of course, but not to be understood as the statement of a general position. The poem is comparable to Dalyell's remarks, to Brown's cartoon, and to the generality of Wilson's hostile observations on the Jews, Judaism, and Israel (which I take to be no more than a series of "remarks"). Does this mean that Paulin and the rest are anti-Semites?[65] I am not prepared to say so; the evidence is not conclusive. Still, there is an objectionable glibness about what they have said (or written or drawn), one that indicates a susceptibility to the discourses of English literary anti-Semitism and of anti-Semitic anti-Zionism. They should also have cared more about the complaints of anti-Semitism, which were not ill-judged.

One wants—as a Jew and as an intellectual—to live in a culture where the intelligentsia is ready to say, as was once said by the English novelist and civil servant C.P. Snow (not the most impressive of intellectuals, perhaps, but a representative one): "While there is a single anti-Semite alive, we are proud to be on the other side."[66] Intellectuals should be glad to make this declaration and to do so understanding what it means. Yet it is hard to imagine such a declaration having any appeal for the generality of England's intellectuals today.

# 7

# Playground for Jihad?

## The Case of Great Britain

*Robert S. Wistrich*

On September 11, 2002, an extraordinary meeting took place at the Finsbury Park Mosque in North London to "celebrate" the first anniversary of the bombing of the World Trade Center in Manhattan. A thousand British Muslims were gathered inside this "holy place" to learn about this "Towering Day in History," to quote the organizers. The assembly was protected by a force of about five hundred British Metropolitan Police while a dozen or so menacing-looking men wearing kaffiyehs stood on the mosque's steps to stop unsympathetic journalists from entering. The meeting adjourned twice for prayers, and the crowds, led by the muezzin, flowed into the courtyard. The star speaker, Sheikh Omar bin Bakri Mohammed, head of the Al-Muhajirun (The Emigrants, a radical Islamist group) is a Syrian-born cleric who explained to his enthusiastic audience the "lessons" of September 11, 2001—preaching jihad against all "corrupt regimes," including those of the United States and Britain, as well as their secular lackeys in the Middle East. The meeting was chaired by the Egyptian-born Abu Hamza, who not only presided over the mosque but openly celebrated the events of 9/11; he told the press that Saudi Muslims financed the event in the hope that it would create an organization that better represents "the real views of Muslims in Britain."[1]

Hamza's mosque has for some time been a training station on the route for young men embracing jihadist Islam and then graduating into secret training camps and programs in Britain and abroad. Many of the four thousand British Muslims who received training from the Taliban, al Qaeda, or other terrorist groups came from Hamza's North London congregation, which has contact with many militant Muslim networks abroad. Hamza himself never denied his support for terrorism and armed struggle, and his adopted son participated with five other British Muslims in a thwarted attack in the Yemen in 1998, primarily directed against British diplomats, including their families, homes, and offices in the country. Hamza also reportedly recruited the British Muslim convert Richard Reid, the "shoe-bomber" who on December 22, 2001, tried to blow up an American Airlines flight from Paris, bound for Miami. The imam has further been implicated in the theological brainwashing of Zacarias Moussaoui, arrested in the United States for conspiring with the murderers of 9/11.

For the leadership of al Qaeda, terror attacks on any Western targets and on Western Jews are by no means to be confined to the United States. Sheikh Bakri and other Islamist radicals made this clear when they branded Britain, like the United States, as "evil" for striking back at Afghanistan and al Qaeda bases. The extremists seem unconcerned at the undeserved shame their threatening rhetoric brings to the majority of tolerant, law-abiding British Muslims.[2] Their efforts to import Muslim Judeophobia from the Middle East to Britain and Europe have not passed unnoticed and have undoubtedly led to a serious deterioration of relations between Muslims and Jews. The Anglo-Jewish community has protested, for example, that some of London's Arabic-language newspapers, by their defense of Palestinian suicide bombings and of al Qaeda's call to kill millions of Americans, incite attacks on their children and on synagogues and other Jewish institutions. Mike Whine of the Community Security Trust (which is responsible for protecting Jewish buildings in Britain) points to the fact that in the past few years Muslims have become "so wound up by what they have heard in the mosque or what they have read that they have gone out and attacked the nearest Jew."[3]

The extremists who carried out the slaughter of 9/11 have tried to carry out more attacks since then and will try again and could succeed despite the improved alertness of police and security services in the United States, Britain and other nations. Britain's then home secretary, David Blunkett, observed back in September 2002 that "a real threat" existed in his country, issuing a stark warning against complacency: "The UK and its interests overseas remain a target for al-Qa'ida terrorists who will almost certainly seek to carry out further terrorist attacks, drawing on the network which they have already established."[4]

In Britain, alone, there are several dozen suspected al Qaeda activists and hundreds of supporters; they pose a threat both there and as part of an international terror network. After all, it was to Richard Reid, the British-born would-be shoe bomber, that al Qaeda turned to exact revenge for the Taliban's fall and the loss of Afghanistan.[5] More important, one of the leading ideologues of al Qaeda, the forty-four-year-old Abou Qutada (his real name being Omar Mahmoud Uthman), a Palestinian and political refugee from Jordan, lived in Acton, London, for eight years, until the passage of the newly strengthened antiterrorism bill in Great Britain. Qutada was arrested several times by the British authorities, fled the country, but has now once more been apprehended. He is considered by some experts to be the heart and brains of al Qaeda in Europe. In an interview with CNN in October 2001, he expounded on his reasons for preaching against the West. He accused it of having plundered the resources of the Muslim people (*oumma*), of causing the deaths of many thousands of innocent people in the Middle East and Afghanistan; Muslims were only protecting their religion and ethics against outside domination, and Osama bin Laden's actions were perfectly understandable since Americans controlled his own country—Saudi Arabia and its corrupt regime.[6]

Britain's European partners have long been concerned about its role as "a perfect haven for Islamic radicals looking for young Muslim recruits. Bin Laden's associate Khalid al-Fawwaz had already established a "media office" there in 1994, on behalf of the Saudi millionaire-dissident. In 1998 al-Fawwaz and two Egyptian militants were arrested under U.S. extradition warrants (for involvement in the U.S. embassy bombings in Africa), and they are still in jail. The fact remains, however, that despite the new British legislation, a significant number of supporters of terrorism live freely in "Londistan," even though they are wanted by the Americans and the French as well as by Egyptian, Jordanian, Yemeni, and other Middle Eastern governments. One has to wonder if it is this British "tolerance" that has kept Great Britain free (for the moment) from terrorist attack, as was claimed by the Saudi Arabian academic Mohammed al-Masari, who helped set up a London press office for bin Laden.[7]

British "tolerance" is all the more remarkable since Sheikh Bakri has periodically made threats against British leaders whom he regards as legitimate targets for assassination—beginning with John Major during the Gulf War of 1991 and more recently against Prime Minister Tony Blair. Bakri has, moreover, recruited British Muslims to fight abroad in places such as Kashmir, Afghanistan, Chechnya, or Palestine. He claims to be closely linked to the International Islamic Front for Jihad against the Jews and Crusaders, created by bin Laden, which actively supports Hamas and the Palestinian Islamists—recruiting militiamen, collecting funds, and sending volunteers to Jordan to infiltrate the West Bank and join the Intifada.[8] Three years ago, he published a letter to bin Laden on his Al-Muhajiroun Web site.[9] It stated: "We are an Ummah of Jihad and beyond doubt we have been chosen by Allah to rule the world if we hold to his command. . . . The opportunity is here and we must not pass it by. . . . The war is our war, and the enemy is our enemy." He urged bin Laden to act decisively against the West, especially the United States, "for a new dawn is near at hand." The objectives of this Islamic jihad included "bringing down their airlines," occupying their embassies, and forcing closure of their banks. Sheikh Bakri's radical ideological doctrine, like that of his London colleague, Sheikh Abu Hamza al-Masri, is replete with Holocaust denial and rabid hatred of Jews and of Israel, "the cancer in the heart of the Muslim world."[10]

At the same time, in the missionizing vision of the jihadists, Jews, Christians, and other non-Muslims may choose to keep their faith as long as they agree to live under the all-encompassing authority of Islam—the only universal religion, allegedly capable of establishing peace and harmony. Bakri, Abu Hamza, and Anjem Choudary (one of the UK leaders of the al-Mujahiroun and chairman of the Society of Muslim Lawyers) share a common loathing for the West and its values, a loathing they have never disguised.[11] Moreover, virtually all of the British-based fundamentalists openly support bin Laden, and some—like the Jamaican convert to Islam, Abdullah el-Faisal—have been accused of touring Britain and openly preaching death to the Jews.[12] During a recent rally of these extremists in Trafalgar Square, Abu Hamza (head of the Supporters of Sharia) said the 9/11 atrocities were "an American-Zionist plot to blame the Muslim world." Banners denounced Israel as "the UK and America's illegitimate child" and proclaimed: "From individual to superpower Islam destroys every other thought, idea and system of life."[13]

In February 2003, Abu Hamza was finally banned from preaching at the London mosque, which, during the preceding decade, he had turned into a base for radical Islamism. However, it was not the government, police, or municipal authorities but the Charities Commission that removed him from his position as imam of the Finsbury Park Mosque for preaching hatred and delivering inflammatory sermons. Hamza predictably denounced this ban as "another example of the oppression against Islam" provoked by any criticism of the United States or Israel. He then caused further revulsion by calling the *Columbia* space shuttle disaster on February 1, 2003 (in which eight astronauts, including an Israeli, Col. Ilan Ramon, died) "an act of God." The Almighty, according to Abu Hamza, had punished the "trinity of evil" represented by the space shuttle passengers—Americans, a Jew, and a Hindu.[14]

At the end of February 2003, el-Faisal was convicted in London's Old Bailey criminal court of soliciting murder and of three counts of inciting racial hatred. This was the first prosecution in Britain of a Muslim cleric and also the first time that jurors of particular religions (Jews and Hindus) were excluded by the judge, at the request of the defense. On tapes of el-Faisal's lectures (on sale at specialist bookshops in Britain), he can be heard encouraging young Britons to travel to terrorist training camps in Afghanistan, both before and after 9/11. He had promised that those who died during a "holy war" would not feel any pain and would go to heaven, where they would enjoy the favours of seventy-two virgins. "We believe in the bullet, not the ballot," he told the impressionable youngsters whom he sought to recruit. In one speech, he urged them: "People with British passports, if you fly into Israel, it is easy. . . . Fly into Israel and do whatever you can. If you die, you are up in Paradise. How do you fight a Jew? You kill a Jew. In the case of Hindus, by bombing their businesses."

At his trial, el-Faisal—who received his Islamic education in Saudi Arabia—declared that he had nothing against Americans and Britons but that he was "appalled by the American government and their support for the Zionist state of Israel"; he was no less "appalled by the British government's support for America." He also claimed to have been against the killing of innocent civilians on 9/11. However, overwhelming evidence produced at his trial demonstrated that he had incited his audiences to wage jihad on all nonbelievers by terrorizing and killing them. Like many other radical Islamist clerics, el-Faisal blamed the Manhattan massacre on the United States and the Jews.[15]

For the Jewish community in Britain, there is particular cause for concern. The increasing number of violent incidents recorded against Jews since October 2000 have been mainly caused by Muslims or Palestinian sympathizers, who are sometimes non-Muslims. A blatantly anti-Semitic Arab and Muslim media with its sources of inspiration in the Middle East combined with the left-liberal obsession—and at times demonization of Israel in the British media—have helped create this environment. The call to arms of jihadist organizations, much of it directed against Israel, all too easily mutates into anti-Semitism around the world—not least in Britain. The UK-based *Azzam Publications*, for example, denounced the "Jewish-controlled media . . . predominantly biased against the Muslims," which manipulates minds to convince the public of the legality of Zionist crimes.[16] Al-Muhajiroun, advertising a rally for al-Aqsa, proclaimed: "The day of judgement will not come until the Muslims fight the Jews and the Muslims kill them." A series of posters bore an almost identical hadith: The "final hour will not come until the Muslims kill the Jews."[17] Sheikh Bakri "urge[d] Jews in the UK and elsewhere not to show any support for the Israeli regime, whether verbal, financial or physical, or they may allow themselves to become targets for Muslims."[18]

While incitement from the Far Right has decreased in Great Britain, the promotion of hatred against the Jews that comes from the Middle East and radical Islamic groups is steadily growing. This requires much more effective action from the government, police, and courts, but it also needs a reassessment of Muslim-Jewish relations. Muslims, too, are victims, of racism and Islamophobia in Britain as elsewhere. This is what makes the participation of some fanatical Islamists in anti-Semitism all the more saddening and deplorable—especially as the Anglo-Jewish community has been involved with Muslims in a common struggle against racism in the past.

But, as Malise Ruthven has written, "Islam is programmed for victory—its religious institutions were predicated upon the attainment of imperial power." It is no coincidence that fifteen of the nineteen World Trade Center bombers were Saudi nationals—holding to a brand of Islam that is viciously intolerant, not only of other religions but even of other strains of Islam. In his analysis of jihad, Ruthven cites the famous "Sword Verse" of the Koran, in which Mohammed instructs his followers to "kill the polytheists [nonbelievers] wherever you find them."[19] Christians and Jews might be spared, so long as they honoured their Scriptures, but they must remain second-class citizens. In the early twenty-first century, extremist Muslim preachers in Britain, as in the Middle East, have unfortunately revived and radicalized those verses of the Koran that can all too easily be made to justify the unspeakable. As a result, Islamists are now a danger to everyone, to Jews, to Christians, to themselves, and to Muslims in general.[20]

The British media—like its counterparts in France and Germany—radically distorts the Israel/Palestinian conflict by ignoring the power of religious fanaticism. Very little attention is paid by the media to the intoxicating impact of Islamism, with its crazed ideology, culture of martyrdom, and violently anti-Semitic hatred.[21] Instead, terrorism and Islamist "suicide attacks" are explained away as a product of the general misery induced by Israel's policies. It was such facile assumptions that led the British prime minister's wife, Cherie Blair, to remark at a charitable event in London a few years ago that young Palestinians "feel they have got no hope but to blow themselves up." Not only was the comment unfounded, but it was particularly offensive since it was made only hours after a Hamas suicide bomber blew up a bus packed full of Israelis, including schoolchildren, killing nineteen and maiming many more.[22] The profiles and the statements of the bombers themselves tell a very different story, one in which "martyrdom" killings are a strategic choice and an exalted act of religious self-sacrifice. The many terrorist acts perpetrated across the globe in the name of Islam have not produced a major backlash against British Muslims. On the contrary, the prevailing "antiracist" form of political correctness has ensured that their religious beliefs enjoy an astonishing level of immunity from criticism. This makes a frank discussion of the role of Muslims in the propagation of hate literature and violence against Jews more difficult. But radical Islamic organizations like the semi-clandestine Hizb-ut-Tahrir (HUT: Party of Liberation) as well as the al-Muhajiroun have been active for more than a decade, inciting hatred against Jews and Israel on British campuses.

Among the young Muslims converted to religious extremism at Abu Hamza's Finsbury Park Mosque were two British-born suicide bombers, Asif Mohammed Hanif from West London and Omar Khan Sharif from Derby. Both of them had also been markedly influenced by the al-Muhajiroun group, accepting Sheikh Bakri as their "spiritual" guide. In May 2003, the twenty-one-year-old Hanif blew himself up and killed three civilians when he detonated an explosive belt at a beachfront bar in Tel Aviv.[23] It appears that the Anglo-Pakistani bomber had studied for several months in Damascus, where he may have developed links with Hizbollah or al Qaeda.[24] The cause of Palestine no doubt provided an emotional rallying point for his act; after all, Hanif must have assumed he would be killing Israeli Jews and then heading for heaven. However, he might just as easily have killed Arabs or foreign tourists—as in fact also happened.[25] Evidently this possibility does not trouble the sleep of the bombers once they have been mobilized for global jihad.

The case of Omar Sheikh, another young Anglo-Pakistani terrorist and former London School of Ecomomics student who masterminded the gruesome beheading of the American Jewish journalist Daniel Pearl in Karachi in February 2002, was already an early warning signal of what might be lying in store. Sheikh, too, was a well-educated "Englishman" from a comfortable middle-class immigrant family—as much the child of British culture as of radical Islam. Once he metamorphosed into a Muslim militant, he could more openly hate the Jews, read *Mein Kampf*, and quote from the Koran as circumstances required.[26] Sheikh had already been radicalized in the mid-1990s by the Bosnian massacres in Europe. His militancy was reinforced by a spell in the Afghan training camps of al Qaeda and by his return to Pakistan—a major ferment of Islamic fundamentalism and a hotbed of "anti-Semitism without Jews."

How many more Sheikhs or Hanifs are there among the outwardly peaceful and law-abiding population of two to three million Muslims in Britain today? Does the fact that 80 percent of them originate from the Indian subcontinent (Pakistan, Bangladesh, India) and not the Arab world diminish the danger of a new anti-Semitism, developing in Britain, that is able to draw on Koranic sources?

Unfortunately, this is far from certain. The growing library of Islamist books and videos that feeds the militant imagination is blooming against a background of disaffected Pakistani youth and the presence of many Muslim radicals who were granted asylum in Britain during the 1990s. During the Salman Rushdie affair of over a decade ago, fundamentalist anti-Westernism, full of puritanical disgust for "American" popular culture and sexual license, had already begun to attract a significant following. It was helped by the dominant role played by fanatical mullahs and clerics in spreading their antidemocratic jihadist ideology through the mosques. Not only rabid anti-Semitism but the repression of women and extreme homophobia were further facilitated by lax British immigration laws and a judicial system that placed no obstacles in their path. The present generation of marginalized Muslim youth in the big cities is highly susceptible to militant propaganda. The videos to which these young Muslims are exposed feature a message of worldwide Islamic persecution. They implicitly endorse terrorism, and (along with books glorifying jihad) they often blame the Jews for corrupting the beliefs and morals of Muslims. In other words, Western freedoms are being exploited in countries like Britain to spread a bigoted, antidemocratic message.

"Londistan" has indeed become a major world capital of political Islam in the last decade through the unique diversity and range of its Arabic newspapers, magazines, and publishing houses—not to mention its flourishing network of bookshops, mosques, and community centres.[27] The Islamists have taken full advantage of British citizenship and democratic liberties for their anti-Western goals, reaping the benefits of London's centrality at the hub of global finance, electronic media, Internet services, and mass communications technology.[28] A critical mass of Algerian, Tunisian, Egyptian, Saudi, Syrian, Iraqi, and Palestinian exiles have in fact been able to act freely as oppositional groups and organize themselves in order to try to undermine the many oppressive regimes in the Arab Middle East that have persecuted them.[29] Above all, London has become the nerve center for global jihad;[30] and as we have seen, it is a favorable terrain for the radicalization of British Muslims.

This is less surprising when one recalls that 40 percent of British Muslims surveyed in a *Sunday Times* poll after 9/11 believed that bin Laden was "justified" in his war against the United States and supported those of their core-ligionists from Britain who volunteered to fight with the Taliban against the Western allies.[31] Bakri has shrewdly played on this emotional sympathy with al Qaeda's war against the United States and Western "Judeo-Christian" civilization. He shares the fundamentalist worldview, propagated by the Palestinian Sheikh Abou Qutada that the "war of civilizations" is a reality. It is, therefore, the mission of Islam to defeat the United States and the West in order to ensure its own global hegemony.[32]

A Koranic-based Judeophobia, imported from the Middle East to Britain and fused with the anti-Semitic mythology of the *Protocols of the Elders of Zion*, continuously feeds this psychology of ressentiment toward the West. However, for Islamists like Qutada, Bakri, Hamza, and Choudary, Britain and the West are mere pawns controlled by the "Zionists." As for Israel itself, it is invariably portrayed as a "cancer in the heart of the Muslim world,"[33] one that can be eliminated only by radical surgery.

Radical Jew-hatred linked to the Palestinian cause is obviously an important part of the Islamist mobilization strategy designed for British Muslims, even though most of them have family roots in Pakistan, India, and Bangladesh. The issue of Palestine has great emotional power even *beyond* the Arab community, a resonance that the more moderate Muslim Council cannot afford to ignore. This has become increasingly evident since the new Intifada caught fire in October 2000. Thus, though the Palestinian problem is not a *national* issue for radical Islamists in Britain, it has been skillfully exploited as a revolutionary prologue to the long-term aims of global jihad. Al-Mouhajiroun synthesizes its call for "the black flag of Islam to fly over Downing Street" with the liberation of Palestine and the jihadist demand to "dejudaise the West."[34] The highly inflammable cocktail put together by these and other Islamist groups combines jihad, the dream of a worldwide caliphate, Koranic indoctrination, and classical Judeophobia.

As a result, radical young British Muslims grow up on a diet that combines the emotive issue of Palestine, Jewish "control" of Islamic holy places, and fury at the racism they encounter in British society.[35] There is no doubt that such incendiary propaganda has increased the physical danger to British Jews, especially since the Iraq war. In the first quarter of 2003, eighty-nine malicious acts were aimed at the Jewish community—an increase of 75 percent over the previous year. In most cases, these incidents were linked either to Iraq or Palestine. As Mike Whine, director of the Community Security Trust, has put it: "The Iraq war fed anti-Semitism because groups from across the political and social spectrum alleged that the war was fought for 'Zionist interests.'"[36] In as many as 100 of the 350 anti-Semitic incidents that occurred in Britain in 2002, there was strong evidence of an anti-Israel motivation.[37] This was more than double the number of incidents—48—in which far-right allegiances were involved.[38] Many of the incidents showed that perpetrators automatically identified Jews with Zionism and Israel.[39] A rise of 15 percent in violent assaults on Jews in 2002 also reflected the spillover effect from the Middle East.[40] Anti-Israel and Islamist activists were noticeably more conspicuous than previously in instances of abusive or threatening behavior toward Jews. On British campuses, this grew directly out of the campaign to turn the boycott of Israeli goods into a Student Union policy, enforced by a combination of pro-Palestinian and Islamist groups. At the University of Manchester, after one such debate on the boycott, a brick was shoved through the window of a Jewish student residence, and a poster in Arabic was stuck to the door of the building; it read "Slaughter the Jews." A week earlier the General Union of Palestinian Students had distributed a leaflet in which Jews were described as "vampires."[41] Similar leaflets, also quoting from the Koran, were left on cars outside a London school, denouncing the "Zionist Crusader conspiracy to control the world and propagate evil."[42]

Such Islamist propaganda generally asserts that the Jews run the world economy and that they dominate the United States and the Christian world while also seeking to subvert and undermine Islam. Though no reliable studies exist regarding anti-Jewish feelings among British Muslims, there is little doubt that substantial segments of the community do sympathize with the Palestinians, are very critical of U.S. and British policy, and feel alienated by the racism of Western society.[43] It is clear that the demonization of Israel is not merely a radical fringe phenomenon. The Muslim Council of Britain, for example, justified its boycott of the official British Holocaust Day commemoration by evoking the (imaginary) "genocide" of the Palestinians.[45] The same spectacle was repeated in January 2005, on the sixtieth anniversary of the liberation of Auschwitz. Furthermore, even moderate British Muslims who profess to be alarmed at "Islamicized" anti-Semitism and admit its cancerous growth in their own community seem unable to transcend self-serving myths and half-truths about their own history. For example, they will uncritically repeat the idyllic notion that Jews always prospered and reached spiritual heights under benign Muslim rule; that only Muslim "protection" can guarantee the security of Jews; that intransigent Christianity allied to right-wing Zionism is the source of all evil in the Middle East; or that anti-Semitism is a foreign growth in Islamic culture, solely provoked by Israel's violent behavior.[45] The ultimate price for Muslim acceptance of the Jewish nation in the Middle East, even for most moderates, appears to be the dismantling of Israel and a return of Jews to their pre-emancipatory *dhimmi* status of being a "protected" and subjugated people.[46]

For example, Fuad Nahdi, publisher of the Muslim magazine *Q-News*, has repeated the untenable argument that Zionism is solely to blame for the growth of anti-Jewish feelings in the Muslim world. Typically he looks to "critical voices" among Jews (that is, anti-Zionists) to ensure that all Palestinian and Muslim demands are met by Israel without any explicit recognition of the right to a Jewish state; and he hints that if these demands are not met, radical Muslims are likely to target Jews in large numbers. The majority of militant British Muslims evidently see no distinction between Jews and Israel. The Jewish state's actions toward the Palestinians—systematically misrepresented as a form of "ethnic cleansing"—have become the measure for judging British Jews.[47] This way of thinking is already halfway to anti-Semitism, and it has become increasingly accepted in mainstream British thinking.[48] Thus, a well-known Jewish journalist, Mitchell Symons, recently noted in the *Daily Express* that Britain was no longer any different from Germany when it came to desecrated Jewish cemeteries, "hate-crimes," and verbal insults against Jews: "Synagogues and Jewish schools in this country are on the highest alert against terrorist attacks, Muslim fundamentalists preach hatred against Jews and Arab publications, openly on sale, spew out anti-Semitic poison. Isn't there *anyone* in a position of power who's prepared to make the connection between these two facts? And can you imagine the reaction of the police and the State if it were the other way round and Jews were attacking Muslims?"[49]

This last comment is much more than merely a rhetorical question. Even the mildest rebuke of Muslim behavior is liable to be attacked as "racist." When Foreign Office Minister Dennis McShane, speaking in his Rotherham constituency, sensibly suggested that the Muslim community in Britain choose between supporting terrorism or the "democratic rule of law," the remark aroused a storm of protest.[50] The secretary-general of the Muslim Council of Britain (MCB) said his community was "shocked and dismayed," adding that Britain should be pressuring the United States to act against Israel, not invoking the threat of terrorism.[51] Some Jewish spokesmen also criticized the Minister's remarks as "offensive,"[52] even though McShane has been outspoken in calling for tough countermeasures against *both* Islamophobia and anti-Semitism. Trevor Phillips, chairman of the Commission for Racial Equality (himself from the black community) has also pointed out that anti-Semitism as well as Islamophobia are on the rise. However, Phillips, to his credit, specifically deplored the fact that critics of Israel's policies were actively fomenting anti-Semitism. He bluntly called on the British Home Secretary to deport Islamic extremists.[53] After the horrific car bombs in Istanbul and the burning of a Jewish school in a Paris suburb, even the *Guardian* conceded that "a new anti-semitism is on the march across the globe."[54] Its editorial on November 18, 2003 acknowledged that the Anglo-Jewish community had good reason to feel "unsettled, uncomfortable and fearful" following random attacks on schools, synagogues, and cemeteries. It noted that "all Jews are now seen by some extremists as legitimate targets," including ultra-orthodox Jews who do not even recognize the State of Israel. And it also recalled that Jewish peace activists (themselves opposed to the invasion of Iraq) had been beaten up in large anti-war demonstrations in London and Paris the previous year: "Their victims were targets just because they are Jews."[55] The editorial concluded with a belated appeal, all the more ironic in the light of its barely disguised hostility to Israel: "Could not the liberal left, which in an earlier era vigilantly sought to protect Jews from prejudice and bigotry, rediscover its old values?"[56]

# 8

# The Retreat of the Strong State and the New Anti-Semitic Mobilization in France

*Pierre Birnbaum*

Officials at the highest levels of government concede that anti-Semitism is dangerously on the rise in contemporary French society. At the annual dinner of the Representative Council of French Jewish Institutions (CRIF) in May 2001, then prime minister Lionel Jospin, speaking to an audience that included nearly all the members of his government, stated that "we will no more tolerate acts of anti-Semitism than acts of racism." When he stressed "the government's determination to combat anti-Semitism in all its forms," the CRIF's president did not hesitate to respond that "we are confronted with anti-Jewish hatred. We fear for the safety of Jews in France."[1]

Two years later, on May 27, 2003, Jacques Chirac, the president of the Republic, marked the sixty-seventh anniversary of the CRIF with a combative speech in which he hammered home the same message, reinforced by the impressive surroundings of the Elysée Palace:

> Today you are no longer alone. In the fight against anti-Semitism, France is with you. For it is indeed France that is under attack on its own soil. It is indeed France that is insulted when a synagogue burns on French soil. It is indeed France that is humiliated when a Jewish child living on French soil is obliged to change schools in order to escape the taunts, intimidations, and insults of classmates. The Republic owes all its children the protection of the law. Anti-Semitism is contrary to all the values that France holds dear. It cannot be tolerated. Anti-Semitic acts must be combated unremittingly and punished with the utmost severity. . . . We will allow no apologies for crime and hatred. France is not an anti-Semitic country.[2]

A few months later, when a Jewish school was set ablaze in the Paris suburb of Gagny, President Chirac "firmly" condemned "this intolerable criminal
act." For the first time, he received the leaders of a wide range of Jewish
groups, to whom he stated that "when a Jew is attacked, it must be understood
that all of France is attacked. Our Jewish compatriots have for centuries made
France their home. Anti-Semitism is contrary to all French values. I count on
all Frenchmen to be vigilant in opposing it."[3] Finally, on January 31, 2004,
Prime Minister Jean-Pierre Raffarin addressed the CRIF in the presence of most
of the important ministers of his government and issued another declaration
every bit as resolute as those that had preceded it:

> I know that the Jews of France are particularly worried about the unacceptable preva-
> lence of anti-Semitic acts. France is of course not an anti-Semitic country. To be sure,
> there is a residue of anti-Semitism on the extreme right. There is also an anti-Semitism
> of resentment, which has emerged among people who do not feel integrated [into
> French society], people conflicted about their identity, who are creating absurd cate-
> gories and developing a logic of hatred. I intend to combat this anti-Semitism not only
> by enforcing the law as needed but also by taking preventive steps. Tonight I wish to
> restate one simple point as forcefully as I can: it is intolerable for a citizen of France
> to be attacked because he is a Jew. You can nevertheless rest assured that the whole
> country is concerned and that my entire government is mobilized against this hydra,
> whose many hideous heads regularly reappear. . . . As long as anti-Semitic acts are com-
> mitted, we cannot rest easy, because France bears the wounds.[4]

The repetition of such staunch declarations by the highest officials in
France indicates the urgency, the almost dramatic character, of the surge of anti-
Semitism that the country has experienced in recent years. To be sure, France
is not anti-Semitic, and the vast majority of the French reject such behavior, as
the president and successive prime ministers have hastened to point out, as if
in response to alarmist criticism stemming from abroad, especially from the
United States, as well as Israel, which has made no secret of the fact that it has
set up a system to receive French Jewish immigrants similar to that established
in the past to receive Russian Jews wishing to leave the Soviet Union. Indeed,
French Jews have been urged to make their aliyah without delay, and Michael
Melchior, Israel's deputy minister for foreign affairs, has not hesitated to
embellish his statements with such unfortunate rhetoric as "France is the worst
of the Western countries when it comes to anti-Semitism,"[5] a formula that rei-
fies the nation unduly while transgressing the bounds of acceptable criticism.

Nevertheless, it is true that Jewish synagogues, schools, stores, and cemeteries have been the targets of brutal attacks in France ever since the tragic

events at Carpentras, where Jewish graves and remains were desecrated in May 1990, and indeed well before that, for more than twenty-five years in fact, hence predating the Intifada. Going back all the way to 1980, Jewish cemeteries have been destroyed year after year throughout France, Jewish synagogues have been attacked with Molotov cocktails, and Jewish stores have been looted and covered with anti-Semitic graffiti, while throughout this period the general public remained largely indifferent. Newspapers inevitably dismissed such stories with a few lines relegated to inside pages, even in cases such as synagogue burnings where catastrophe was narrowly averted.

Between September 1, 2000 and January 31, 2002, sixty-seven synagogues were the targets of incendiary devices, stonings, or violent incursions. France is not anti-Semitic, but as the official report of the National Consultative Commission on Human Rights recognizes year after year, anti-Jewish acts now account for the majority of its human rights violations: In 2002, 193 violent anti-Semitic acts were reported, accounting for 62 percent of the violations registered that year.[6] The commission soberly noted that in 2003, "anti-Semitism continues to be very apparent in French society," as evidenced by 588 anti-Semitic incidents, including 125 violent acts (70 assaults, 49 acts of vandalism on Jewish property, and 6 cases of arson) and 463 threats (in the form of insults, graffiti, and pamphlets). The official commission report went on to note that "these statistics clearly indicate that the violence against the Jewish community is taking root and growing more serious."[7]

These figures, as impressive as they are, understate the extent of the phenomenon, since many anti-Semitic attacks take place on the street, in public transportation, and in schools and are not reported even if they permanently traumatize their victims. A climate of evil seems to be spreading, provoking "serious anxiety among French Jews."[8] It is impossible to keep track of the dozens of synagogues and religious schools that have been attacked, set ablaze, destroyed, or simply vandalized over the past few years. Teachers have been attacked and children subjected to veritable persecution in elementary and secondary schools.[9] Many students have been obliged to change schools, while groups of Jewish students have been attacked on the street, in school buses, and on the soccer field, to the point where Joseph Sitruck, the chief rabbi of France, advised Jewish children to hide their skullcaps and conceal their Jewish identity when out in public: "Suddenly they find themselves back in time immemorial."[10] The Union of French Jewish Students and the antiracist organization S.O.S.-Racisme have published a long list of anti-Semitic attacks that is staggering to read: Page after page recounts assaults accompanied by exclamations of "Filthy Jew!" "Death to the Jews!" "Hitler our savior!" "Drown all the Jews!" and "Long live Palestine!"[11]

The number of anti-Semitic acts has been growing rapidly for some time. In May 2004, Nazi symbols and slogans (swastika, SS symbol, "Juden Raus," "Ein Volk," "ein Reich," "ein Führer" and so on) were written in red on 127 graves in the Jewish cemetery of Herrlisheim, in Alsace and subsequently scrawled on the Jewish memorial of Verdun, built to commemorate the death of Jewish soldiers during World War I. Add to that any number of widely reported anti-Semitic "slips" by a variety of well-known personalities, including Abbé Pierre (a Catholic priest and advocate of the poor who let it slip that he believed the number of Jews killed in the Holocaust had been exaggerated), the comedian Dieudonné (who dressed as an elderly Orthodox Jew in a satire of alleged Jewish mistreatment of Palestinians), to the writer Renaud Camus (who remarked that in his view there were too many Jewish journalists working in French broadcasting). It is almost as if "the Jewish question" were making an unexpected comeback, fueled by traditional fantasies coupled with the myth of Israel as a threat to world peace. As Moïse Cohen, the president of the Jewish Consistory of Paris, remarked to that group's convention, such an upsurge of anti-Semitism in France is "unimaginable sixty years after the Shoah."[12]

Arson, vandalism, and attacks on Jewish children and teachers used to be the work of the extreme Right in France, but today these offenses are more likely to be committed by youths of North African descent living in run-down housing projects on the outskirts of big cities. Nearly all the people arrested and tried for such crimes come from the immigrant community, although some are French citizens. Hence, there is no denying the fact that the situation in Israel has contributed to the surprising upsurge in anti-Semitic activity by encouraging these youths to identify with the activists of the Intifada and to think of themselves as being at war with French Jews, whom they perceive as having no choice but to identify with Israel. So nowadays, it is increasingly common to hear the old cry of hatred "Death to the Jews!" being shouted out in the streets of Paris and of provincial cities such as Strasbourg, where "the Synagogue of Peace seems to be in a state of war."[13] Nothing of the sort had been heard in France for at least fifty years, since the 1950s, when the followers of Pierre Poujade stooped to such slogans.

These cries, reminiscent of the pogroms, can now be heard in demonstrations against Israeli policy or the war in Iraq organized by extreme left-wing groups or antiglobalization activists who reject the "cosmopolitan, capitalist, and American" globalization of the economy. To be sure, such slogans are the exception in demonstrations of this sort, yet they are nonetheless intolerable. In short, "anti-Jewish hatred" is erupting everywhere, fueled in France and elsewhere by the tragic conflict between Israelis and Palestinians. On March 22, 2003, large numbers of people demonstrated in Paris in solidarity with the people of Iraq, and the event ended with a violent assault on a group of young Jews. This in turn led to a crisis among the Greens when a Parisian official belonging to the Green Party declared that "by encouraging the distinction between anti-Zionist and anti-Semitic, the Left is encouraging anti-Semitic speech and action."[14]

In some segments of the North African immigrant community, anti-Semitism is commonplace, although its scope is limited and it is openly condemned by some Muslim leaders, who have spoken out against "cowardly and outrageous attacks on Jewish places of worship."[15] It feeds on a variety of sources, some of them quite surprising. For instance, when the National Assembly voted almost unanimously to ban the wearing of "conspicuous" religious symbols in public schools, prohibiting not only the Muslim veil but also large crucifixes and Jewish skullcaps, demonstrations against the law erupted throughout France. One of the most extreme Muslim leaders, Mohammed Latrèche, led a parade of some ten thousand demonstrators through the center of Paris; some of the demonstrators carried large signs proclaiming that Zionism was a form of Nazism. He did not shrink from responding directly to the words of the president of the Republic: "You said that the Jews have been in France for two thousand years, Mr. President. Do you think we're going to wait two thousand years? We expect an apology from you." And then he added: "We are anti-Zionists. We are true anti-Zionists. Just as we opposed Nazism, we oppose any ideology based on social discrimination." This declaration had little to do with the ostensible purpose of the demonstration, which was to protest the law against wearing religious symbols in the public schools.

Jewish integration into French society is endlessly denounced on the grounds that the good fortune enjoyed by Jews makes the miserable treatment of Muslims that much more glaring. Thus, a doctoral student whose parents were immigrants from North Africa noted during the demonstration in question that "the protest is coming together. A law against the veil will be taken as a law of exception. This is what I call the Crémieux spirit." The reference is to Adolphe Crémieux [1796–1880], a French Jew who served as minister of defense and who in 1870 won approval of the so-called Crémieux Decree granting French citizenship to the Jews of Algeria. The French colonization of

Algeria is constantly invoked as historical background to the present difficulties, as if the only way to achieve decolonization in the minds of protesters were to rewrite history and rescind the Crémieux Decree, which Algerian Muslims experienced as a humiliation because it integrated Algerian Jews into French society. It is as if Jews and Muslims explained their persisting civic inequalities in terms of rival histories, which have abruptly come into conflict long after the Crémieux Decree, the end of the tragic Algerian War (1954–1962), and the subsequent exodus from North Africa to France. As a result, debate on many issues has been complicated by allegations of Jewish "influence," often based on unbelievably crude and fantastic versions of the *Protocols of the Elders of Zion*. It is common, for instance, to hear that "the Jews have everything"[16] and to see Jewish influence blamed even where Jews clearly are not responsible for the alleged discrimination; for instance, France's leading rabbis came out in favor of *allowing* the veil to be worn in school!

Another grievance has to do with the fact that a number of Jews served on the Stasi Commission, which was charged with looking into the issue of religious symbols in the schools. Even though these Jewish commission members were selected for their professional expertise in regard to the relevant laws, rumors of a Jewish conspiracy began to circulate. Allegedly, the purpose of this conspiracy was to combat the presence of Muslims in France. In many respects, these rumors were reminiscent of the wild allegations launched by intransigent Catholics at the turn of the twentieth century, when the issue was the separation of church and state. At that time, Jews were accused of undermining France's Catholic identity, even though the laws at issue, then as now, were passed nearly unanimously by the nation's representatives in the National Assembly for the purpose of strongly affirming the secular character of public space in the French Republic—what the French call *laïcité*, a word for which there is no adequate equivalent in English.[17]

The sheer number, frequency, and repetitive character of anti-Semitic acts, words, taunts, and caricatures have reawakened old fears and encouraged an undeniable tendency on the part of Jews to withdraw from public space and retreat into private life and the family circle. The incomprehension on the part of non-Jews is so great and their indifference so shocking, that old social bonds are dissolving, and Jews are increasingly socializing with one another. Jews resent and reject the tendency to tolerate and even justify anti-Semitism by invoking psycho-sociological explanations or interpretations involving poverty and social exclusion for which Jews are in no way responsible. They feel cut off, condemned to internal exile, maimed in their very identity, and obliged to refrain from public speech. Thus, many of them suffer from what Hannah Arendt called *acosmia*, worldlessness, a condition of silence and inaction signifying death to the world.[18] Over the dinner table, with family and friends, French Jews are often anxious enough about the current situation that they speak constantly of exile and escape, although most of the time in a sarcastic tone and without really believing what they are saying, since the vast majority of French Jews embrace an assimilationist view of Judaism and feel completely integrated into French society. Few have ever seriously considered the idea of leaving. As the director of the French equivalent of the United Jewish Appeal remarked, "People have been shaken, and a fissure has opened up. What is new is that this hasn't affected only the 30 percent who are active in the life of the Jewish community but others as well who are farther from the active center."[19] Many French Jews feel as if they have embarked on a never-ending journey to some fearful heart of darkness.[20]

The emotion that gripped the whole of French society at the time of the desecration of the Carpentras cemetery has vanished. At the time of that incident, nearly a million people representing all shades of opinion and all parts of the political spectrum turned out almost spontaneously to express their revulsion at anti-Semitic acts of any kind. By contrast, in April 2002, following a series of violent anti-Semitic acts, only "the Jewish community marched en masse in Paris from République to Bastille and in the provinces." Marching with the protesters were three minor presidential candidates: Corinne Lepage, Alain Madelin, and François Bayrou. Neither of the major candidates, Jacques Chirac and Lionel Jospin, took part in the demonstration.[21] Farewell to Carpentras? Farewell to solidarity with the Jews of France? Memories of the post-Carpentras demonstration remain fresh: The streets of Paris around the Place de la République were flooded with people, and the huge crowd, relaxed but resolute, unambiguously proclaimed its rejection of anti-Semitism and disgust at the desecration of a Jewish cemetery. President François Mitterrand was there along with countless other political leaders of every stripe, who made a point of being seen. Feelings ran high throughout the country. Nearly every politician, religious leader, and editorial writer expressed "solidarity with the Jewish community.[22] Times have certainly changed. Although protesters still carry banners proclaiming "Synagogue burned! Republic in danger!" the Republic seems to have averted its eyes.[23] Rabbi Josy Eisenberg has voiced his bitter regret: "We pray for the Republic every Sabbath. Weren't we praying for a Republic that was somewhat imaginary? Didn't we make Marianne [the female symbol of the Republic] out to be more beautiful than she was?"[24]

Apart from a few belated though sonorous and powerful statements from official sources rejecting anti-Semitism in all its forms and a few editorials in major newspapers, public silence on the subject has been deafening of late. In this climate, 2,566 French Jews left France in 2002 to settle in Israel, while an unknown number of others left for Canada or the United States. To be sure, the number of departures to date has been small, but nothing comparable has been observed since World War II. This emigration of French Jews attests to the nervousness of the Jewish community, which for the first time since World War II finds itself grappling anxiously with the possibility of exile. The extent of this anxiety is dramatic, as evidenced by surveys showing that 20 percent of French Jews say they have decided to make their aliyah to Israel, while 81 percent say that they would be happy if their children decided to settle in Israel.[25]

Are these signs of a veritable mental earthquake, a profound upheaval in the French intellectual landscape and in French perceptions of the nation and citizenship? Perhaps what is ultimately at risk is the marriage between France and the Jews sanctified by the French Revolution and the happy outcome of the Dreyfus Affair. Are new attitudes toward Zionism suddenly casting doubt on the most firmly established principles of Franco-Judaism, which has generally been hostile to any movement that threatens to undermine national unity?

The increasingly fragile position in which French Jews find themselves has been exacerbated by the persistence of a populist anti-Semitism of the extreme Right, which has solidly implanted itself in the French political landscape. On the night of February 4, 2002, a statue of Captain Alfred Dreyfus, the symbolic focal point of this older anti-Semitism, was covered with anti-Semitic graffiti. A few days later, on February 8, a small ceremony was held in front of the newly cleaned statue, from which the words "filthy traitor" and a Star of David had been removed. Among those present were Bertrand Delanoë, the Socialist mayor of Paris; Roger Cukierman, the president of the CRIF, along with other officials of that organization; representatives of the Dreyfus family and a few other participants. The call for "vigilance" pronounced on that occasion was not echoed by the media or government. The statue itself had already been moved a number of times from locations considered "too visible." Its official inauguration had had to wait until opposition from various quarters had been overcome, opposition attesting to the persistence of certain prejudices and denials. It was finally assigned a discreet place at the intersection of the Rue du Cherche-Midi and the Boulevard Raspail, where it gradually melted into the urban landscape. Amorous couples whisper sweet nothings at its base, taking no more notice of its significance than the pedestrians who hasten past. That it has now become a target of anti-Semitic attacks that appear to draw on the slogans and passions of the past is inevitably reason for surprise and worry.

It is as if the political anti-Semitism of the late nineteenth century has survived intact, while in the meantime recent polls show that the extreme-right-wing National Front Party led by Jean-Marie Le Pen continues to do well despite fractious internal dissension; the party consistently attracts about 16 percent of those polled. The April 2002 presidential election stunned everyone when Le Pen finished second to Chirac and ahead of Socialist Prime Minister Jospin in the first round of voting. The National Front also did well in the regional elections of March 2004, and despite the fact that elections of this type tend to disfavor populist parties, the National Front attracted roughly the same level of support nationally and garnered as much as 30 percent of the first-round vote in certain regions where Jews are particularly numerous, such as Alsace and certain *départements* in the southeastern part of the country. These results have also heightened fears among French Jews, who are well aware of tenacious anti-Semitic sentiment among supporters of the far Right. This can be seen in National Front publications and public statements, in which metaphors introduced by the radical Right in the late nineteenth century are recycled, as well as in the party's fondness for German marching songs and its outspoken opposition to Israel as an instrument of "cosmopolitan capitalism," accused of being corrosive of national identities. The National Front's vehement hostility to North African immigrants in France should not be allowed to conceal the permanent influence of an anti-Semitism that is deeply rooted in the traditions of the intransigent radical Right. The fact that one French voter in four identifies with ideas defended by Le Pen, while only 42 percent of the French deem his positions unacceptable, can only increase the anxiety of French Jews, who are well aware that the extreme-right movement is solidly implanted in certain parts of the country.[26]

The current outbreak of anti-Semitism, one of the worst in recent French history, stems in large part from the impact of conflict in the Middle East and the aftermath of the attacks of September 11, 2001. It was as if two forms of anti-Semitism, stemming from two distinct sources but drawing on identical imagery, had come together; as if antagonistic political currents could for a moment combine in unified hatred of Jews, of Israel, and of their dominant U.S. allies; and as if the alliance of which some had dreamed in the 1990s between the populist extreme Right and Islamist groups had briefly come to life in the form of a common rejection of Jews, wealth, and capitalism. A single redemptive force had brought two "imagined communities" of contradictory inspiration together: on the one hand, a community of intransigent Catholics dreaming of a purified nation purged of all immigrants, recent or ancient, and defending a distinctive cultural code; on the other hand, a community that saw itself as part of the *umma*, the community of Muslim believers, hostile to all Jews and enlisted in the media-propagated crusades of Osama bin Laden directed, in the French case, exclusively against Jews. Does this mean that these two rival forms of anti-Semitism could briefly reinforce each other, as two identity-based nationalisms combined to undermine the status of French Jews, who could no longer count, as they had in the past, on the support of the French state? Were French Jews now faced with two opposing movements, while the government and the public remained indifferent, leaving the Jewish community vulnerable to a fatal blow against the old French model of integration?

In today's world, Jews are primarily oriented toward one or the other of two dominant centers, each of which claims to embody to perfection the possibility of a full Jewish existence: the United States and Israel. In the United States, Jews have found a haven of peace and tolerance, a "homeland" that stands as a model of Diasporan existence, a modern Babylon that adds the further blessings of liberal democracy. Although it is true that pluralism, individualism, and various forms of assimilation threaten the durability of Jewish identity, the primary challenge probably comes from U.S. Jews' participation in a profoundly multicultural social space in which relations between different cultural groups are far from regulated. In Israel, the question of multiculturalism is equally vexing, even though the society conceives of itself as exclusively Jewish: It has proved necessary to reinvent the relations between state and religion and the links between Jewish citizens and their distinct cultures and identities in order to make them more egalitarian without relinquishing their special tie to Judaism in favor of a mere community of citizens. These challenges are not insurmountable, even if they do call many preconceived ideas and certainties into question and point toward a future that is rather difficult to imagine as well as toward a new conception of public space capable of accommodating cultural differences.[27]

Apart from these two centers, Israel and the United States, the only other significant model for the future of Jewish society is France. In the countries of the former Soviet Union, the importance of Judaism is diminishing by the day, as a thousand-year history in which much of Jewish culture was forged draws gradually to a close. The same can be said of the Muslim countries, from Morocco to Yemen. That leaves Great Britain, Hungary, Argentina, and above all, France, whose symbolic importance in modern Jewish history is crucial because of the role of the Enlightenment and the French Revolution in forging a model of Jewish emancipation. In today's Europe, the fate of the French Jews therefore turns out to be crucial as an alternative to the two major centers of Jewish life: Israel, a state in which Jewish culture dominates, and the United States, which is basically a pluralist society with an important communitarian element. In contrast to Jews in both of these societies, French Jews have, over the course of a lengthy history, placed great weight on the importance of their privileged relationship with a strong state cast in the role of a liberator of minorities. They have traditionally maintained a vertical alliance[28] with the state, which has used its power to keep particularisms under control and to banish collective identities from the public space while at the same time bestowing legitimacy on each sect.

Since being granted citizenship during the French Revolution, most French Jews have enthusiastically embraced the republican contract, which limits religious and cultural expression to the private sphere. As zealous supporters of the emancipating Republic, French Jews ceased to exist as a nation and did not oppose the broadest possible extension of the rule of *dina de malhuta dina* (the law of the land is the law). Like their fellow citizens, and in particular their fellow Catholic citizens, who bore the brunt of the secularization of public space that gradually called into question the Christian character of French society, they were obliged to bow to the state's assertion of control over marriage and adapt to state regulation of religion through the consistorial system established by Napoleon. Deeply integrated into French society, benefiting from rising social mobility thanks to republican meritocracy, tapped to play leading political roles of great symbolic importance, and identified with zealously pro-republican Jews who rose to eminent positions as ministers, deputies, generals, prefects, state councilors, and appellate judges, the Jews of nineteenth-century France remained faithful to the republican ideal despite the Dreyfus Affair and outbreaks of anti-Jewish violence. They fully assumed their role as citizens of France. Integration did not cause their cultural identity to vanish, though expression of that identity was limited to the private sphere.

Throughout the nineteenth century, French Jews found ways to remain Jewish, avoiding mass conversion, self-hatred, and marriage outside the faith. It is true, however, that state domination of society, implicit in the logic of the strong state, accentuated the decline of Jewish life and Jewish studies. The benefits achieved through integration in the public sphere entailed costs in the form of a loss of collective consciousness and diminished creativity in Jewish culture. The impact of what was called "Jewish science" in Germany, although not negligible in France, was relatively limited.[29]

In many respects, therefore, it is fair to say that the Jews of France developed a model of Jewish life in the Diaspora compatible with the French model of the state, namely, that of a strong state with universalistic norms further accentuating the vital function of the vertical alliance. Although some Zionist thinkers condemned this model and accused French Jews of serving a nation-state that submerged their identity, French Jews in reality proved every bit as capable as their non-Jewish fellow citizens when it came to preserving their own culture and memory, their own values and specific forms of sociability. Though deprived of territorial enclaves, they nevertheless managed to preserve a milieu of their own and to keep faith with their own history while fully embracing French citizenship and integration into the life of the nation. Thus, for Jews as well as non-Jews, a state-centered national ideology has been able to coexist with particularistic faiths and cultures with less conflict than is often assumed. Despite the feverish rhetoric of certain critics, the Republic has generally done well by Jews as well as Catholics, by Bretons as well as Berrichons.[30]

In recent years, however, this model has been decried by political theorists who have rediscovered the influence of communal cultures. The model is said to threaten the survival of each community's collective identity by reinforcing the power of a nation-state dedicated exclusively to the cult of reason. This argument has often been brandished by the nationalist Right, which rejects the model spawned by the French Revolution in favor of a national identity rooted in the remote past. Lately, however, it is more common to find it invoked by a Left no longer under the influence of Marxism, which took no account of "tribes," nations, or cultures. "Culturalists," such as Charles Taylor and Will Kymlicka, insist that each nation has its own specific character, its own true personality, and for them the French model of the rationalist nation-state has become a kind of bête noire; they overlook its actual capacity to leave particularistic cultures intact. The theorists of multiculturalism thus fail to recognize how flexible the French model is in practice. Rather than submerging particularistic cultures, it has largely succeeded in combining its unifying rationalist principles with respect for cultural differences.[31] By contrast, theorists of the public sphere influenced by the work of Jürgen Habermas acknowledge the French model as an ideal type of a post-nationalist discursive community of rational citizens capable of setting their particular cultural allegiances aside. This philosophical tendency invokes the French model of rational citizenship to construct the global concept of a European public sphere not tied to potentially irreconcilable historical and cultural traditions. But just as the theorists of multiculturalism fail to perceive the high level of de facto tolerance for different identities in the French model, the post-nationalist public-sphere philosophers fail to see that they overestimate the republican character of French society.[32]

The ambivalence of the general model is apparent in any consideration of the history of French Jews. As citizens of the nation at large without any territorial niche of their own, they were able to preserve a collective consciousness without constituting, as they had before the Revolution, a "nation within the nation." In contrast to the U.S. model, however, they were unable to achieve what has been called a "Judaization of their exile." Once the Jewish enclaves in Alsace and Lorraine and neighborhoods of Jewish immigrants such as the Marais in Paris disappeared, the French Jewish "homeland" became simply the nation itself, at least until fairly recently. In the wake of the decentralization laws of 1981, however, French Jews joined with other French citizens in rediscovering their regional "roots" and cultures, as well as in cobbling together various revivals of traditional religious life, as public expression of communal cultural forms increasingly gained legitimacy. This resulted in a sort of "communitarization from below," as certain publicly visible political and consistorial entities entered into public debate as representatives of French Judaism.

Signs of an increased Jewish presence in the public sphere became unmistakable. The social practices of relatively recent Jewish immigrants who had come to France in the wake of the decolonization of North Africa also called more attention to the Jewish presence, as did the somewhat paradoxical and unexpected "regeneration" of traditional French Judaism, which manifested itself in the appearance of Hebrew letters on storefronts and the expansion of Jewish schools, paralleling the expansion of Catholic private schools in the same period. In France as in the United States, it became increasingly common for Jews to wear distinctive clothing, such as skullcaps. This was especially noticeable in certain neighborhoods and suburbs of Paris (such as the Nineteenth and Twentieth Arrondissements, Sarcelles, and Créteil) and in certain other cities, such as Strasbourg. There were even efforts to establish symbolic markers designating certain portions of public space as "religious zones." Major religious celebrations such as Torah Day drew upwards of thirty thousand people, and large demonstrations were organized in support of Israel and around other issues of concern to Jews. Taken together, all these things meant that the Jewish presence inside France was now impossible to ignore—a sort of "nation within the nation" compatible with the vision of Mirabeau but not with that of Abbé Henri Grégoire.

At the same time, the state has set about in a surprisingly deliberate way to bring about "communitarization from above" by recognizing as a legitimate part of the public sphere one community after another. Corsica, for instance—a French *département* with separatist tendencies—has been granted certain privileges at odds with French law. This demonstrates a certain "Girondization" of French society (to use a term that harks back to the Jacobin-Girondin split in the French Revolution, when the Jacobins sought to impose centralized authority and the Girondins advocated a certain local autonomy). While this may be a source of cultural enrichment, it poses certain difficulties for a nation-state based on the logic of universalism. In this effort of "communitarization from above," the state has been abetted by the national press, whose insistent use of the word "community" has pounded home the idea. Jewish circles have been particularly affected by this, as the highest officials of the government as well as the mass media constantly invite Jews to think of themselves as constituting an organized community. These efforts in turn reinforce the "communitarization from below," which gains daily in legitimacy and visibility owing to this backtracking by the state. Although "communitarization from below" affects all collective cultural identities in France, it has been particularly disruptive for Jews, who are urged to turn away from militant citizenship and to establish instead communal organizations that many French Jews reject.

Because French Jews have been recognized by the public authorities as constituting a legitimate community, many have lately been trying to re-create an "imaginary community" within the society and to establish for themselves a "homeland" within the nation. In so doing, they are turning away from the state and calling into question their traditional vertical alliance with the authorities. Like their fellow citizens, they seem more willing than in the past to subscribe to the logic of association or even market individualism, which is proving attractive to elites formerly devoted to the state. Emulating other Frenchmen, the Jews of France seem to be gradually accepting the logic of a weak U.S.-style state dominated not only by the market but also by associative and communitarian ideas that serve as justification for various forms of multiculturalism and affirmative action. Thus, the republican model itself has been shaken. This is true for all citizens, but the impact on French Jews has been especially significant, since they have been forced to forsake their traditional vertical ties to the state and enter into horizontal negotiations or conflicts with other groups.

Even if Jews still call on the state regularly to intervene and protect them, they suddenly find themselves more alone, almost isolated, and perceived as a special-interest group ultimately without much influence, given that they represent less than 1 percent of the population of France. In the instrumental terms of U.S. politics, their influence as a voting bloc offering party loyalty in exchange for specific communal advantages is therefore extremely limited, especially now that the political parties are increasingly willing to adjust the ethnic makeup of their candidate lists to broaden their appeal. In the past, when the logic of the strong state and militant citizenship prevailed, Jews found themselves at the symbolic heart of French politics, and their prominence in the pro-republican parties earned them the enmity of nationalists bent on attacking the Republic.

Today, with the decline of the state and the general shift of emphasis to civil society, there is a consensus that the Republic forms the backbone of the nation, and this has caused the Jews to lose some of their centrality and, initially at least, some of their vulnerability. Political anti-Semitism, which was linked to the role Jews played in the republican state, could only decline, and it was this political anti-Semitism that accounted for some of the most serious outbreaks of anti-Jewish sentiment of the nineteenth and twentieth centuries, from the Dreyfus Affair to Poujadism and even to the popularity of Le Pen. But a new social anti-Semitism has come to the fore. Nearly all the families that had provided generations of "state Jews" to France have turned their attention elsewhere, and the remaining state Jews have become more discreet as the Jewish "community" has become more visible. It is as if the effects of the Vichy government's betrayal of its high-ranking Jewish officials were still being felt today, impelling French Jews to withdraw from the public stage and retire to less exposed niches within the society—indeed, as if intrusive memory itself were compelling Jews to quit the public sphere in favor of the private.

Yet the Jews of France cannot escape history that easily, and today they are bearing its full brunt. They have lately been plunged into a historical situation that baffles them because its sources are so different from what they have dealt with in the past. The abandonment of the logic of the state has had unanticipated consequences that may become permanent, leaving Jews vulnerable in a France that has become a pluralistic nation no longer offering the protection of the republican model. The costs of that model—a degree of submerging of particularistic cultures—were offset by the benefits. Now the costs and benefits are different. Americanization—at least in the limited sense of a legitimation of cultural pluralism—is bringing with it unanticipated consequences of its own, reviving forms of competition and potential conflict that had largely been attenuated by the consolidation of the nation-state. The risks are all the more real because the French political imagination, shaped by the nation-state, is still hostile to the common U.S. assumption of multiple allegiances and diverse loyalties. American society was constituted by successive waves of immigration from many different countries, and Americans take it for granted that there is no fundamental incompatibility between adherence to the constitutional values on which the U.S. political system is based and persistent strong attachments to far-off countries of origin, even if some citizens may feel discontent or bitter if they see U.S. foreign policy as unjust toward their native land. Such frustrations have never led to internal clashes, however, except perhaps in some instances of nineteenth-century hostility toward Catholics. To be sure, there have been clashes, violent at times, between African Americans and Asian Americans, Latinos, and Jews, but these have had to do mainly with competition for scarce economic resources. They do not, for the most part, reflect politics stemming from affinities external to U.S. society. The tensions in question in no way reproduce conflicts between foreign societies to which U.S. citizens are entitled to feel legitimate attachments stemming from their cultural background. Each group sees the United States as its "homeland" while retaining its own foreign allegiances and memories.

Things are not necessarily the same in today's France, even though French society like U.S. society is composed of successive waves of immigrants. In fact, France and the United States are the two foremost examples of immigrant societies in the world today, but France long sought to integrate its immigrants, whereas the United States, despite its "melting pot" ideology, preferred to respect each individual's multiple identities. According to a number of U.S. sociologists, the paradigmatic American has a "hyphenated" identity such as "Italian-American" in which the left-hand term takes precedence over the right, so that the repository of shared values is minimal. In France, almost no one believes in multiple allegiances. Indeed, the idea that French Jews could be loyal citizens of France while asserting ties to Israel is a source of astonishment and even anxiety, whereas no one makes an issue of this in the United States, where all cultural groups retain deep ties to their country of origin. As a result, the abrupt decline of the strong state in France and the rise of particularisms in the public sphere has left imaginary communities suddenly facing one another—imaginary communities with no empirical reality or collective capacity, deeply heterogeneous, insubstantial, and composed of myriads of individuals with contradictory values. Hence, it is by no means certain that "as France becomes multicultural and multiethnic at the beginning of the twenty-first century, the history of French Jewry moves from the margins to the center."[33] On the contrary, one might argue that Jews, now merely one minority group among others, are abandoning their traditional vertical alliance with the state, which protected them from hostile masses and placed them at the heart of Franco-French conflict.* Rather than moving toward the center, they may be led to banish themselves to the periphery and retire from the stage of history, thereby relinquishing the leading historical role they have played since the nineteenth century in the French model—one of a number of possible routes to emancipation.

If we compare the anti-Semitic incidents of 1898 at the climax of the Dreyfus Affair with those of 2000–2004, the differences we see are indicative of the profound transformation that has occurred.[34] Today, in contrast to 1898, we do not find thousands or even tens of thousands of people thronging the streets of Paris and smaller cities throughout France screaming vile slogans and clamoring "Death to the Jews!" Of course, as noted earlier, such cries can once again be heard in the streets of Paris, but furtively directed at a passing rabbi or other Jew. This is nothing like the tumult of 1898, when angry crowds howled in hatred and heard their words echoed by mass-circulation newspapers and politicians with a national audience. Outspoken rejection of a Jewish presence in French society was then part of the French political landscape. Some people wanted to deny citizenship to Jews and exclude them from the public sphere, even to destroy them or expel them from France. The public dimension of today's anti-Semitic mobilization is nothing like this. The streets are generally calm. There is no permanent threat of collective anti-Semitic action. Even if Le Pen appears to have achieved a durable hold over a part of the French electorate, the nationalist and populist press has abandoned its overbearing tone, and its circulation has shrunk to a fraction of what it once was, while the national media of all political stripes severely condemn anti-Semitic rhetoric. Thus, nothing comparable to the old anti-Semitism exists except the acts themselves: The number of people injured is smaller, and the number of attacks on synagogues and schools is smaller still. To be sure, communitarization has made the Jewish presence far more visible, and attacks are now likely to target not

---

\*　The conflict born in 1784 and appearing since that time until the middle of the twentieth century between Republican and the conservative Catholics.

Jewish-owned stores but synagogues and schools in the Paris suburbs and provincial cities. Now, in contrast to the late nineteenth century, anti-Semitic acts are not accompanied by a flood of propaganda in the form of tabloids, songs, caricatures, and even toys. They are limited to direct attacks on property and people, including Jewish students and teachers, who are assaulted, insulted, and molested.

France is not living in a state of siege as it was in the days when the police and army maintained order by mounting constant patrols, charging demonstrators, and standing guard outside buildings. France remains peaceful. Nothing seems likely to disturb the peace. Public order is not threatened, not even by the repeated cases of arson in synagogues, which have gone up in flames one after another, or the attacks on individuals, which are not just rumors. A profound change has taken place in the mode of anti-Semitic expression. Anti-Semitism no longer has deep roots in social movements influenced by Catholicism, which has itself lost much of its own influence because of a general erosion of religious sentiment as well as the Church's decision to support the Republic and withdraw its support from various antirepublican factions.

Hence, the present differs from the era of the Dreyfus Affair in that the nation appears not to be very concerned by the recent surge of anti-Semitism, which poses no threat to national institutions or to the republican regime. Thus, we are probably witnessing a decline of anti-Semitism of a strictly political kind directed against a strong state perceived to be an instrument of the Jews in their alleged effort to de-Christianize French society. The correlation between a strong state and political anti-Semitism as a specifically political mode of reaction retains its heuristic value, but its significance cannot help but diminish when the state's power over society recedes and the government gives freer rein to the expression of traditional anti-Semitism inherent in society itself and reflecting prejudices and fantasies about Jews.[35] The state is not now speaking with the same clear and firm voice it has as in the past, as in late 1898, for example, when French elites finally awoke to the fact that it was the Republic itself that was threatened. The state is still not very active in arresting those who attack Jews and their institutions, and the courts have hardly been quick to impose stiff sentences. Apart from a few incidents that made headlines, the press has generally relegated stories about such attacks to inside pages, where they are lost among articles about traffic accidents, injured dogs, and pedophiles. Meanwhile, some French Jews sense that their current and future position in French society is threatened and that the full-fledged citizenship they have enjoyed since adhering to the republican pact is now in peril. Having become a small minority group, they sense that they are no longer shielded by the protective umbrella of a state that seems to be allowing various social forces to go their own way. It is as if the much-bruited "Americanization" of France has led to the adoption of broad political strategies conceived not in terms of far-reaching political platforms or worldviews but as a means of maximizing voter support at the polls in closely contested elections.

In this respect, Pascal Boniface's report to the Socialist Party, drafted early in 2001, has proved disastrous, especially since it was not rejected out of hand by the party leadership. It is likely that similar reports have been written by strategists for the parties of the Right eager to win the votes of French citizens of Muslim descent, as if they formed a homogeneous bloc whose support could be secured only by a shrewd decision to take a critical stance toward Israel. Such an instrumentalization of politics is incompatible with the idea of a public space of citizens in France, yet there can be no doubt that such an instrumentalization has taken place.

Boniface is the director of the Institut de Relations Internationales et Stratégiques. His report, prepared as an internal memorandum to Socialist Party leaders, was entitled "The Middle East, the Socialists, International Equity, Electoral Efficacy." It contains some astonishing passages. The effect of the "link between the struggle against anti-Semitism and the all-out defense of Israel," the report argues, has been "to provoke irritation with the Jewish community" and

> to isolate it at the national level. . . . By using its electoral influence to win impunity for the Israeli government, the Jewish community stands to lose in the medium term. The community of Arab and/or Muslim descent is also organizing, and in France at any rate it will soon wield enormous influence, if it doesn't already. . . . The perception that Socialist policy on the Middle East is not balanced confirms the Arab-Muslim community's sense that its views are not taken into account or are even rejected by the Socialist camp. The situation in the Middle East and the timidity of Socialists in condemning Israeli repression are forcing French Muslims to react defensively by asserting their own identity, and no one—Jew, Muslim, Christian, or pagan—can be happy about this. Of course it is better to lose an election than to lose one's soul. But to put it bluntly, if we put the Israeli government and the Palestinians on the same plane, we risk losing both. Is supporting Sharon worth losing in 2002? It is high time for the Socialist Party to abandon a position that, in seeking balance between the Israeli government and the Palestinians . . . does not serve—indeed, it disserves—the medium-term interests of the Israeli people and the French Jewish community.[36]

The effects of this attempt to inject identity politics into the French electoral arena can be seen in the Third Arrondissement of Paris and in the suburb of Sarcelles, where candidate lists reflect the fact that these districts are home to a Jewish population. It can also be seen in the Thirteenth Arrondissement, where the lists reflect the presence of people of Asian descent.

It gets worse with each new election in Paris, Lyons, Marseilles, and Roubaix, when the parties nominate French citizens whose names suggest that they are of North African descent. All this points toward an ethnicization of politics,[37] which to one degree or another all the parties must recognize as they seek the votes of a minority group comprising some four to six million individuals and representing at the very least a million voters whose support may well prove decisive. By contrast, the Jews of France number only five or six hundred thousand, and they are even less of a political force owing to the fact that, apart from their common rejection of Le Pen and his National Front, their votes are dispersed among the parties. On the whole, moreover, they reject the ethnic strategy and deny that there is such a thing as "the Jewish vote."[38] They vote in much the same way as their non-Jewish compatriots. Furthermore, it is by no means certain that French of Muslim descent are susceptible to the ethnic appeal, which may well put off those eager to follow the republican path to emancipation and unwilling to vote as a communitarian bloc.[39] Nevertheless, the Boniface report, with its legitimation of an ethnicity-based campaign strategy, marked a turning point. Of little importance in itself, this incident was nonetheless powerfully symbolic; in addition, it sparked intense polemics that influenced the way people think.

Insignificant as the Boniface report is in itself, it may nevertheless mark the beginning of a new era, since it basically sets forth a communitarian policy that favors one "community" at the expense of another. Both communities are judged in terms of their probable influence in the next national elections. The party's commitment to moral or ideological imperatives is devalued, and the universalist character of a public space in which citizens are supposed to act in keeping with their values and not their allegiance to a nation within a nation is seriously undermined. As Elie Barnavi has pointed out, "The Jewish community is thus no longer an aggregate of individual French citizens whose fight against anti-Semitic prejudice should be of concern to the entire national community. . . . It is reduced to a 'nation' in the pre-revolutionary sense, a nation well advised to adopt a defensive posture if it does not wish to reawaken old demons."[40] The Boniface report in effect essentializes collective identities that are in fact volatile, contradictory, and increasingly internalized in the imaginations of individuals themselves. It appears almost to justify the current surge of anti-Semitism by holding the Jews responsible for what the writer considers to be their immoderate attachment to Israel. It thus condemns the very principle of a full-fledged plural citizenship in the public sphere by asserting that ties external to the nation are perfectly legitimate if rooted in the citizen's own memory and history. Must French Jews, who have only recently grown accustomed to addressing their enemies openly in the public space and to making their desires and concerns known, resign themselves, as in the past, to whispering among themselves,[41] to making inaudible comments on the events that torment them without expressing their hopes and expectations? Must they resign themselves to renouncing an essential part of their citizenship, to keeping a low profile, to hugging the walls, to keeping their convictions and loyalties to themselves for fear of finding themselves ostracized as in the past and treated as a separate nation—in a word, to being reified? In their heart of hearts, are they coming gradually but inexorably to think of themselves as pariahs of a new type, even though they are full citizens of a liberal nation in which the rights of citizens are guaranteed by law?

The current surge of anti-Semitism directed at Jewish citizens of France cannot be tolerated. Those citizens are reacting, moreover, not as a community or "nation within the nation" because they know full well that such a reaction would be alien to the republican pact. If anti-Semitism is to be controlled—and more than ever, this is the task not of outside parties but of the state, which has for too long remained dispiritingly silent—it is time to overcome fears of expressing multiple solidarities yet without allowing foreign conflicts to be transposed into the national space. Precisely because "the law of the Republic is the law," it is important that the law protect, and soon, all citizens who respect it while keeping faith with their own memories and cultures. Citizenship is in no way incompatible with identity, and identity is in no sense a justification for the numerous acts of anti-Semitism against French Jews in recent years. French Jews did not question their integration into the Republic in spite of the anti-Semitism they encountered at the time of the Dreyfus Affair; they tried to forget their betrayal by the Vichy regime in view of the German presence and the indispensable assistance offered to Jews by other Frenchmen; and they have always considered all of France to be their natural "homeland," in which they were free to exercise all their rights as citizens; but the current situation threatens to put them on a tightrope, in a position that is precarious because it embodies a multiplicity of intensely felt loyalties. The state's sudden retreat and the rise of particularism in the public sphere has brought imaginary communities abruptly face-to-face. The implication of all this may be that the Jews, now reduced to the status of one minority among others, have no choice but to withdraw from their traditional alliance with the state, from the familiar vertical alliance that used to protect them from hostile masses while affording them a prominent but dangerous place at the center of Franco-French conflict. This divorce, though barely noticed, is already taking place, yet French Jews have no idea what their fate will be in a transformed public sphere in which horizontal alliances cannot be taken for granted.

—Translated by Arthur Goldhammer

# 9

# Esau Can Change, but Will We Notice?

*Konstanty Gebert*

They noticed my *kippa*, my skullcap, almost immediately. "Dirty Jew," they jeered. "Dirty kike." Loud, spiteful voices. There were four or five of them, youngsters, on the escalator behind me. The escalator was chock-full, but people just pretended they did not hear, did not see. No one reacted. The ride down to the subway station dragged on, but fortunately nothing more violent happened. They jostled me at the landing, but if not for their ridicule, I probably would not have even noticed. What hurt was not so much what these youngsters said or did but the fact that nobody else did anything. This was my third experience of its kind in a week, and I was getting edgy.

But what else can one expect if one lives in Poland and runs around in a kippa, you might ask. Fair enough—and over the last dozen years or so I have had a few nasty incidents, although probably fewer than you might think. Almost never, however, when harassed, did I have to confront the perpetrators alone. With just a few exceptions, passersby would react, express support, engage my assailants. The escalator experience was of a different kind. But then again, this was Paris, not Warsaw. And, to be fair, my timing for visiting in a kippa was probably not best chosen: it was late March 2003, the beginning of the Iraq war, which French public opinion vehemently opposed. Some saw a "Zionist plot" behind the U.S. strategy. Poland was less critical of the war, and for once it did not seem that Poles were blaming the Jews.

The difference between France and Poland was striking. Although personal experience is never a sound basis for drawing general conclusions, I could not avoid thinking that it was indicative of a sea change in social attitudes in both countries. Anti-Semitism, long in the Jewish mind indelibly attached to Poland, is no longer prevalent there. At the same time, it no longer is beyond the pale in France, the country of Émile Zola and human rights. Both developments are surprising, though probably not to people who have been closely following local developments. And both seem to indicate that although freedom from hate is never assured anywhere (but then, which freedom ever is?), Amalek need not remain Amalek forever.

Most of Poland's track record in contemporary Jewish history goes from bad to devastating to repugnant. There seems to be a logical progression from the officially sanctioned anti-Semitism of the interwar period to the horror of the Shoah and on to the obscenity of the postwar pogroms and anti-Semitic campaigns. Nor was much dissent heard from the Poles themselves, which seemed to indicate that they approved or at least, did not disapprove. As former Israeli prime minister Itzhak Shamir succinctly put it, "They suckle anti-Semitism with their mothers' milk." When, in a meeting with him, I criticized this statement, saying that no Jew has the right to be racist, he replied, in perfect Polish, "Polish peasants murdered my father and his family when they were hiding from the Germans. What would you have me say?"

Nothing. There is no counterargument to suffering and pain. Relatives of mine, hiding during the occupation on the Aryan side in Warsaw, eventually returned to the ghetto, where they felt safer because there were no Poles there to denounce them to the Germans—and then, of course, they ultimately perished in Treblinka. But I also had a grandfather who survived on the Aryan side by hiding in a Polish village. Two dozen people, almost all of them non-Jewish, were involved in his rescue. HaShem was willing to save Sodom if ten righteous people could be found there. I will not be more demanding than he.

Yet I believe we need to place our suffering in context in order to understand its reasons. Understanding, contrary to the French saying, does not necessarily lead to forgiveness, nor am I willing to forgive in somebody else's name. But it is a necessary prerequisite of any intelligent debate and action. We can hardly remain satisfied with the vision of Esau remaining hostile forever. Esau is no Amalek.

In the interwar period, anti-Semitism, though dominant, was not the only attitude in Poland toward Jews, either in public opinion or in government circles. Liberals, Socialists, and Communists would protest anti-Semitic measures, hold demonstrations, and express solidarity. Police would often act against anti-Jewish mobs, occasionally causing loss of life. Nor were Jews the only group singled out for discrimination: Ukrainian villages were raided by the police and army in search of real and imaginary terrorists; dozens of villagers were killed, and thousands were incarcerated. Other minorities also suffered. Interwar Poland was an authoritarian state getting worse—and yet it was better than its neighbors east and west (though not south), as the steady flow of refugees, Jewish and not, attested.

Under the Nazis, anti-Semitism increased, and most Jews could at best count on a callous indifference to their fate from their neighbors; interest would more often be malign than benign. Yet this was not the reason the Germans put their death camps in Poland; they were totally indifferent to what the Polish *Untermenschen* approved or disapproved of. The horror of Jedwabne—a village where in the summer of 1941 at least several hundred Jews were murdered, most of them burned alive in a barn—was committed by Poles, however, not Germans. Nor was it an isolated case: More than a dozen similar massacres are currently being investigated by the Polish Institute for National Remembrance. Yet all these massacres occurred within a few days of one another, in a restricted radius of some fifty kilometers, and in a province that, even before the war was known for the extreme anti-Semitism of its Catholic hierarchy and the political influence of the fascist-like ONR (Obóz Narodowo-Radykalny) party. Conditions elsewhere in Poland were milder, though hardly satisfactory, and no new Jedwabne-like incidents have been so far identified elsewhere in the country. With the great public visibility that the story of the Jedwabne massacre attained during debates after the case was publicized by Jan Gross's book *Neighbors*,[1] one can safely assume that had there been other similar cases, they would by now have been revealed. Jedwabne is not characteristic of the fate of Jews in Poland under Nazi rule.

The Kielce pogrom of 1946, in which forty-six Jews were murdered by a Polish mob incensed by a rumor that Jews were kidnapping Christian children to make Passover matzos with their blood (in July, no less!), however, is characteristic of the situation of the Jews in immediate postwar Poland. Though no other massacre in Poland in the first two postwar years was as bloody, violence was widespread and systematic. Jews, seen as supporters of the Soviet-imposed Communist regime, could not feel safe anywhere; the government eventually gave them arms for self-defense. This violence, however, took place within the framework of a bloody civil war, which claimed at least thirty thousand lives, and of the general lawlessness of the postwar years. Human life was dirt cheap, and Jewish life was cheaper than most. One cannot overlook the fact, however-er, that existing Jewish organizations had supported the regime, which was legitimately seen by a majority of Poles as illegitimate, thus involving the Jewish community in a bloody political conflict. Anti-Jewish violence had subsided by 1947, but anti-Semitic feelings flared up again in 1956, when a de-Stalinization campaign concentrated on the only too real crimes committed by secret police functionaries of Jewish origin, conveniently overlooking crimes perpetrated by those who were ethnic Poles. Finally, in 1968, a combination of the repression of a student democracy movement and an interparty power struggle led to the expulsion of some twenty thousand Jews from the country. But here again, the motivation was in part political: Some old Jewish Communists were clinging to posts that Aryan young wolves wanted to have, and some of their children were active in the student movement that the young wolves' secret police bosses had just crushed. This particular campaign, therefore, is as much part of the wider history of internal Communist Party power struggles as it is part of the wider history of anti-Semitism in Poland.

All this, however, should not obscure the fact that throughout, a unifying anti-Semitic ideology held sway, singling out Jews as objects of hatred. Precise accusations would vary from having killed God through being allied with communism to resisting communism, but clearly no other group was branded and affected as were the Jews. This was not a specifically Polish ideology, however: it was a European one, and its manifestations could be seen all across the continent, from Russia to Spain. Its impact was always more severe in an unfree society; one could therefore expect that if an independent and democratic Poland were to come into being, the country's attitude toward its Jewish citizens would change. And this is precisely what happened after the transition of 1989.

Actually, the change preceded Poland's democratic transition. The generation born after World War II, which came of age in the seventies and became the backbone of the democratic opposition, developed a keen interest in "things Jewish." In part, this was due to curiosity about a subject that had become taboo, but in greater part, it signified a moral reaction to the distortions and manipulations of both the Communist authorities and of the dominant part of the unofficial narrative. A Jewish publishing boom emerged, first—and this, in the light of later, less promising developments, needs to be remembered—in Catholic publications and publishing houses. In fact, a segment of the Catholic Church, under the impact of Vatican II that belatedly started having an effect on the country's faithful, opened itself to Jewish issues and Jewish concerns. There was no proselytizing involved; instead, there was a genuine interest in "things Jewish" and moral outrage at their occlusion. This in itself was a breakthrough of historical proportions. The Church had been responsible, through traditional Catholic theological teaching, for much of the anti-Semitism of the past, endorsing political anti-Semitism as a matter of course. Given this legacy, statements contained in the Catholic Cardinal August Hlond's pastoral letter of 1936—which condemned Jews for all sorts of evils, from white slavery to dishonest business practices to communism, and advocated separating them from "Polish" society but condemned resorting to violence to achieve these ends—were to be seen as a positive step. This position even apparently worsened after the war, with Hlond explaining the Kielce pogrom as an understandable if deplorable popular reaction to the "Jew-Communist" power grab. Later, however, Hlond's successor, Primate Wyszynski, obliquely condemned the anti-Semitic campaign of 1968.

Subsequently, the Solidarity movement, which emerged in 1980, championed the rights of all Poles, whatever their ethnicity or religion; in a touching example, in 1981 the local chapter in the small town of Pulawy placed all remaining Jewish monuments "under the protection of the Union." Yet Solidarity, which represented the nation organized, included all stripes of political opinion, anti-Semites included. During the union's first congress, some delegates, soon ironically dubbed "true Poles," enquired into the ethnic origins of their political opponents within the movement. Later, a prominent regional leader railed against "traitors with changed names" who "should be hanged outright."[2]

This orientation remained a permanent feature of the union's political makeup. Less visible in the underground years that followed the military coup of 1981, it reemerged after 1989, in statements made by Lech Walesa in his presidential campaign ("I am 100% Polish, which is more than some other candidates can say"[3]—an allusion to his chief rival Tadeusz Mazowiecki's falsely presumed Jewish origins), in overtly anti-Semitic declarations by Solidarity leaders at the Ursus tractor plant, a historical birthplace of the union, and in anti-Semitic sermons delivered in Gdansk by Father Henryk Jankowski, the movement's chaplain. Yet the same Lech Walesa, visiting Israel in 1991, departed from prepared remarks in his speech given at the Knesset to condemn and ask forgiveness for any suffering the Jews had experienced at the hands of Poles. Solidarity was also widely present at unofficial ceremonies for the fortieth and forty-fifth anniversaries of the Warsaw ghetto uprising, held under martial law; one of Solidarity's leaders, future defense minister Janusz Onyszkiewicz, even served time for the crime of reading aloud a message of support from the union's underground leadership.

The issue of Polish-Jewish relations, past and present, remained very much in the forefront of public debate throughout the nineties. Crises such as the protracted struggle for the removal of the Carmelite convent from the grounds of the camp at Auschwitz and its aftermath, the "war of the crosses"; public statements such as those by Father Jankowski, already mentioned; and debates about the degree of Polish factual and moral coresponsibility for the fate of the Jews in World War II, ensured that it stayed there. And while foreign opinion, especially that of U.S. Jewish observers, understandably concentrated on expressions of unadulterated anti-Semitism ("The Star of David is contained within the sign of the swastika"[4]—Father Jankowski, sermonizing on the responsibility of the Jews for World War II), the fact remains that the debate was not only between anti-Semites and Jews but cut across Polish society, with a substantial—and growing—segment of it overtly and actively opposing and condemning anti-Semitism.

Furthermore, two key elements of contemporary anti-Semitism—historical revisionism and anti-Zionism—are markedly weak in Poland. Parliament passed a law penalizing the denial of Nazi or Communist crimes, and—in the only case of public revisionism—Darius Ratajczak, a young historian at a provincial college, promptly lost his job when he started publicizing the writings of Roger Faurisson and his ilk. Faurisson is a French researcher, a literary critic by profession, who maintained that the gas chambers never existed; Ratajczak claimed to be publicizing Faurisson's work solely to give his own students an appreciation of what he claims is a legitimate historical controversy. The law worked in this case, but it is not always so efficient: The prosecutor's office, acting on a citizen's complaint, did indict Father Jankowski for "incitement to national and ethnic hatred," but a judge threw the case out of court, quoting "the low social threat" such behavior supposedly entails.

This shameful ruling needs to be seen in context. Another judge threw out a suit brought by a black victim of a racist beating against the publisher of a pamphlet of antiblack jokes, ruling that "Poles have a sense of humor" and can differentiate between joke and reality. The Polish judiciary still has a ways to go.

Attitudes toward Israel are particularly interesting. Perhaps unsurprisingly, sympathy for the Jewish state has always run relatively high in Poland, owing both to the Polish origins of its founders and to the geopolitical stance it adopted. After the Six-Day War, Warsaw wits quipped happily: "Our Jews beat their Arabs!" A knee-jerk reaction to government propaganda ensured the abiding unpopularity of the Palestinian cause: I myself, writing in the underground press in the eighties about international affairs, was accused of anti-Semitism for the statement that the Palestinians' goal of self-determination might be legitimate even if the methods used to bring it about are not. My critic was a right-wing commentator, also underground and not known for any special sympathy to Jews. But he and parts of the Polish nationalist Catholic right wing somewhat distortedly saw in Israel what they wanted Poland to become: a militarily strong, politically independent, fiercely nationalistic, and religious state that acts as it pleases, pulls no punches, and responds to uppity neighbors with overwhelming force. This phenomenon remained isolated on the world scene until the rise to prominence of the U.S. Christian Right. Not to be outdone, the Left saw in the Jewish state an incarnation of its socialist/liberal dreams. In addition, many non-Jewish Polish families simply had friends there.

It should therefore not come as a surprise that the first major foreign policy decision of Poland's first non-Communist government, in the fall of 1989, was to reestablish diplomatic ties with Israel, which had been severed by the Communists in 1967. Poland was also very active in the United Nations, working for the repeal of the shameful "Zionism Is Racism" resolution that the Communist government in Warsaw had earlier strongly supported. Finally, when direct flights from the Soviet Union to Israel were not yet possible, Poland acted as way station for the Russian aliyah, terrorist threats notwithstanding. This pro-Israel stance has been maintained: Poland's voting record in the United Nations, including on the Human Rights Commission, is, on issues of concern to Israel, good to excellent, European Union pressure notwithstanding. Poland is an importer of Israeli weapons, a deal politically too sensitive in many other democracies, and the Polish media's coverage of the Middle East is much more balanced than that of the mainstream press in the United Kingdom, France, or Italy.

This does not mean Poland's foreign policy is one-sided. Poland maintains traditionally good relations with the Arab world, supports Palestinian self-determination, and informally grants the PLO mission in Warsaw the status of an embassy. Nor is criticism of Israel, at times unjustifiably harsh, absent from the Polish media and public scene. But as a Jew—and a supporter of Israel—I feel comfortable with the position my country has taken. And where else can an Israeli ambassador, his face immediately recognizable from untold dozens of TV appearances, go dancing in a street crowd, welcomed and cheered, his bodyguard lost far behind? This is standard fare at the yearly Cracow Jewish Culture Festival, itself one of the biggest manifestations of Jewish culture on the continent. Its (non-Jewish) organizers were asked to repeat their performance in 2004 in the Marais, the Jewish quarter of Paris.

But more than anything else, the Jedwabne debate is probably the most emblematic illustration of current Polish attitudes. The publication of Jan Gross's *Neighbors* in 2000 in Poland had the effect of a bombshell. Whereas in prior debates the "defenders of Poland's interest and honor" knew they were trying to make the best of a bad case, occasionally slipping into outright falsehood and denial when they argued that Poles had played no adverse role in the Shoah—and most everybody was aware of this—this time, Poland honestly did not know. Although the Polish Jewish community had preserved the historical memory of the massacre and its implications,[5] non-Jewish Poles were utterly ignorant of the case. Not only that, but the story ran contrary to basic beliefs about the course of Polish history: The actions at Jedwabne were what others (Ukrainians, Russians, Germans) did to Poles, not what Poles did to others. The result was shock—and catharsis. The Institute of National Remembrance, Poland's Yad Vashem, did its own investigation and endorsed most of Gross's findings. Its director, Leon Kieres, mercifully a Pole of unimpeachably Catholic peasant stock and a beacon of moral probity, was attacked in Parliament as a "stooge for non-Polish interests". Responding earlier to his critics, in a statement that will not be forgotten, he stated: "I do not, as a Pole, feel responsible for what happened in Jedwabne, but I feel guilt for it. If I am attacked for feeling that, and for saying it out, I reply: No-one has the right to deny me the feeling of guilt for what happened on July 10, 1941." Slightly over 50 percent of Polish public opinion endorsed the Institute's findings entirely, only a minority rejected them outright, and a full 33 percent expressed the belief that Poland should ask forgiveness of Jews for the crime, they themselves being willing to personally sign such a statement. This was almost certainly post-Communist Poland's most important debate to date: Of those polled, 85 percent said they are familiar with it, a salience probably reached only by the debate on abortion.

The political impact was not less impressive. On June 10, 2001, the sixtieth anniversary of the massacre, President Aleksander Kwasniewski went to Jedwabne and delivered a moving speech, condemning the murder and asking for forgiveness and reconciliation. As a post-Communist and—again falsely—rumored to be of Jewish extraction, he was by some denied the legitimacy of speaking in the name of the Polish people (which, incidentally, had elected him by a healthy majority and continues to give him high approval ratings). Responding implicitly to the challenges, he powerfully said that he was speaking "in the name of all those whose conscience has been moved" by the crime. Israeli ambassador Shevach Weiss, in his speech, remembered the martyrs burned alive in the barn in Jedwabne and then went on to say, "But I also remember other barns"[7]—like the one in which, when he was a child, he and his parents had been hidden from the Germans by Polish and Ukrainian neighbors during World War II, in what was then eastern Poland. It was a high point of Polish-Jewish reconciliation.

Yet the anniversary event was not attended by some who should have been present. The Solidarity prime minister, Jerzy Buzek, was not there, preferring instead to host, that same evening, a commemorative concert in a Warsaw church. In his speech, he stressed the power of art to overcome suffering. I told him that I—a former underground Solidarity activist like himself—was ashamed to see that it was the former Communist Kwasniewski who had the moral courage to say what had to be said. More striking still was the absence of the Catholic Church. Cardinal Józef Glemp had justified this absence by fears of "political instrumentalization." The Church had held its own expiatory ceremony more than a month earlier. At a special Holy Mass, bishops in simple black penitential cassocks knelt on the stone floor of Warsaw's All Saints Church to ask of God forgiveness for the crime at Jedwabne, which had been committed by Christians. The televised event was impressive, the emotion palpable. And yet the impact would have been greater had forgiveness been asked not only of God and had the church not been almost empty: Only half of Poland's bishops participated, though all had come to Warsaw on that day to participate in a meeting of the Episcopate. Not many other faithful chose to attend, though the Mass had been well-publicized and open to all; in front of the church a small group of protesters, who condemned this Catholic sellout to presumed Jewish pressure, also attracted little attention. The rabbi of Warsaw, Michael Schudrich, declined an invitation to attend, since the event took place on the eve of the Jewish holiday of Shavuot, but a clever observer noted that the Mass ended well before sunset and that therefore the rabbi could have made it.

Another reason why the rabbi and other members of the Jewish community (we decided to treat the invitation extended to the rabbi as addressed to all of us) decided not to be there was that this particular church also houses Warsaw's most extensive library of anti-Semitic literature, from the *Protocols of the Elders of Zion* to *100 Lies of Jan Gross* (true, the most offensive titles were that day not on display). Yet another reason had to do with a series of statements by the primate of Poland in which he denied the existence of anti-Semitism in prewar Poland ("Jews were simply disliked because of their bizarre folklore,"[8] he said) and wondered when the Jews would finally ask forgiveness for the evils of communism. I volunteered to give him satisfaction on this last count, expressing willingness to apologize to him for Jakub Berman, the Jewish member of the Polish Stalinist Politburo in charge of the secret police, if he would apologize to me for Boleslaw Bierut, the ethnic Pole who was president of Stalinist Poland. To date, my offer has not been acted upon. All this had led to the absence of the Church hierarchy at the Jedwabne ceremony. And though Catholic friends have since protested my statement that the Church itself was absent—we were there, they correctly say, and we too are the Church—my disappointment at this moral failure remains undiminished, especially since the Church had, over the previous ten years, made considerable and laudable efforts to come to terms with its past.

This situation illustrates well the ambiguities of the Polish Catholic Church when confronted with the legacy of anti-Semitism. On the one hand, the sale of the *Protocols* and other such trash is unfortunately not limited to that particular Warsaw church. They can be bought in many Catholic churches nationwide, and the Catholic daily *Nasz Dziennik* often engages in anti-Semitic polemics, often accompanied by vicious denunciations of the Jewish state. Radio Maryja, a fundamentalist broadcaster with mass appeal, whose programs are reminiscent of those of Father Charles Coughlin's in the United States in the thirties, has not been shut down or condemned by the Church for the presence of anti-Semitism in its broadcasts, though the Church has sharply condemned its insubordination to ecclesiastic authority for Radio Maryja has clearly Lefebvriste leanings. When outraged Catholic laity recently called on Church authorities to ban the sale of such books, their request was denied— on grounds of freedom of expression, no less. One wonders if the Church would therefore approve, for example, distributing the magazine of the Polish gay community on Church premises—or even the Jewish magazine that I publish. Cardinal Glemp, in his statements, seems to express a mainstream Catholic consensus.

On the other hand, those who condemn anti-Semitism are certainly not marginal. Poland is one of the few Catholic countries in which the Church has set up an annual day of Dialogue with Judaism. The first chairman of the Episcopate's Commission on dialogue with Judaism, Bishop Henryk Muszynski, had been an almost successful contender, against Cardinal Glemp, in elections for chairman of the Episcopate a few years back. In 2004, he was expected to run again, and so was his successor on the Commission. Both are considered good friends by the Jewish community, both had in the meantime been promoted within the hierarchy, and both were considered serious contenders. This is a clear indication that reaching out to Jews is not an impediment to a successful ecclesiastic career, a statement that in a hierarchical institution rings louder than the publication of books on the necessity of dealing with the past and building a dialogue with the Jews—and there is no shortage of those, either. Furthermore, these books, which also include volumes on Judaism by Polish and translated Jewish authors, are put out by established Catholic publishers, whereas the publishers of the *Protocols* and such are marginal or anonymous.

The Church is also beginning to deal very specifically with the issue of Christian responsibility for anti-Jewish violence. A pastoral letter of the Episcopate, published early in 1992, asked forgiveness for such acts. A number of priests have published books and articles in mainstream Catholic journals dealing in detail with the blood libel and Church-incited pogroms. The Catholic majority has certainly not yet interiorized this knowledge, but denial is giving way to moral unease. And certainly a cornerstone of much of prewar Catholic preaching, the belief that only a Catholic can be a true Pole, has taken a beating from which it will not recover. A minority—from 15 to 30 percent of the general population, according to different polls—still believes Jews are not "truly" Polish and would deny or limit some rights, and even larger percentages might express unease with what they perceive as "excessive Jewish influence" in the life of the nation or with the prospect of having a Jewish neighbor, boss, or son-in-law. These results, unfortunately, do not differ from what is found in other European nations. More to the point, never has any political action been undertaken to attempt to implement such bias, de jure or de facto. In a nation that has begun electing immigrants, including Africans, to local posts, racialism, though still present in people's minds, is a losing proposition.

The Jedwabne debate—frank, honest, and largely devoid of denial—and the powerful anniversary ceremony marked a turning point in Polish-Jewish relations. Joanna Tokarska-Bakir, a cultural anthropologist, whose essay on the Jedwabne case deservedly won Poland's prestigious Essay of the Year award, concluded that this debate puts an end to the myth of Poland's innocence, the cherished historical illusion that Poles have always been victims, never oppressors. "Some things simply cannot be seen from close by, and especially from within. One of them is the Polish obsession of innocence. The rules which govern Polish public and private debate, which is controlled by this compulsion of innocence, are another . . . How does the Poles' knowledge of themselves and of the Holocaust translate into Polish innocence? . . . Our memory is a place in which there are no Jews . . . It is worthwhile to ask why our memory is capricious and fails us over causes which seem to be just and morally incontrovertible . . . This Polish unmerciful and traumatic anti-Semitism of good and gentile people, which closes shut the issue of the Holocaust even before it is raised, which exaggerates each unfair Jewish comment and dismisses each fair one—it is not the result of a traumatic experience? Is the Holocust not, from the view-point of many elderly Poles, a perfidious Jewish and German dirty trick, which once and for all cuts away the return to Soplicowo*? The myth of Soplicowo played a fundamental role when [Poland's] independence was being recovered. But since we are home back again, it has become a dangerous delusion."[9] No similarly deep and wide-ranging debate has taken place in any of the other Nazi-occupied countries, France emphatically included. My non-Jewish Polish friends, incidentally, are less thrilled with it than I am. Having known nothing about Jedwabne, they registered a deep moral shock at reading Gross's book, and expected from the debate a moral release it could not have provided. Jews, on the other hand, had always known about the facts—and what shocked them, in a positive sense, was the frankness with which the Poles came to terms with that knowledge.

Or, should I say, most Poles. A survey of anti-Semitism, released in the summer of 2003, as compared to a similar survey conducted eleven years earlier, cast some cold water on what might have been overly hasty optimism. The percentage of those agreeing with a set of traditional anti-Semitic stereotypes (Jews as Christ-killers and the like) remained stable at 11 percent, contrary to predictions that it would decline assuming that those endorsing such beliefs would simply die out. Apparently, enough of such hatred is still being peddled to poison younger minds. On the other hand, the percentage of those rejecting such statements rose from 55 to 59 percent. More worrying, however, is a marked increase in the percentage of those agreeing with a set of modern anti-Semitic statements (such as "Jews have too much power") from 17 to 27 percent, while the percentage of those opposed actually declined, from 38 percent in 1992 to just 32 percent in 2003. This last set of results may be due to the fact that while in 1992 attitudes toward Jews were shaped mainly by the past, both by accumulated biases and by the recognition of their existence and the desire to overcome them, contemporary attitudes are being shaped by recent events. These include the use of anti-Semitism in current Polish politics, a series of demands made by different Jewish bodies on Poland (property restitution, pressures that amends be made for evils of the past), and a growing if still man-

---

\* The name of a Polish manor and the literary symbol of Poland's innocent past.

ageable hostility to Jews as a result of policies of the Jewish State that are perceived as unacceptable.

These polls should, however, be seen in the broader context of other polls. It is possible to believe that "Jews have too much power in Poland" and yet sincerely condemn the Jedwabne massacre, to support the right of free speech for anti-Semites without necessarily being anti-Semitic oneself, to sincerely condemn anti-Semitism and yet be against having a Jewish son-in-law. Expressions of public attitudes will vary depending on the kind of stimulus that triggers them, so the overall picture need not necessarily be consistent. What is important, however, is the declining percentage of those who, when confronted with different kinds of anti-Semitic statements, express no opinion on them. Attitudes toward the Jews have become an index of a wider set of opinions, on democracy, tolerance, modernity, and the like. The Poland that is rejecting anti-Semitism does so because it wants to rejoin Europe. And this is where paradox can strike. For the Europe that rejected anti-Semitism as long as the generation of witnesses of the Shoah was alive seems—if the example of France, as discussed in this book, is to be considered relevant—to be adopting a more tolerant attitude toward this historically central element of European identity. If the postwar period of condemnation of anti-Semitism eventually appears to be a sixty-year aberration in the two-millennia-long history of European anti-Semitism, then the Poles, in their valiant attempt to finally exorcise the horror, will appear out of sync with Europe once again.

This, however, is not a foregone conclusion. Yet to say that the Jewish reaction to the profound changes in Poland over the last fifteen years has been muted would be an obvious overstatement: There has been almost no reaction. Some may say, to be sure, that the belated endorsement of decency—and as I have illustrated above, a spotty endorsement at that—deserves no applause. On this I beg to differ: Decency is far too scarce a commodity for Jews or anyone else to afford the luxury of ignoring it. My fear, however, is that we have simply become too attached to the vision of the immutability of Amalek to allow facts to stand in our way. But if so, we do it at our own peril.

# 10

# Telling the Past Anew: Recent Polish Debates on Anti-Semitism

*Jaroslaw Anders*

Not long ago, I returned from Warsaw, my native city. I visit it approximately once a year and have developed a habit of spending the first day after the transatlantic flight walking the streets and reading the writing on the walls: homemade posters, pasted leaflets, graffiti. I have noticed that over the last few years this form of public discourse has been undergoing a series of noteworthy transformations. The standard fare of anti-Communist and anti-Semitic slogans, often lumped together, as they often were in Poland, has been gradually replaced by a more diverse array of public resentments. "SLD [the ruling post-communist coalition] = KGB," "EU = Communism," "EU = Fascism," "Good president = dead president," "Anarchy yes," "Class war goes on," "God hates faggots," "God hates bigots," "Women—be free," "Nobody is illegal." An occasional swastika, a Star of David dangling from a gallows, seemed less conspicuous and somehow less menacing in the midst of this new democracy of political gibberish.

Many Polish intellectuals seem to agree. My Warsaw friends were quick to point out that in Poland, anti-Semitism is no longer an idea capable of mobilizing masses for political action. It survives, they say, at the most as a mindless reflex among the most primitive social groups and is indistinguishable from other kinds of public idiocy. They claimed it is devoid of real content and therefore no longer dangerous. I was assured that those who scribble on the walls hardly understand the meaning of the slogans they use. They are people who feel left out during the social and economic transformations taking place in their country, and they merely vent their general frustration by spitting insults at everybody they can think about—from the European Union and the United States to . . . yes, the Jews.

Within the Polish Catholic Church, we still hear admonitions that the "obsessive" evoking of the problem of Polish anti-Semitism is divisive and offensive to national pride, and that it is distracting Poles from other, more important problems. When the Polish primate, Cardinal Józef Glemp, visited Israel in 2000 and called Polish Catholics to resist all manifestations of anti-Jewish sentiment, Archbishop Józef Michalik of Przemyśl responded that attributing anti-Semitism to Poles creates unnecessary animosity, breeds hatred, and can result in "immeasurable evil." In other words, talking about anti-Semitism is worse than anti-Semitism itself.

In Church circles, this reluctance to deal with past and present anti-Semitic tendencies in Polish society may be understandable considering the Church's own unedifying record. But the tendency to de-emphasize, even ignore, the historical, psychological, and moral gravity of the issue also exists among the secular, liberal intelligentsia. It is as if anti-Semitism dissolved right in front of our eyes in the malodorous cesspool of other prejudices, obsessions, conspiracy theories, and phobias—the irrational, endlessly mutating mental waste of modern mass society. People of good will and moral sensitivity in Poland seem resigned to the fact that in today's acrimonious, coarse public discourse, anti-Semitism is just one of many unsavory, offensive idioms. Besides, they point out with sad relief, Polish feelings about the Jews hardly matter any more because there are practically no Jews left in Poland.

The last statement is painfully true. Before World War II, there were about 3.5 million Jews living in Poland, constituting close to 10 percent of the country's population. In the eastern parts of Poland and in some big cities, the proportion was much higher. But more then 90 percent of Polish Jews perished in the Holocaust. A majority of the estimated 350,000 survivors subsequently emigrated to Israel or to the West. Today, the number of Jews in Poland is estimated at five to ten thousand in a total population of close to forty million. Those figures, however, are highly speculative and primarily count those who belong to Jewish religious communities or cultural organizations. Despite the admirable efforts of a handful of organizers of Jewish cultural and civic life in Poland, like Konstanty Gebert, the publisher of a Polish-language Jewish monthly *Midrasz*, the rich, multifarious Jewish presence in Poland belongs to the past.

And yet Jews in absentia remain a strange irritant for the Polish collective psyche. When debates on Jewish or, to be more specific, Polish-Jewish subjects do take place, they erupt with uncanny, edgy intensity as if the past was still very much determining the present. Perhaps in some special way it still is. Many observers have marveled at the peculiar Polish phenomenon of anti-Semitism without Jews (or even without anti-Semites, because no one would freely admit to being one). There is, in fact, a whole slew of mostly marginal but vocal groups that make anti-Jewish rhetoric an important part of their official programs. The most significant among them is Liga Polskich Rodzin (LPR; League of Polish Families), an extreme-right political party commanding 40 of 460 seats in the Polish Parliament. Its youth wing, Młodzież Wszechpolska (All-Polish Youth), is active in Polish schools, organizes "white power" rock concerts, and has even won a number of seats in Poland's local governments. The Polish populist peasant movement Samoobrona (Self-Defense), whose popularity suddenly spiked on the eve of Poland's joining the EU, is ideologically more vague than LPR, but its local chapters maintain contacts with extreme-right nationalist and anti-Semitic groups.

The number of violent anti-Semitic incidents in Poland is relatively low—much lower than in France, Germany, or even Great Britain—but there is a visible proliferation of anti-Jewish pamphlets and publications. Although rarely seen in reputable bookstores, they can be obtained, for example, in many government-leased newsstands as well as in some churches. Many of these publications come from the presses of the notorious Leszek Bubel, the publisher of the *Protocols of the Elders of Zion*, and of a 'helpful pamphlet', *Poznaj Żyda* (How to Recognize a Jew). One of the main sources of distribution of anti-Semitic literature is the Antyk bookstore located in the beautiful All Saints Church in Warsaw, which stands on the border of the former Warsaw Ghetto facing Europe's only Yiddish theater. Despite protests from some Catholic youth organizations, the Church hierarchy in Poland has refused to close the bookshop down.

Amid colorful, increasingly Western-looking Warsaw stores and chic cafés, those images are like the sudden, cold whiffs of decay occasionally reaching the passerby from the yards of Warsaw's half-abandoned, crumbling tenements that survived the city's near total destruction by the Germans in 1944. How deep does this shameful, lingering stench penetrate the Polish social fabric?

More systematic analyses of contemporary Polish attitudes toward the Jews yield a rather contradictory answer. A poll conducted in July 2000 by Poland's Center for Public Opinion Research (CBOS) showed that about 70 percent of respondents had no personal contacts with Jews but that 55 percent had heard anti-Semitic remarks.[1] Three-quarters of those questioned supported punishing, or at least publicly denouncing, anti-Semitic activities. More than half of the predominantly Catholic sample agreed with Pope John Paul II's statement that "Jews are our elder brethren in faith." Another study conducted in 1994 and compiled by a Polish sociologist, Ireneusz Krzeminski, indicated that about 17 percent of Polish respondents show most of the attitudes and beliefs associated with the notion of anti-Semitism.[2] This is roughly as much as in other developed societies. But Poles seem to be very receptive to something that may be called "casual" or "accidental" anti-Semitism. The same study showed that 60 percent of respondents chose at least one reply indicating anti-Jewish sentiments. Younger people were relatively free of such sentiments, but animosity against the Jews was strongest among the generation that grew up during or immediately after World War II. The majority of Poles who had personal contacts with Jews describe them as positive. Anti-Jewish attitudes in Poland seem to be passed along primarily in the private domain—within families and groups of friends. When asked whether Poland is an anti-Semitic nation, 35 percent of Poles said no, 21 percent said yes, and some 30 percent chose an evasive answer.

This strange jumble of opinions is evidenced during periodic public debates about past and present Polish-Jewish relations, whose participants tend to split into almost equal camps of accusers, deniers, and obfuscators. The most recent case was a debate sparked by the publication of Jan Gross' shocking book *Neighbors*[3] about a pogrom committed by Poles in the eastern town of Jedwabne in the first days of Nazi occupation. The heated exchange of opinion in the Polish media lasted over a year. Although ostensibly about the debate, it offered interesting insight into Poland's present-day complexes, anxieties, and myths that lie at the core of the Polish national identity.

In May 2000, a small Polish publishing house brought out this slim volume by a New York based Polish historian, Jan Gross, telling the story of the horrific incident known to historians but hardly mentioned in public debate. Gross's book, subsequently published in the United States, created a shock of disbelief among Poles used to seeing themselves as noble martyrs of World War II unblemished by collaboration with the Nazis. What proved particularly hard to accept for the large number of those participating in the public debate was Gross's assertion that the crime was possible because of a deep residue of Polish anti-Semitism, for which all Poles of that time partly bear the blame. While acknowledging that the German presence in Jedwabne was probably the catalyst of violence and that therefore the tragedy was "but an episode in the murderous war that Hitler waged against all Jews," the author summoned his compatriots to collective reckoning. "We must be clearheaded enough," he wrote, "to remember that for each killing only a specific murderer or group of murderers is responsible. But we nevertheless might be compelled to investigate what makes a nation (as in 'the Germans') capable of carrying out such deeds."[4]

Some Poles, mostly on the extreme Right, summarily rejected Gross's account as yet another example of Jewish anti-Polish slander. Antoni Macierewicz, former dissident and later activist of several rightist political groups, called Gross's book a part of "a campaign of hatred directed at Poles and Poland" by international Jewry "declaring a journalistic and propaganda war against us." In Macierewicz's view, the campaign had an ulterior, materialistic purpose. It was supposed to create "conditions for the recovery of property that belonged to the Jewish community, murdered by the Germans on Polish soil."[5]

On the other end of the spectrum were those who exhorted their compatriots to accept the fact that anti-Semitism was a shameful and often criminal part of Polish history. A Polish sociologist, Hanna Swida-Ziemba, wrote that even the Holocaust did not change the anti-Jewish attitudes of many, perhaps the majority, of Poles. She also agreed with Gross that the responsibility for acts of violence against Jews extends to "all bearers of anti-Semitic views in Poland and—indirectly—to those who were indifferent, who did not oppose them."[6] But a considerable number of participants in the debate, while accepting the basic facts of Gross's account and condemning the perpetrators, struggled to prove that the events in Jedwabne, although horrifying, had little to do with "Polish anti-Semitism." Some suggested that the real motive for the massacre was robbery because "Jews controlled all stores and warehouses." Others claimed that the town's population must have been coerced by German soldiers or by a small pack of Polish thugs. Still others questioned the reliability of eyewitness testimonies or hinted that a massacre could take place only because of the victims' passivity.

The debate also revived the old argument about "Jewish anti-Polonism," as supposedly parallel and morally equivalent to "Polish anti-Semitism." The allegation that Jews are culpable of irrational, visceral hatred of Poland and things Polish and tend to blame Poles rather than the Germans for the Holocaust was already current in the Polish nationalist underground during the Nazi occupation, and curiously, it has survived until the present day. When Roman Polanski's film *The Pianist* opened in Poland, one critic remarked sarcastically that we finally have a movie about the Holocaust that shows that "not all Poles were bad, and not all Germans were good."

One of the current permutations of the belief in Jewish anti-Polonism that surfaced during the Jedwabne debate was the charge of widespread Jewish collaboration with the Soviets, who invaded together with Germany under the Ribbentrop-Molotov pact, and later with the Moscow-imposed Communist regime. The Polish primate, Cardinal Glemp, stated in a homily in May 2001: "We wonder whether Jews should not acknowledge that they have a burden of responsibility in regard to Poles, in particular for the period of close cooperation with the Bolsheviks, for complicity in deportations of many of their fellow citizens, etc. The fact that Poles also took part in these repressions does not exclude the fact that the leading role was played by officers of the UB (Security Police) of Jewish descent."[7]

The myth that Jews played a prominent role in the repressive organs of the Communist regime (neatly combining the image of the Jew as a disseminator of the Communist plague with that of the Jew as eager persecutor of Polish patriots) was frequently invoked during the Jedwabne debate as an implicit extenuating circumstance for the perpetrators of the massacre or as a handy way of changing the subject. In an essay published in one of Poland's largest dailies, *Rzeczpospolita*, Tomasz Strzembosz, a distinguished historian at Lublin Catholic University, claimed that although nothing could justify the savagery of the crime, what happened in Jedwabne was possibly not an eruption of anti-Jewish hatred but an act of political retribution. While quoting mostly oral testimonies of local Poles, Strzembosz accused Jews in the eastern parts of Poland of enthusiastic reception of the Soviet invaders, active collaboration with the Soviet police, betrayal of Polish resistance fighters, spontaneous violence against Polish neighbors, and even armed uprisings against Polish authorities. "If they did not regard Poland as their homeland," wrote Strzembosz about Poland's Jews, "they did not have to treat it as an occupation regime and join its mortal enemy in killing Polish soldiers and murdering Polish civilians fleeing to the East. They also did not have to take part in fingering their neighbors for deportations, those heinous acts of collective responsibility."[8]

It is entirely possible that there were Jews among Soviet collaborators and oppressors in Jedwabne. Although Communists were a small minority among Polish Jewry and religious Jews considered communism a heresy, some Jews might have greeted advancing Soviet troops as protectors. Some might have even used the time of the Soviet rule to settle accounts with their Polish tormentors. It should be remembered that before the war, the local Polish governments were run mostly by the virulently anti-Semitic Endecja National Democratic Party, which openly called for the removal of Jews from Polish lands. But the frequent Polish claims of alleged Jewish "overrepresentation" and unique viciousness in the organs of Communist repression have never been borne out by any material evidence. If anything, historical records show that Polish Jews were also prominent among the victims of Soviet repressions. In any case, it takes an anti-Semite to see a Jewish Communist, or a Jewish traitor, as someone acting on behalf of all the Jews.

The Jedwabne debate also revealed that many Poles still believe that Jews possess an inordinate influence on public opinion in the West. Even some of those who accepted the main premises of the Gross book and called for national reckoning were visibly irked by the fact that *Neighbors* appeared in the United States, where, they assumed, it would be used to damage Poland's image. Jan Nowak-Jezioranski, one of the most respected political analysts and a hero of the Polish wartime underground, stated honorably that Poles should face the horror of Jedwabne without looking for moral loopholes. But he followed his appeal by cautioning his readers that "we have both friends and relentless enemies among American Jews." He also called for "immediate preventive action to limit the damage caused to Poland by the world reaction to the news of the massacre."[9]

Such oversensitivity may be characteristic of a nation in transition, struggling for respect and recognition in the global community. But it also betrays a skewed view of what really constitutes a "national image." It is not the past itself but the way the past functions in the present public discourse that makes or destroys the reputation of a community. Needless to say, few are ready to condemn contemporary Americans for slavery, the Indian massacres, or even, more recently, the Jim Crow laws, unless, of course, someone tries to defend the "good name" of the United States by launching "preventive actions" or diminishing the horrors of those events.

Perhaps one of the most surprising, and perhaps also symptomatic, statements during the debate came from Adam Michnik, a hero of Poland's democratic opposition, a prominent liberal intellectual, and the editor of the largest Polish newspaper, *Gazeta Wyborcza*, which distinguished itself in numerous battles against nationalism, bigotry, and intolerance. In an emotional op-ed article published simultaneously in *Gazeta* and in the *New York Times*, and in a subsequent polemic with Leon Wieseltier in the *New Republic*,[10] he emphasized his personal disbelief, shock, and revulsion at the events described by Gross. But, as if heeding Nowak-Jezioranski's call for preemptive action, he asked rhetorically, "Do Poles, along with Germans, bear guilt for the Holocaust? It is hard to imagine a more absurd claim." In fact, neither Gross nor any of the serious defenders of his book, in Poland or abroad, made such a claim. Further on, Michnik complained that "Polish and foreign newspapers" write about the murderers, and pass in silence those who rescued Jews. Again, the salvo was aimed at a purely imaginary target. Almost all accounts mentioned the facts that many Poles risked their lives to save their Jewish neighbors and that Polish names predominate in the Jerusalem memorial to Righteous Gentiles. Michnik also hinted at Jewish culpability toward Poles by calling the Jews to reckon with the "darker side of Jewish memory" as a "prerequisite to understanding Polish-Jewish relations." And finally, the Polish intellectual protested against what he saw as burdening Poles with "collective guilt and collective responsibility." "When I hear a call to admit my Polish guilt, I feel hurt the same way the citizens of today's Jedwabne feel when they are interrogated by reporters from around the world," he wrote.[10]

Coming from a prominent public figure and a historian, that last statement seems a peculiar misreading of the meanings of "guilt" and "responsibility" as they functioned in the debate. Of course, nobody was expected to admit his or her personal "guilt" in crimes committed by somebody else a long time ago. Such an act of contrition would be emotionally false and morally meaningless. But some who spoke on the subject, both Poles and Jews, did ask Poles—all Poles—to think strenuously about the past, to acknowledge the true nature and hidden sources of its evils, and perhaps to reach an understanding of how such events could have happened among people not much different from themselves. In that and only that sense they were asked to "take responsibility" for the future of their nation, not its past.

In many respects, the debate on Jan Gross's book was encouraging and reassuring. It showed that an increasing number of Poles were ready to assume such a responsibility. But it also showed that the subject of anti-Semitism still discomfits many Poles, inducing them to change the subject, to turn the tables, to grope for extenuating circumstances, or to subconsciously slip into old, discredited stereotypes and prejudices.

What causes such painful contortions? The endless obsession about the Polish "image" disguises the fact that what really matters to many Poles is not how others view them but how they must view themselves. Simply speaking, the whole subject of Polish-Jewish relations contradicts the canonical Polish memory, the established narrative of innocent, heroic sufferers—the romantic tale of a noble nation withstanding the overwhelming forces of history.

Krzemiński's research revealed that 78 percent of Poles believe they were more often the victims in history than were the members of any other nation.[11]

But during the brutal Nazi occupation, the Poles encountered something unexpected, something that obviously did not fit the narrative. Together with their own considerable suffering, they were forced to witness the unimaginable suffering of others. In fact, two wars were being waged in Poland at the same time: a war against the Poles and a war against the Jews. These wars were separate, yet they were interwoven into a bewilderingly horrifying tapestry of human fates and human choices. As events demonstrated, it was entirely possible to be a hero in one war and a passive bystander, a hostile onlooker, or even an active collaborator in the other. There were Polish heroes who saved Jews and Polish henchmen who tormented and betrayed them, and between those two extremes there stretched a vast area of ambiguity, of moral and emotional opacity, of actions and inactions whose motives were often obscure and unnameable.

Testimonies of Jewish survivors repeatedly mention the hesitation with which they approached even those Poles whom they considered their friends and whom they would trust unreservedly under less-extreme circumstances. Perhaps even Poles saw themselves in those years as strange, clouded, unknowable—not at all like the bright and simple nation that they knew from their prayer books and their national legends.

This realization should have marked the long overdue end of innocence, but the romantic legend of Polish purity in suffering was surreptitiously revived after the war. The Communist oppression seemed to call again for the old, simple self-image of the Pole as a saintly athlete of martyrdom. Memories were being erased by the Communist propaganda machine, but they were also suppressed by the Polish psyche unaccustomed to dealing with moral complexities. Perhaps it was the decades of stifled and distorted memory that produced the angry defensiveness and awkward elusions, the pointless recriminations and irrational fears even among people of clean hands and those who were themselves free of anti-Semitic sentiments.

It can be argued that since 1989 the Polish nation has been living through the trauma of recovered memory as its past—including the buried past of Polish-Jewish cohabitation—is finally becoming accessible. Poles face the task of rebuilding their self-image—in fact, their whole identity as a modern nation and part of the international community—in new, unprecedented circumstances. Perhaps the main task of Polish intellectuals, who are living through their own crisis of identity, should be to help in that endeavor, to show that political freedom is inseparable from the duty of intellectual freedom and that intellectual freedom requires, among other things, an uncompromising, clear-eyed view of one's past. Polish feelings about the Jews and the Polish-Jewish past may matter little to the Jews, but they should matter to Poles. As Gross stated in his book, a big lie lodged in the collective biography of a nation tends to warp everything that comes afterward. "Poland is not an exception in this respect among European countries. And like several other nations, in order to reclaim its own past, Poland will have to tell its past to itself anew."[12]

That is the task for intellectuals. But intellectuals seem tired, and not only in Poland. The mood of unconcern that settles in as soon as the latest heated debate peters off exists in numerous local permutations. Each country seems to have its own version of this exhaustion. In Poland, as the Jedwabne debate demonstrated, it is the concern about Poland's "good name" and assertions that the Poles should apologize to the Jews only when the Jews apologize to the Poles. In Germany, it is a sense of exhaustion by the moral revolution that the German nation has undergone since World War II and rising calls for unburdening the nation from the weight of its history, allowing it to finally become a "normal" country. (A normal country, it seems, is one that may be allowed a certain, reasonable amount of anti-Semitism without the rest of the world reaching for the panic button.) In France and some other European countries, anti-Jewish slogans became part of the "anti-imperialist," "antiglobalist," pro-Third World, and, of course, pro-Palestinian rhetoric of the Left. In his book *La nouvelle judeophobie* (The New Judeophobia)[13] a French scholar, Pierre-André Taguieff, describes the infatuation of the French leftist intellectuals with the figure of the young Arab rebel, who became the new antiestablishment, antibourgeois icon with his anti-Western and anti-Zionist (often *classically* anti-Semitic) harangues.

But the moral demobilization in the face of rising anti-Semitism cannot be explained only by specific political circumstances in today's Europe. It is not easy to pinpoint the real cause of this seeming weariness, this lack of a sense of urgency. An obvious explanation, of course, is the passage of time that moves us further and further from the experience of the Shoah, which demonstrated both the infinite evil and the mysterious uniqueness of the phenomenon of anti-Semitism. We believe we have learned the lesson well, but perhaps because of that we also believe that we do not need to subject ourselves to any more tests; we are free to occupy ourselves with something else. A new generation is coming to the scene, both in Eastern and Western Europe—the second generation that has no personal experience with the war and the Holocaust.

For this generation, it is difficult to perceive the Jews as a vulnerable, powerless, mostly pacifist people. Now the Jews have their own country, it is said, their own army, and their own politicians, who make wise or stupid decisions. And yes, sometimes they may evoke irrational negative feelings . . . like everybody else.

I think this shift in perception is mostly good, but it is also somehow desensitizing. It is so easy to forget or to deny that the negative feelings about Jews invariably surge from the same buried sources that have been lying in wait for decades and generations, and that they immediately fill the same old capillary system in the collective subconscious. In the meantime, our memory becomes an artifact. It turns into the ritual of commemoration. Our emotional responses also become ritualized—we go on making Holocaust movies, we go on publishing Holocaust memoirs, but we already know what they contain. We know how we should react, and we react dutifully, decently, and we move on. It all belongs to the past. It is amazing how slowly, how reluctantly, our supposedly well-trained imagination responded to the more recent genocidal attempts in Cambodia, Iraq, Rwanda, or right at our doorstep in the former Yugoslavia. It is strange and unsettling to realize how difficult it was to feel compassion, to make the connection, to say that, yes, it is happening again.

But anti-Semitism has always posed a certain problem for intellectuals, especially liberal intellectuals. Ruth Wisse, devoted a whole book to the subject: *If I Am Not for Myself: The Liberal Betrayal of the Jews*[14] where she argued, quite persuasively, that the phenomenon of anti-Semitism is a negation of classical liberal beliefs about the mitigating rationality and goodness of man, about social progress, and about the perfectibility of human relations. The Holocaust, said Wisse, was a negation of those beliefs. What is more, it proved that liberalism could not save the Jews. The failure brought about a crisis within the soul of liberalism, and the most prominent reaction to it was glossing over or denying the fiasco. Writing about the curious insensitivity of contemporary liberals, especially in Europe, to the mortal threat to Israel and Israelis, she said: "Anti-Semitism discomforts liberals by forcing them to abandon their pacific, generous, optimistic view of the world in order to take account of a specific, aggressive, and declared intention of destroying—yet again—the Jews." As a result, the "inconvenient Jewish variable" is sacrificed to the purity of liberal ideals. "The more virulent anti-Semitism grows, the more ordinary people are inclined to wish it away."[15]

But perhaps the root of the problem reaches even deeper. Despite thousands of books written on the subject, despite hundreds of interpretations, anti-

Semitism remains, in my opinion, very much a mystery. It is remarkably impervious to intellectual analysis. The enigma starts with its phenomenology: What is it and how does it exist? Is it one continuous phenomenon or a sequence of phenomena? Is it homogenous or composite? Is it an idea, a belief, perhaps an ideology, an emotion, a mental illness, a flaw of character? We know about its uncanny durability, its mutations, its many disguises, its ability to adapt itself to every set of social conditions, to attach itself to almost any idea, to serve as a catalyst for the most fantastic, warped ideological constructs. But how does it begin, where does it come from, how and where does it enter the mind of an individual, or the body politic? Of course, there are many ingenious answers to those questions; but each of them, to my mind, leaves out an important chunk of reality. The moment we define the object of our analysis, its outline starts to flicker, and the thing itself slips from our grip. Part of the weariness, the irritability that I notice among some of my intellectual friends, not only in Poland, may be due to this frustration, a sense of failure in what is the main task of an intellectual: to understand and by understanding to expose, to disarm, to render harmless.

This weariness may be part of a larger syndrome. Obviously, we are not living at the end of history, but it sometimes feels as if we are living at the end of the history of ideas. Of course this end, like so many other "ends" before, will eventually prove to be just a transition. But this is where we are: It is harder and harder to pretend that the world cares much about ideas and, to paraphrase W. H. Auden on poetry, that ideas make anything happen. The revolt of the masses, which José Ortega y Gasset diagnosed in 1929, is again gaining momentum. Resurgent anti-Semitism is certainly one of its components, but intellectuals seem to believe, perhaps rightly, that this time they have little to contribute. The heroic era of intellectualism, with all its moments of glory and moments of infamy, appears to have come to an end. We are but sad, resigned observers, memoirists, readers of scribbling on city walls, writers of minority reports. We even start to celebrate our ineffectiveness as a virtue in the mode of the nineteenth-century Eastern European intelligentsia. We try to keep our distance because we have been wrong before, we have been chastised for our errors, and also because too passionate an involvement in anything today looks awkward and sometimes even ludicrous.

I do not wish to conclude in either lament or exhortation. The phase of intellectual weariness, discouragement, impotence about anti-Semitism and about so many other things is probably just a phase. I also do not anticipate catastrophic events, especially of the kind that intellectuals would be capable of averting.

Experience teaches us that social and political catastrophes are averted and human lives are saved by moral character and courage rather than by intellectualizing. But I do see the need for vigilance and watchfulness, because the toxin of anti-Semitism is spreading again, and we never know when and how it may overwhelm our natural immunity. I see the need for compassion, which is emotional comprehension of an experience of the other, especially if it is a terrible, unimaginable experience—like that of Shoah. Of course, it is as unachievable a goal as we can imagine, but a goal, nevertheless, to which we have a duty to strive (especially Germans and Poles, though for different reasons).

But perhaps all this is not a task for intellectuals *as intellectuals*. It is a task for moral and courageous people. Perhaps, when faced with the mysterious, unattainable, appalling, debasing fact of anti-Semitism, we need not more ideas but—here I quote the Nigerian writer Wole Soyinka describing Nelson Mandela—"the unselfconscious manifestation of uncluttered humanity." It sounds very old-fashioned, perhaps naïve, but "uncluttered humanity" may still be our best chance.

# 11

# Anti-Semitism in the Spanish-Speaking World

*Enrique Krauze*

In the historic center of Mexico City, there is an old square near the cathedral and the Palace of Government. It is called the Plaza de Santo Domingo, and the children of Jewish immigrants used to play there during the thirties. They did not know that three hundred years earlier, some of their remote predecessors, the "crypto-Jews," had been burned alive there during the autos-da-fé, not far from the School of Medicine, which had been the headquarters of the Spanish Inquisition.

In the Central Archive of the Mexican Nation are hundreds of records dealing with the vibrant crypto-Jewish community (the Marranos) who once lived in the capital of New Spain. Working with them, I found items of great interest, like the story of a family called the Riveras, consisting of the mother, Doña Blanca, and her five daughters. Brought before the Inquisition for secretly practicing Jewish rites, each one of these six women embodied a different response to anti-Jewish persecution, ranging from a heroic defense of their beliefs to craven apostasy. The records include the so-called prison conversations, discussions between the prisoners recorded by hidden spies of the Inquisition. One can hear the voices of the Riveras intimately detailing the rich texture of the crypto-Jewish life, marked by fear, secrecy, evasion, and—here in prison facing the prospect of a horrible death—their desire for revenge. Doña Blanca and some of her daughters would eventually be burned at the stake.

The parents of those Jewish children who played in the Plaza de Santo Domingo had come to Mexico from Eastern Europe, where many of them had experienced anti-Semitism. They had rapidly discovered, sometimes to their surprise, the tolerant character of Mexican society. They had been broadly accepted by the common people, the middle class, and officials of government. Certainly the word "Jew" continued to have many of the negative connotations it had acquired in Spain, and in some parts of the country, there existed (and still do) certain pockets of anti-Semitic feeling, primarily in the west, where a war of religion, called the Cristiada, had been fought in the 1920s between extreme right-wing Catholics and the fiercely anticlerical government of President Plutarco Elías Calles. But for the most part, the medieval prejudices of Spanish anti-Semitism did not prevail in Mexico. One of the most important reasons for this was the strong Mexican tendency toward *mestizaje*, race-mixing (a characteristic in which Mexico was very different from a country like Peru or Argentina). In Mexico, the notion of "otherness" and the prejudice against the other became meaningless because almost everyone mixed with the other. Another important reason for this tolerance was the early victory of the liberals over the conservatives in the mid-nineteenth century, which brought about a state and a constitution erected on secular foundations and true civil liberties (very different from Spain). It remains so until this day.

In 1924, the very same year that the United States imposed a quota on immigration, the government of General Calles issued a formal invitation to the Jews of Eastern Europe, urging them to come to Mexico. Tens of thousands came, and most of them rapidly prospered in business, industry, and the liberal professions. With the rise of Nazism, anti-Semitism did increase in Mexico but never posed any significant threat to Mexican Jews. A group of Mexican fascists called the Camisas Doradas (Gold Shirts) harassed Jewish street-peddlers, and some intellectuals—partly driven by strong anti-U.S. feelings—became pro-Nazi. Sadly, one of them was José Vasconcelos, the most important Mexican writer and thinker of the first half of the twentieth century, who founded a virulently anti-Semitic and pro-Nazi magazine called *Timon*. During the seventies, after decades of philo-Semitism in government and intellectual circles (based on genuine compassion linked to the Holocaust and sympathy for the liberals of the State of Israel) a new, more subtle kind of anti-Semitism began to rise in Mexico and the rest of Latin America. It was an anti-Semitism of the Left, which was angered by the Israeli occupation of the West Bank and Gaza. Mexico voted for the U.N. resolution that equated racism with Zionism. But in Mexico itself, none of this ever translated into persecution. Symbolically, for forty years, Mexican television had a single dominating news anchorman, with the easily ethnically identifiable name of Jacobo Zabludovsky.

In South America, Argentina, with its large Jewish population of some two hundred thousand, was the great exception to tolerance, but it was also a country whose capital, Buenos Aires, was marked by a Jewish cultural vitality second in the Western Hemisphere only to that of New York. Throughout the modern history of Argentina, there have been anti-Semitic incidents fueled by the ultranationalist parties that often had very strong pro-Nazi sympathies. This, of course, was further fed by the influx of many Nazi refugees after World War II. During the ferocious military dictatorship of 1976–83, an attempt was made to exterminate all those whom the generals considered leftists (including such groups as the Argentine psychiatric community). It was a persecution that can legitimately be compared to that of the Nazis—not, of course, in numbers, though those were large enough, but for its unspeakable cruelty. Many Jews who were left-wing militants, or who were accused of being so, or who were even relatives of those accused, would die in the secret prisons dedicated to torture and murder or would be thrown alive from airplanes into the ocean. Sometimes the electric probes of torture would be applied in rooms decorated with portraits of Hitler. The liberal newspaper editor Jacobo Timmerman—who was not a leftist but who "disappeared" (or maybe was just "taken prisoner") for daring to publish in his newspaper the names of kidnap victims—was tortured almost daily for months and only survived because his torturers had decided that he was one of the mythical "Elders of Zion" and they believed they could extract important information from him. He describes one session in which he lay under the electrodes for hours, wearing the hood that the Argentine torturers used as a standard procedure and splashed with water to increase the intensity of the pain. In that session no questions were asked. He experienced only the application of electric shocks while listening to constant choruses of the word "Jew! Jew!" But the terrorist attack of 1994 against the Jewish community center of Buenos Aires stemmed from a newer Muslim anti-Semitism and seems to have been orchestrated from Iran. There is an element of this kind of anti-Semitism in contemporary Chile, where the Palestinian population numbers about three hundred thousand and the Jews only fifteen thousand. Here again, the source of discord lies in the policies of the State of Israel. But in countries like Costa Rica, Peru, and Uruguay, Jews have flourished in various sectors of society, including the political realm. Even in Venezuela (where President Hugo Chávez has flirted with some radical Arab countries), currently there does not seem to be serious reason for alarm. In general (and with the important exception of Argentina, but not constantly or totally even there), the five hundred thousand Jews of Latin America have been an exception to the long history of anti-Semitic persecution.

There has always been something artificial and borrowed about the character of Latin American anti-Semitism. During World War II, Jorge Luis Borges wrote, "Hitler does nothing but exacerbate a pre-existing hatred; Argentine anti-Semitism has become a bewildered facsimile that ignores all ethnic and historic issues."[1] Borges (a defender of the Jewish people) was referring to a much-generalized condition in those countries where those last names of a secret "Judeo-Portuguese strain" were abundant.

\* \* \*

The case of Spain is another story because Spain was one of the original cradles of anti-Semitism. In that story, the Jew represented precisely the non-assimilated other, expelled yet present as a specter. Following this idea, a revealing book by Gonzalo Álvarez Chillida has been published in Spain, a book that is of no less significance than the classic works on this topic that have been published in other countries of Europe and that deserves immediate translation into English: *Anti-Semitism in Spain. The Image of the Jew (1812–2002).*[2] Each element of the title is significant, because the strangest thing about the Spanish case is that anti-Semitism survived despite the fact that for five centuries there have been no Jews in Spain. What remained is precisely its "image," a Gordian knot that for almost two centuries has formed part of the (characteristically Spanish) debate about the "being" and "historic mission" of Spain.

One of the saddest aspects of the book is the description of the deeply rooted and stable character of the anti-Jewish prejudice in the popular mentality, which is not mysterious at all when one considers that the Jewish presence on the peninsula ("the Golden Age" in Jewish historiography) lasted seven centuries. Maria Moliner's dictionary of Spanish usage defines the word *judiada* (roughly, in English, "jewing") in this way: "An unjust and badly intentioned action enacted against someone." The word *ladino*, originally used to designate the population and the Castilian-based language of Balkan Sephardic Jews, came to signify a person who is "astute and sly, who works with quickness and dissimulation in order to achieve what he wants."[3] Both words continue to be used. The variations of the degraded image of the Jew in popular sayings and refrains are impressive: "Jew, little shame, little conscience, and lots of game"; "For everything that they are shown, both Jews and cats claim it their own",

"To trust a Jew, absurd are you." There are many more. Clearly, these sayings refer back to the old medieval catalog that J. Tratchemberg and others studied, but they do so with a peculiar Spanish literary accent. Stained in his origin, the Jew is mean-spirited, malicious, vindictive, rich, usurious, and in the end, diabolic. The Jew's physical appearance is dual: large-nosed in the case of men, beautiful in the case of women. The image appears throughout the rich collection of medieval poems and stories; it shows up in songs and couplets, rites, legends and customs, some of which made it to Mexico. In Mexico's War of Independence, the popular army that followed the leader Miguel Hidalgo would pull down the pants of their Spanish victims seeking "the 'tail', the infamous sign of the Jew." "Spitting—say some—is a thing that only Jews do," as are selling and speaking naturally and unabashedly about money. In the famous Burning of Judas that takes place during Holy Week, there appears (in Spain and Mexico) a tailed devil, representing the disciple who betrayed Jesus, which ends up in the bonfire. And the most persistent of all of the incriminating mythologies is, of course, that which posits the Jews as a god-killer.

"Time has made customs with as much patience and measure as it has taken to create mountains," wrote Benito Pérez Galdós, the greatest Spanish-language novelist of the nineteenth century, "and only time, working day after day, can destroy them. Mountains are not destroyed by the tips of bayonets."[4] In political and ideological terms, Spain's modern history from the Cadiz Constitution of 1812 until the fall of Francisco Franco in 1975 can be seen as, essentially, a complex battle of the liberal conscience (in all of its forms, from moderate to radical) against the solid mountain of absolutist and integrationist forces, as well as against the political and religious customs of the country. The Jewish issue has always been relevant because it is tied to crucial experiences of Spanish history: the decree of expulsion in 1492 and its consequences in the economic history of the empire, the role of the Inquisition, the "purity of blood" codes and their social effects, the nature of the Counter-Reformation and therefore of the Catholic religion (exclusive and excluding) in the forging of a national unity, and the international trajectory of Spain. There is a "pure" Spain that views its theological-political roots as the essence of its "being" and its providential destiny among nations. For this sector, which at some points in time composed the majority, the image of the Jew was always negative; Jews were hatchers of conspiratorial plots that were meant to subvert the established order and achieve, from the shadows, world domination. Freemasonry, the French Revolution and its vicissitudes, and democracy were seen as Jewish creations. In Spain and its provinces (with the partial exception of Catalonia, which resented its own otherness and identified itself at times with Jewish alterity), entire libraries were formed based on these themes and consumed by the reading public. Newspapers and magazines were published; theatrical works were written; novels, poems, treaties, countless lectures and sermons were given; an authentic mountain of cultural production was indebted to, in one way or another, *The Island of the Monopantos*, written in 1650 by the classic writer of the Spanish golden age, Francisco de Quevedo. This strange, repulsive work was written against "the infernal ilk" of Jews and the *conversos*, Jews who, whether under force or for strategic reasons, converted to Christianity ("vermin, enemies of light, friends of darkness, filthy, stinking, disgusting"), whom Quevedo imagined gathered together on an island in the Black Sea for the purpose of dominating the world. It was a direct precursor to the anti-Jewish literature of the nineteenth and twentieth centuries. In its intense hatred and its practical recommendations Quevedo's influential work is comparable only to *Mein Kampf* by Adolf Hitler: "Throwing them out and destroying them is the only possible measure to take, since punishing them is not an option . . . May they perish, my lord, all of them and all of their works."[5]

But in contrast to that Spain, things began to give way gradually yet irreversibly, leading to the other Spain, the liberal Spain. Even though Spain was the heart of the Counter-Reformation, it was also the country where the word "liberal" was used as a noun for the first time (in the anti-Napoleonic militias of 1808). Beginning even before the Cadiz Constitution, during the time of the Bourbon Enlightenment, these liberal tendencies worked to modify the ideas and customs, laws and institutions, prejudices and memory of the Spanish people. An obvious precursor was Goya, in some of his engravings against the Inquisition, specifically *Through the Lineage of the Hebrews* and *Zapata Your Glory Will be Eternal*. The word "Hebrew," taken from the Old Testament, is used to ennoble the term "Jew," and the pose of the hostage Zapata—a doctor from Murcia accused of heresy—is similar to the *Ecce Homo*. The process of change was slow and gradual. The Spanish Inquisition was abolished in 1813, and the Constitution of 1837 (during the government of Juan Álvarez Mendizábal, disdainfully called "Rabbi Juanón" because of his distant, *converso* ancestry) did the same with the statutes of "purity of blood." Freedom of worship was not legislated, however, until 1867. One incident of special interest was the discovery of the Jews of Tetuán by the Spanish armies of occupation in Morocco in 1860. There they were, intact, cheering on the troops no less, and speaking an archaic form of Castilian Spanish, the direct descendants of those

Jews of Spain, expelled nearly four centuries earlier. This encounter with Sephardic roots coincided with the vindication, albeit partial, of a socially segregated group on the island of Mallorca, the chuetas, who were also descendants of the expelled Jews of 1492. Despite having adopted the Catholic religion centuries before, they suffered permanent discrimination and found refuge in a tenacious practice of endogamy. The champion of the liberal cause was the orator and historian Emilio Castelar, who in addresses, speeches, and acerbic polemics (above all, after the "Glorious Revolution" of the First Republic in 1868), praised the spirit of tolerance of Alfonso X (called "the Wise"), rejected the image of the Jew as a god-killer, refuted the charge of Jewish ritualistic crimes, and lamented the expulsion of the Jews in 1492 that provoked the loss of men of the stature of Baruch Spinoza and Benjamin Disraeli.

This process of liberalization through which Spain sought out the gradual separation of the sacred and the profane coincided with the publication of pioneering works of historiography, most notably Amador de los Ríos's *The History of the Jewish Spaniards* (1877). Although many of these works maintain certain racial or religious biases, the general tendency was to legitimately reincorporate the Jews into Spanish history. The defining characteristic of this trend was its ambivalence, which can be seen frequently in the work of Don Marcelino Menéndez y Pelayo, the greatest nineteenth-century scholar of Spanish cultural history. Around 1880, while writing as a moderate Catholic, he praised Quevedo's *Monopantos* and the Inquisition for stopping the "Jewish infection"; at the same time, he compared Maimonides to Saint Thomas of Aquinas and rejected the statutes of "purity of blood" for being anti-evangelical. In literature, the same thing happened: others (Mariano José de Larra, José de Espronceda, Gustavo Adolfo Becquer) wrote variations of the old Jewish theme that Lope de Vega addressed, the tragic love of the beautiful Jewess Raquel and King Alfonso VIII of Castile, and in sketching out the Jewish male figures they did not refrain from using the old images of avarice and cruelty. But in contrast, Benito Pérez Galdós wrote at least three moving works (*Glory, Mercy*, and *Aita Tettauen* in his celebrated *National Episodes*) that are a decisive declaration in favor of religious tolerance and which treat their Jewish characters with immense piety, respect, and dignity, pitying their misfortunes without falling into sentimentalism. This clear tendency toward the vindication of Jewish heritage as an integral part of the national being of Spain was accentuated in 1881, when because of the tsarist pogroms, the government of the liberal Práxedes Mateo Sagasta issued a declaration that had few practical consequences but that carried a great symbolic weight: "Your Majesty as well as the government will receive Jews of Russian origin, opening for them the doors of what was their ancient homeland." Toward the end of the century, and before the end of the Spanish Empire, the famous "Generation of '98" instinctively sought the integration of lost fragments in the ocean of time—the Sephardic heritage. Their desires were translated into action through the creation of university positions, institutions, and publications dedicated to their interests. In fact, this attitude became naturalized in Spain and came to characterize the nation for several decades.

The ranks of the Right never lowered their guard. Influential in ecclesiastical, political, and educational spheres, these actors, beginning in the final decades of the nineteenth century, added new wine to the old casks of religious anti-Semitism. New racial determinisms imported from France and Germany were added to the theories of Masonic conspiracy. The Russian Revolution confirmed for many (including the king of Spain, Alfonso XIII) the notion that Bolshevism was nothing more than a disguised version of Judaism. Yet in general, from 1881 until 1931, there was a growing philo-Semitism, to the point that during the government of Manuel Azaña, a Jewish newspaper proclaimed that "the Jew is in style in Spain." Nevertheless, the arrival of Nazism reaffirmed the conspiracy theories and legitimated them in the works of great Spanish writers such as Ramiro de Maeztu and Pío Baroja (and, to a lesser extent, Santiago de Benavente). With the ideological tensions unleashed by the Civil War, as one would expect, the opposing forces returned to the image of the Jew—the republicans in order to exalt it (for example, in the books of Américo Castro, which proposed a third element in Spanish historical identity along with Arab and Christian ones) and the generals in order to defame and distort it. The whole world remembers General Millán Astray's coda, in that famous speech to which Miguel de Unamuno responded with aplomb shortly before dying. But few remember the words that preceded that coda: "The Jewish Moscovites wanted to shackle Spain in order to convert us into slaves, but we must fight against communism and Judaism. Viva death!"[5] The ambivalent saga of Spanish Jewry presented a major surprise to Millán Astray and other manifestly anti-Semitic generals: having lived side by side with the Sephardic Jews of Morocco, Generalisimo Franco always was moderately philo-Semitic for one other reason—he had *converso* blood.

During World War II, Franco gave a limited right of passage (not of residence) to those persecuted by Nazism. Consequently, thousands of Jews were saved. One of his diplomatic agents merits a mention apart from this: Ángel

Sanz Briz, who, in an effort similar to that of Raoul Wallenberg, saved 2,795 Jews by handing out Spanish visas in Budapest. Once in the postwar years, General Franco resented Israel's coolness toward his regime, a resentment reflected in Spain's votes on Israeli issues in the United Nations, and he did everything possible to "protect" the Spanish public from the truth of the Holocaust. The truth, however, made its way into Spain starting in the early sixties, and became much more widely known with the democratic transition. It was democracy, in reality, that revealed anti-Semitism for what it always had been, an ideological weapon between irreconcilable factions that were in dispute—like those in the fratricidal struggle in the painting by Goya—over the soul and power structure of Spain. When the historic cycle ended in 1975, the new generations understood that there was no need to unleash a holy war over ideas. It was simply necessary to compete, and for that the old conspiracy theories did not work. The political parties—the PSOE (Partido Socialista Obrero Español) and the PP (Partido Popular)—were able to attribute their differences to a number of irreconcilable issues but they were linked at least to a singular contract of political coexistence, tolerance, and democracy. The modest liberal utopia had triumphed and anti-Semitism subsided.

Something had changed at the popular level as well. Time, patiently, had revealed the age-old anti-Jewish prejudices. Many towns began to rescue their old Jewish neighborhoods and refurbish and beautify them. Some were proud of this past. Sephardim went back to being a part of Spain, five hundred years after the decree of expulsion. But this story—like many others—does not have a happy ending: On March 2, 2002, the Episcopal Conference announced that it would ask the Holy See to begin the process of canonizing of Isabella the Catholic. And news of this sort is not coming only from the extreme Right. For the first time there are new forms of anti-Jewish sentiment from the Left, and they are serious. Because of the Palestinian-Israeli conflict and the ties between Israel and the United States, old ideas have begun to circulate again. There is a perception that from Washington—the "island of Monopantos"—a "new Jewish conspiracy to rule the world" has been put in motion. Beyond the criticism of U.S. policy in the Middle East (including the critique of Jewish officials in the Bush administration) and also beyond the reasonable objections to the attitude of the Israeli Right toward the Palestinians, influential sectors of the traditionally liberal Spanish press have started to echo, perhaps unconsciously, old anti-Semitic reflections: an unbalanced and skewed handling of information, a condemnatory emphasis, the equating of the entire Jewish community with that of Israel, the portrayal of Israeli society as being one and the same as the Israeli Right, and the scandalous conflation (openly put forth by José Saramago) of Palestinian refugee camps with the extermination camps of Auschwitz—are these not sufficient signs of the return of the demons of anti-Semitism?

Spanish ambivalence toward the image of the Jew continues, and perhaps it always will. In the final pages of his monumental work *The Jews in Modern and Contemporary Spain*, the historian Julio Caro Baroja speaks of Jews as "a people with a neurotic character" and of Spain as a nation "dominated by a unitary spirit." As such, he compares "what happened" in Spain at the end of the fifteenth century with what "has happened in Germany during the first half of the twentieth century," and he sincerely asks himself: "On whom should the blame be placed?"[6] In other words, the six million Jews (among them, a million children) exterminated by the Nazis, in part, shared the blame for their fate. Fortunately, there have always been other voices to defend the multicultural identity of Spain and the deep traces of Sephardim in the press, in books and in academia. In the end, who will win the battle for the soul of Spain, the Inquisition or tolerance, Quevedo or Pérez Galdós?

# 12

# Anti-Semitism and the Vatican Today

*David I. Kertzer*

Debates over what made the Holocaust possible continue to trigger a defensive reaction in many parts of the Western world. What is at stake is not simply a historical question—important as that is—because what also lies close to the surface here is a tenacious brand of anti-Semitism today. Unfortunately, among the places where such a reaction can be found is in circles close to the Holy See, notwithstanding all the efforts Pope John Paul II has made to improve relations between the Catholic Church and the Jews.

In 1998, the Vatican released a historic report that addressed the charges of the Holy See's involvement in the forces that led to the Holocaust. The commission that authored the document—"We Remember: A Reflection on the Shoah"—was responding to a request made eleven years earlier by the pope. The report framed the issue plainly:

> The fact that the Shoah took place in Europe, that is, in countries of long-standing Christian civilization, raises the question of the relation between the Nazi persecution and the attitudes down the centuries of Christians towards the Jews.[1]

In his statement of March 12, 1998, which appears as the preface to the report, the pope himself stressed how crucial it was for the Vatican to come to grips with what had really happened. He wrote, addressing himself to the Commission's chair, Cardinal Edward Cassidy:

A longer version of this chapter appeared as "Anti-Semitism and the Vatican: On Anti-Semitism, Anti-Judaism, and the Holocaust," *Kirchliche Zeitgeschichte/Contemporary Church History*, 16 (2003): 76–91.

It is my fervent hope that the document: *We Remember: A Reflection on the Shoah*, which the Commission for Religious Relations with the Jews has prepared under your direction, will indeed help to heal the wounds of past misunderstandings and injustices. May it enable memory to play its necessary part in the process of shaping a future in which the unspeakable iniquity of the *Shoah* will never again be possible.

The report's authors echoed the pope's emphasis on the crucial importance of reaching a clear-eyed view of this catastrophic past and the Church's role in it. They wrote: "The common future of Jews and Christians demands that we remember, for," they added, quoting the pope himself, "there is no future without memory."

Yet those who hoped that the Vatican would use this occasion to face the Church's uncomfortable past with clear eyes were to be disappointed. While acknowledging that "sentiments of anti-Judaism in some Christian quarters . . . led to a generalized discrimination" in the past, the report never acknowledges any role of the institutional Church itself in such discrimination. But more crucially, the report attributes the demonization of the Jews that lay at the heart of modern European anti-Semitism to forces that had nothing to do with the Church.

The document does this in part by making a fundamental distinction between anti-Semitism and what is termed, by contrast, anti-Judaism. The latter, which, according to the Vatican report, typified the attitudes of many sons and daughters of the Church, is attributed to a religious antipathy to the Jews. Jews were subjected to discrimination because they were viewed as the killers of Jesus and because of their stubbornness in refusing to abandon their religion. Yet, we are told, modern anti-Semitism is of an entirely different nature, entailing not religious antipathy but, rather, an antagonism based on negative political, economic, and racial characterization of the Jews. "We Remember" begins its section "Nazi Anti-Semitism and the Shoah" by stating: "Thus we cannot ignore the difference which exists between anti-Semitism, based on theories contrary to the constant teaching of the Church . . . and the long-standing sentiments of mistrust and hostility that we call anti-Judaism, of which, unfortunately, Christians also have been guilty." And so, we are told, "The Shoah was the work of a thoroughly modern neo-pagan regime. Its anti-Semitism had its roots outside of Christianity."

This is a comforting view for the Church, perhaps, but it bears no relation to what actually happened in Europe in the decades leading up to the Holocaust. As the evidence available not only from the various historical archives of the Vatican but from Vatican-supervised publications of those years clearly demonstrates, the Vatican was in fact energetically involved in the rise of modern anti-

Semitism in Europe from its first appearance in the 1880s. The distinction between Christian anti-Judaism and secular anti-Semitism on which the Vatican's current attempts to deny any responsibility for the Holocaust rest serves only to obscure the historical record. From the beginning of modern anti-Semitism, the Vatican itself promulgated views of the Jews as enemies of the countries where they lived, destroyers of people's welfare, and evil forces who were plotting to conquer Christians and reduce them to their vassals. Later, the Nazis would not only pick up on these economic and political themes but take over many of the traditional Christian "religious" ones as well. What could be a more medieval-Christian manifestation of anti-Judaism than the charge of ritual murder, for example, which held that Jews were commanded by their religion to kidnap, torture, and murder Christian children in order to consume their blood? This charge, which the Vatican-supervised press pushed through 1914, became one of the favorite themes of the Nazi magazine *Der Stürmer* in the 1930s.[2]

"We Remember" likewise fails to mention the Vatican's strong support for the most influential anti-Semitic political party to arise in the late nineteenth century, Austria's Social Christian Party, and its leader, Karl Lueger. Lueger was idolized by the young Adolf Hitler as he was growing up in Vienna, and the anti-Semitic rantings and rallies of the Social Christian Party served as the backdrop for Hitler's developing views on the Jews, as he himself has recalled.[3]

Also missing in "We Remember" is any mention of the links between the Vatican's repeated insistence, from the 1880s through the 1930s, that European governments should not allow Jews equal rights and its support for the racial laws in the 1930s. The Holy See opposed efforts of the various Catholic countries of Europe to grant equal rights to the Jews in the nineteenth century. Where the pope had the power to do what he thought canon law dictated, as in Rome until 1870, Jews were forced to live in ghettoes. They were forbidden from having normal social interaction with Christians and forbidden from going to schools or practicing professions. It is in this context that we can understand why the Vatican and the Church hierarchy in various European countries supported the efforts made in the 1930s to strip the Jews of their equal rights.

Since the publication of "We Remember," historians and other authors who have urged the Vatican to reconsider the denials and obfuscations that lie at the heart of the document have been subjected to strong, often ad hominem attack by Church representatives. The barrage of denunciations from these circles occasioned recently by the publication of my book *The Popes against the Jews* raises a question that I did not previously suspect I would be asking: namely, just how dead is anti-Semitism in the Vatican today? Some of the reactions to my book suggest that opposition to the legacy of the Second Vatican Council is on the rise in influential Church circles. I hope I am wrong.[4]

I should have been forewarned. In early 2001, James Carroll, a former priest and a man whose Catholic identity is precious to him, published his own very personal account of the history of Church anti-Semitism, *Constantine's Sword*. When, shortly thereafter, he was invited to speak at Stonehill College, a Catholic school in southeastern Massachusetts, the diocesan bulletin published a long, denunciatory statement by Sean O'Malley, the bishop of Fall River. O'Malley wrote:

> It is very sad that James Carroll, who has made a lucrative cottage industry out of Catholic bashing, is being given a forum to peddle his tawdry notions at a local campus. His patently unfair characterization of Pius XII, indeed of Christianity, is an outrageous assault on the truth. I am shocked and disappointed that some people have deluded themselves into thinking that this presence could in any way further Catholic-Jewish dialogue.

The bishop concluded with the following hope: "I feel sure that serious Catholics and Jews will boycott James Carroll's presentation. I am positive that the important gains made by Pope John Paul II's efforts at Catholic-Jewish reconciliation will not be compromised by Mr. Carroll's rantings."[5] To any who do not recognize the name, O'Malley, subsequent to this diatribe against Carroll and the attack on those who invited him to Stonehill College, has been made the Archbishop of Boston.

That something truly disturbing is going on in Vatican circles in dealing with the Church's historic role in promulgating anti-Semitism has become painfully evident in the campaign undertaken by *La Civiltà Cattolica* against *The Popes Against the Jews*. To understand the significance of these attacks it is necessary to understand the role played by the journal not only today but in the decades leading up to the Holocaust. *Civiltà Cattolica* was founded in 1850 at Pope Pius IX's request as a means of spreading the pope's view of current events and problems of the contemporary world to the Catholic faithful. Published twice a month, it is run by a collective of Jesuits, who write all the articles and who review all drafts as a group to be sure that they fully represent their collective wisdom. Most importantly, both in the decades dealt with in the book, and still today, all articles must be approved by the Vatican itself prior to publication. Drafts of all articles are sent to the Vatican Secretariat of State and five days before publication of each issue, the director of the journal is received at the Secretariat office. There the director is notified of any language that should be changed. The principles on which such directives are based, according to the web site of the journal today, are the following:

1. "conformity of the articles published in the journal with the official teaching of the Church in matters of faith and morals."
2. "conformity or at least not any substantial lack of conformity with the directions being followed by the Holy See in its relations with other states."
3. "propitiousness or lack thereof of publishing such articles in particular situations."[6]

These same procedures were in effect in 1880, at the very time that modern anti-Semitism was first taking shape, when *Civiltà Cattolica* published the first of thirty-six virulently anti-Semitic articles that appeared over the following forty months. A typical passage, from December 22, 1880, warns: "If this foreign Jewish race is left too free, it immediately becomes the persecutor, oppressor, tyrant, thief, and devastator of the countries where it lives." The journal urged that special laws be introduced to keep the Jews in their place and to protect Christian society from the hostility that the Jews harbored "against all human society not belonging to their race." The author went on to observe:

> The Jews—eternal insolent children, obstinate, dirty, thieves, liars, ignoramuses, pests and the scourge of those near and far—. . . immediately abused [their newfound freedom] to interfere with that of others. They managed to lay their hands on . . . all public wealth . . . and virtually alone they took control not only of all the money . . . but of the law itself in those countries where they have been allowed to hold public offices.[7]

Catholics were repeatedly warned that Jews were members not simply of a religion but of a hostile nation, dedicated to using every criminal means imaginable to rob and persecute them. Only by sending the Jews back to the ghettoes could Catholic Europe be again made safe. The articles fully embraced the charges at the heart of modern anti-Semitism. As an 1893 article devoted to the topic put it, the Jewish nation

> does not work, but traffics in the property and the work of others; it does not produce, but lives and grows fat with the products of the arts and industry of the nations that give it refuge. It is the giant octopus that with its oversized tentacles envelops everything. It has its stomach in the banks . . . and its suction cups everywhere: in contracts and monopolies, in credit unions and banks, in postal services and telegraph companies, in shipping and in the railroads, in the town treasuries and in state finance. It represents the kingdom of capital . . . the aristocracy of gold. . . . It reigns unopposed."[8]

This image of the Jewish octopus would later be picked up by the Nazis themselves.

*Civiltà Cattolica* was also active in promulgating the ritual murder charge against the Jews, and it did so well into the twentieth century. In 1914, for example, in connection with the Mendel Beilis case, the journal—its text having been first approved by the Vatican—reported that their recent research had revealed that Jews are taught by their holy texts to regard the blood of Christian children as "a drink like milk."[9]

In light of this and of the fact that *Civiltà Cattolica* championed the racial laws introduced against Jews in the middle and late 1930s across Europe, one might think that today, in the wake of both the Second Vatican Council and Pope John Paul II's call for repentance and coming to terms with sins of the past, the Vatican-supervised journal would recognize and apologize for the pernicious role it played in the development of modern anti-Semitism. What happened in 2002, however, was just the opposite.

In June 2002, under the title "Anti-Judaism or anti-Semitism? The Accusations against the Church and against *Civiltà Cattolica*," the journal offered its response.[10] The author of the piece—although the text was gone over by the entire *Civiltà Cattolica* collective for review before being sent to the Vatican Secretariat of State for its approval—is Father Giovanni Sale. The editorial board member responsible for historical questions, Sale served as the key spokesperson in the Vatican-linked assault on *The Popes Against the Jews*. He broadcast denunciations of the book on Vatican Radio and in a series of interviews in a number of the major daily newspapers in Italy as well as in the second most widely read popular Catholic magazine in Italy, *Jesus*, in a piece boldly titled "The Catholic Church and the Jews: Anti-Judaism Yes, Anti-Semitism Never."[11]

As the title of the *Civiltà Cattolica* piece suggests, the Vatican's continuing effort to distance itself from any responsibility for making the Holocaust possible depends on maintaining the distinction between anti-Judaism and anti-Semitism. In this account, these are two very different phenomena, and whereas the former was linked to the Church, the latter had nothing to do with it.

The June 2002 *Civiltà Cattolica* article begins by claiming: "The distinction between 'anti-Judaism' and 'anti-Semitism' is one that is commonly accepted by most historians, both Catholic and non-Catholic." Sale links this to the official Vatican position on the Holocaust by adding: "The two concepts, furthermore, served as the basis of the document on the Holocaust published in 1998 by the Pontifical Commission for Religious Relations with Judaism, then chaired by Cardinal E. Cassidy, titled 'We Remember: A Reflection on the Shoah.'"

The problem that the Vatican has encountered in clinging to its anti-Judaism/anti-Semitism distinction is that its original rationale—that Catholic anti-Judaism was based on negative religious images of the Jews rather than on the social, economic, political, and racial images underlying of modern anti-Semitism—is so patently false. Even aside from the archival evidence in the Vatican, one only has to read the pages of *Civiltà Cattolica* in the years from 1880 to 1939 to see that it is filled with a demonization of the Jews based on the evil things they were collectively responsible for socially, economically, and politically.

The June 2002 *Civiltà Cattolica* article nonetheless sets out to find a way around this problem. It does this by arguing that there is not one but two forms of anti-Judaism. This enables the journal to avoid having to deny Vatican involvement in demonizing the Jews on the basis of their pernicious economic and political influence and the threat they represented to the well-being of Christian Europe. "In order to understand the attitude of both the Ecclesiastical Hierarchy and *Civiltà Cattolica* on the Jewish problem," Father Sale explained, "it is necessary first to present certain historical considerations." And here he introduced the new definition of anti-Judaism: "From this point of view one must distinguish between a religious or doctrinal anti-Judaism and an anti-Judaism that is, for the most part, produced by considerations of a socio-political nature."

The *Civiltà Cattolica* articles cited above from the 1880s and 1890s were, according to Father Sale, examples of religious anti-Judaism, with the ritual murder charge mentioned as a good example.

By contrast with this *religious* anti-Judaism, the *Civiltà Cattolica* article of June 2002 tells us, "modern anti-Judaism" arose at the time of the French Revolution. As liberal governments in Europe—against the Holy See's wishes—increasingly gave Jews equal rights, Jews became an ever-growing problem from the Church's point of view. "Such liberal legislation, our journal wrote," Father Sale recalled, "made the Jews 'emboldened and powerful, giving them, under the pretext of equality, a position that was increasingly predominant in prestige, especially in the economic sector, in modern society.'" The passage of the Vatican-supervised journal that Father Sale here quoted on the powerful Jews, by the way, came not from the nineteenth century but from a 1928 *Civiltà Cattolica* article.[12]

Here we are finally coming to the crucial issue for *Civiltà Cattolica* and, by extension, for the Vatican today: "Another reason that led to the struggle against the influence that the Jews were rapidly acquiring at the social level," Father Sale wrote, "beyond their preponderance in the economic and financial sectors, was the primary role that many of them had in international Masonry, which was strongly anti-Catholic, and in the modern revolutionary movements, not only in Lenin's Russia but also in the states of Eastern Europe." He continued: "This mode of thinking was nourished by the fact that many of the heads of the European Communist parties were Jewish. The large majority of the members of the Council of People's Commissars, for example, instituted by Lenin after the Russian Revolution of 1917—that is the revolutionary Government of the country—were Jews."

What source does *Civiltà Cattolica* base this last claim on? The footnote cites but one authority: a 1922 article in *Civiltà Cattolica* itself.[13] This charge that the Jews were responsible for the Russian Revolution was in fact one Father Sale had recently revived in seeking to discredit *The Popes Against the Jews*. In the February 28, 2002, issue of Italy's most prestigious daily newspaper, the *Corriere della Sera*, Father Sale responded to a piece I had published there two days earlier.[14] He was eager to defend his own journal from any charge that it was implicated in the spread of anti-Semitism and was offended by my citations of passages from three articles published in 1880, 1893, and 1914. He wrote: "The *Civiltà Cattolica* articles that Prof. Kertzer cites in the February 26 issue of the *Corriere*—it must be stated if they are to be properly understood—were published for anti-Communist ends." He continued, clinging to the anti-Judaism versus anti-Semitism distinction: "The journal battled against Judaism from the religious point of view and, later—along with many Catholics and even liberals of that time—championed the theory of a Jewish-Masonic-Bolshevik plot against Christian society." Yet, rather than regretting the role played by his journal in promulgating this conspiracy theory, he does quite the opposite; he justifies it, continuing: "However, it must be remembered that a large proportion—seventeen of twenty-one—of the members of the Council of People's Commisars that Lenin established following 1917—in other words the country's government—were Jews. It was from this fact that the legend of the equation Judaism-communism was born and reinforced." He concludes: "Therefore it is understandable that the Church, in combating Bolshevism and the atheist doctrine it promulgated, at the same time attacked Judaism as well."

Could *Civiltà Cattolica* and the Vatican not realize that in defending themselves in this way today they are resuscitating some of the core elements of the

Nazis' anti-Semitic campaign? Their charge recalls nothing so much as Adolf Hitler's own language, as in his claim in *Mein Kampf* that "The real organizer of the Revolution and the actual wire-puller behind it [is] the International Jew."[15] Indeed, one of Hitler's main rallying cries against the Jews was that they were responsible for Bolshevism and for the Communist drive to rule the world. Father Sale's eye-catchingly specific charge about the overwhelming predominance of Jews in Lenin's first cabinet, however, has a clear precursor in the U.S. Church as well. On November 20, 1938, just ten days after the devastating anti-Semitic Nazi pogrom that was *Kristallnacht*, the notorious Father Charles Coughlin in his weekly national radio broadcast sought to justify the Nazi attitudes toward the Jews. He explained: "Nazism was conceived as a political defense mechanism against Communism. . . . And, Communism itself was regarded by the rising generation of Germans as a product not of Russia, but of a group of Jews who dominated the destinies of Russia." He then went on: "Were there facts to substantiate this belief in the minds of the Nazi Party, I ask?" Yes, there were: "The 1917 list of those who, with Lenin, ruled many of the activities of the Soviet Republic, disclosed that of the 25 quasi-cabinet members, 24 of them were atheistic Jews, whose names I have before me. The list, published by Nazis and distributed throughout Germany, is as follows. . . ."[16]

This is the company that today *Civiltà Cattolica* and, shockingly, the Vatican itself are keeping.

Perhaps it is worth noting here that according to the major historical expert on this question, the actual count of those of Jewish background among Lenin's first Council of People's Commissars was one: Leon Trotsky.[17]

Having admitted that the Vatican was involved not only in promulgating negative religious views of the Jews but also in demonizing them as plotters against the well-being and safety of Christians throughout Europe, what is left to *Civiltà Cattolica* is to claim that none of this was part of modern anti-Semitism. In short, the Vatican had to abandon its previous attempts to claim distance from modern anti-Semitism by distinguishing it from the Church's earlier demonization of the Jews, which had presumably been based only on religious characteristics. Instead, the current argument, in a nutshell, is the following: It was the Nazis' anti-Semitism that led to the Holocaust; the Nazis' demonization of the Jews was based on racial views that were foreign to the Church; therefore, the campaign of demonization of the Jews undertaken by the Church (which is presented here not as a demonization but for the most part as recognition of an actual pernicious influence of the Jews) was wholly distinct from the anti-Semitism that made the Holocaust possible.

Moreover, according to the 2002 *Civiltà Cattolica* article, the Vatican campaign, which called for treating Jews as second-class citizens and warned of the threat to healthy Christian society deriving from any contact with them, differed from anti-Semitism in another way: "Anti-Judaism responded to the necessity of protecting the ancient '*societas christiana*' which, while it had not existed in Europe for some time, continued in the mind of many men of the Church to still have validity." The article then goes on to explain: "Thus, civil legislation that was approved by States having Catholic majorities, which treated Christians and Jews differently, was considered legitimate, as long as it recognized the duties of moderation and Christian charity toward all." In a footnote, Father Sale further explicated this point in his discussion of Church support for the introduction of Hungary's racial laws:

> *Civiltà Cattolica* support for the racial laws promulgated by Hungary in 1938 is to be understood on the basis of considerations that were not anti-Semitic. Father A. Barbera, author of the article in question, argued that it was the duty of a Catholic State to protect Christian citizens and that granting the Jews equality with Catholics not only damaged the Hungarian State (in distancing itself from its glorious Christian tradition) but would ultimately also damage the Jews themselves, who, taking on important posts in society, would fuel the animosity of the "locals" toward them.

I now see how naïve I was at the time *The Popes Against the Jews* was published. I had hoped then that by providing copious historical documentation to demonstrate the untenability of the distinction between anti-Judaism and anti-Semitism and to chronicle the Vatican's active role in the demonization of the Jews in the decades in which modern anti-Semitism was developing, I would help lead the Church to reconsider the position it took in "We Remember." Just the opposite has happened. Those closest to the Vatican and those regarding themselves as the most loyal defenders of the Holy See have in effect taken the occasion of the book's publication not only to restate the distinction but to undermine those in the Church who have sought to give a different reading to "We Remember." The latter includes Cardinal Cassidy himself, head of the commission that drafted the document. In a November 9, 1998, speech, Cardinal Cassidy said: "In making a distinction between the anti-Judaism of the Christian Churches and the anti-Semitism of the Nazis, *We Remember* does not intend to deny the relationship between these two evils."[18] Yet this is exactly what the Vatican-approved *Civiltà Cattolica* text of June 2002 has done. And rather than using the occasion of the publication of *The Popes against the Jews* to reiterate the Vatican's rejection of the demonization of the Jews and notions of collective Jewish responsibility for various evils, *Civiltà Cattolica* has used the book's publication to resuscitate and defend some of the most notorious of those anti-Semitic slurs.

What is particularly curious is the almost total lack of any controversy or concern expressed about the *Civiltà Cattolica* attack, which passed without any negative public comment by any in the Church hierarchy. It is telling to compare this reaction to the reaction in the fall of 2003 to similar comments expressed by a member of parliament in Germany. In a speech on October 3, 2003, the Christian Democratic deputy, Martin Hohmann, representing a largely Catholic electorate near Fulda, described the Jews as a "perpetrator people" who bore responsibility for the Russian revolution, and he cited Henry Ford's anti-Semitic tract *The International Jew* in support of his position. Such was the outpouring of revulsion to his remarks that the Christian Democratic Party forced him out. It is telling that whereas Hohmann's remarks were viewed by the German Christian Democrats as a great embarrassment, a scandal, the same anti-Semitic message, spewed by the Vatican's most authoritative journal, raised no eyebrows.

The Vatican is playing with fire here, for there are still parts of the Roman Catholic Church in no way resigned to accepting the lessons of the Second Vatican Council. A typical example of this phenomenon comes from Seattle. In its February 12, 2002, issue, the *Seattle Catholic*, which describes itself as "A Journal of Catholic News and Views," turned its attention to *The Popes Against the Jews*. Quoting the book (not quite correctly) as saying that "the church played an important role in promulgating every one of [the] ideas that are central to modern anti-Semitism," the journal went on to offer a listing of these anti-Semitic tenets. "Among these central ideas Kertzer enumerates 'the beliefs that the Jews plotted to control the world, that they were evil conspirators against the public good, that they maliciously controlled the banks and press and that they were behind political movements like Bolshevism.'" Rather than disowning such views, the *Seattle Catholic* wrote that in listing them I have "unwittingly" shown why no apology by the Church for its past behavior is required. The fact is, the *Seattle Catholic* wrote, these are all in fact "unfortunate Jewish tendencies" that the Church rightly combated in the years leading up to the Holocaust.[19]

I imagine that the archbishop of Seattle is less than happy with the material found in the pages of *Seattle Catholic*. Yet what is of serious concern is that the anti-Semitic views found in such crude form here in the network of stridently conservative Catholic organizations that the *Seattle Catholic* represents are today being given respectability by the Vatican itself through the much more subtle language of *Civiltà Cattolica* and other defenders of the Holy See who either deny what the historical record plainly shows or who, in admitting the evidence, seek to reinterpret it by clinging to a distinction between anti-Judaism and anti-Semitism whose historical validity can no longer be seriously defended.

# 13

# Holocaust Denial

*Deborah Lipstadt*

In my book *Denying the Holocaust: The Growing Assault on Truth and Memory*, I devoted a couple of hundred words to David Irving, describing him as a "Hitler partisan wearing blinkers" who "distort[ed] evidence . . . manipulat[ed] documents, [and] skew[ed] . . . and misrepresent[ed] data in order to reach historically untenable conclusions." I wrote that "on some level Irving seems to conceive of himself as carrying on Hitler's legacy." I thought him particularly dangerous because he had a reputation that was independent of his activities as a denier. Irving was the author of numerous books about World War II and the Third Reich. Virtually all aficionados of World War II history knew his name, even if some found his work a bit too sympathetic to the Third Reich. His books were reviewed in major periodicals, and consequently, his Holocaust-denial activities garnered far more attention than those by other deniers.

My words were harsh, but I considered them noncontroversial because Irving had so publicly expressed his Holocaust denial. In 1988, when the Canadian government charged Ernst Zündel with promoting Holocaust denial, Irving testified on Zündel's behalf, telling the court that there was no "overall Reich policy to kill the Jews" and that "no documents whatsoever show that a Holocaust had ever happened."[1] Since then, Irving had repeatedly denied the Holocaust, arguing that the gas chambers were an impossibility and that the Third Reich had no plan to kill the Jews.

I was, therefore, surprised when Irving mounted a libel action against me in the British courts. From a legal perspective, I was at a decided disadvantage. The burden of proof was on me, the defendant, because British law presumes defamatory words to be untrue until the author proves them true. Consequently, had I not defended myself, Irving would have won by default. I would have been found guilty of libel, my book would have been removed from circulation, and Irving could then claim that his definition of the Holocaust had been determined to be legitimate.

There was a certain irony that I found myself in a courtroom in early 2000. I opposed laws outlawing Holocaust denial. (In the United States, the First Amendment renders any such efforts moot.) I believed such laws to be counterproductive. They made denial more—not less—alluring and suggested that the history was so fragile that it needed laws to defend it. Furthermore, I did not believe courtrooms the proper venue for historical enquiry.

Our legal strategy was to argue that Irving used Holocaust denial as a means of spreading anti-Semitism and engendering sympathy for the Third Reich. Our objective was not to prove the Holocaust happened. Our job was to prove the truth of my words, namely, that Irving lied about the Holocaust and did so out of anti-Semitic motives.

Although a major portion of our energies was devoted to proving that Irving distorted the historical truth about the Holocaust, one of our primary objectives was to show that denial and anti-Semitism were inexorably linked one to the other. In Irving's case, we did not know which came first, but we were convinced that they were cut from the same cloth. I was surprised by the number of people who, when they heard about this case, had to be convinced about this point. They had no question but that Holocaust denial was complete bunk; they did, however, often fail to see that Holocaust denial was a form of anti-Semitism.

In Irving's case, proving the link between the two was made far easier by the fact that the court granted us access to all of Irving's correspondence with leading Holocaust-deniers, anti-Semites, and neo-Nazis. It also permitted us to inspect his collection of video- and audiotapes and his personal daily diary. We had asked for this material as part of the discovery process—each side gets to examine the other side's papers and evidence in order to avoid trial by ambush—because we assumed it would reveal his connections with some less-than-savory characters. We also assumed that what Irving said away from the media glare would be more revealing of his true thoughts and motives than would statements crafted for publication.

In 1991, Irving had told a Calgary audience that Auschwitz was "baloney" and a "legend." Then, with a great deal of bravado, he declared his intention to create an organization for Auschwitz survivors, whose numbers, he told his audience, seemed to be multiplying. He planned to call the organization "'Association of Auschwitz survivors, survivors of the Holocaust and other liars . . . A-S-S-H-O-L-S.'"[2]

It was not just what Irving said in these small gatherings that we found significant, but also the way his audience responded. In court, my barrister, Richard Rampton, made a special point of emphasizing the nature of Irving's audience. He noted that when Irving said that "more people died on the back seat of Edward Kennedy's car at Chappaquiddick than ever died in a gas chamber in Auschwitz," they laughed.[3] Irving also delivered a speech at a neo-Nazi rally and march at Halle, a medieval German city that was the birthplace of SS leader Reinhard Heydrich. Rows of skinhead "bullyboys," wearing leather jackets and metal-studded belts, marched in front of Irving. When Irving stood up to speak the crowd greeted him with chants of *"Sieg Heil! Sieg Heil!"*

His audience also laughed when Irving said that Elie Wiesel did a "Cook's tour of the different concentration camps." Irving protested that they were laughing at the "spurious survivors," those "trying to climb on the Holocaust bandwagon." Why, Rampton wondered, would a serious matter such as someone falsely claiming to be an Auschwitz survivor provoke laughter? Irving explained: "Because there is something ludicrous . . . something pathetic about it." Rampton had another explanation: Irving's audience were so "deeply anti-semitic" that they reveled in Irving's words, which were "redolent of animosity, hostility, contempt, spite . . . just like Dr Goebbel's articles."[4]

Irving, we charged, also claimed that Jews caused anti-Semitism. Such was the case when he wrote in his July 1997 *Action Report* "They clamor 'Ours! Ours! Ours!' when hoards of gold are uncovered. And then when anti-Semitism increases and the inevitable mindless pogroms occur, they ask with genuine surprise: 'Why us?'" When Irving was in the stand, Rampton asked him if his statement about Jews clamoring "Ours!" was not the equivalent of "saying anti-Semitism is justified on account of the fact that the Jews are greedy?" Irving insisted that he was not just explaining how the anti-Semite thought. He was putting himself "in the skin of an antisemite." This was not the only occasion on which Irving had engaged in such "explaining." He had given an interview to the filmmaker Errol Morris, when Morris was making his documentary *Mr. Death* about Holocaust-denier Fred Leuchter. "You people . . . have been disliked for 3,000 years. . . . No sooner do you arrive . . . in a new country, then within 50 years you are already being disliked all over again. Now what is it? . . . Is it envy because they are more successful than us? . . . If I was a Jew, I would want to know what the reason is." Irving had told Morris that he was speaking as an "outsider" who "comes[s] from Mars" who, upon arriving on earth, sees the Jews and declares, "as a race, they are better at making money than I am." When Rampton declared that a "racist remark," Irving again insisted he was explaining, not justifying. A racist would say, Irving continued, "these are better people than us, they play the violin better, they make money better than us." This generates envy, Irving continued. He, however, was just "investigating" why people become anti-Semitic.[5]

Sitting in court just a few feet from this man and hearing these words roll off Irving's tongue, so extemporaneously, was chilling. I had been studying anti-Semitism for most of my adult life, but rarely, if ever, had I encountered it so unfettered in such a "civilized" setting. The judge, who had been staring at Irving intently as he made these statements, interrupted and asked him to be a bit more specific about what he was saying. "You say: 'If I was going to be crude, I would say not only are they better at making money but they are greedy.' That is you, Mr. Irving, saying the Jews are greedy, is that right?" Vigorously shaking his head, Irving insisted that he was just putting himself "into the skin of a person who is asking questions about those clever people." The judge wanted more specificity. "You are saying of the Jews, well, they have been disliked for 3,000 years. . . . Then you say: 'Well, I do not know the answer.' . . . But then do you not go on to say . . . Well, look at it at 'as if I came from Mars'. . . . And it appears to me that the reason why they are disliked is because they are greedy'; is that not what you are saying?" Irving insisted that he did not know "*the* reason" why Jews were disliked, but he was suggesting that it may be a "contributing reason." It might also be part of the "endemic human xenophobia which exists in all of us and which civilized people like your Lordship and myself manage to suppress, and other people like the gentleman on the Eastern Front with the submachine guns cannot suppress."[6]

I sat listening to this in amazement. I was less surprised by what Irving said than at how polite this all sounded.

Given my knowledge of Holocaust-deniers and the company they keep, I was not surprised to find Irving had also made some explicitly racist remarks. In a 1992 interview he gave on Australian radio, he said he felt "queasy about the immigration disaster" in Britain. The interviewer asked: "What do you think about Black people . . . on the British cricket team?" Irving replied: "That makes me even more queasy." The judge again intervened and asked Irving if the reason for his regret was "the color of their skin." What was regrettable, Irving responded, was that "blacks and people of certain races are superior athletes to whites." The judge again asked why it was regrettable. Irving replied that he regretted that if someone pointed out the "differences between the species" that was considered racist.[7] I listened in wide-eyed amazement to his use of the word "species." I regretted that my barrister did not question him about it.

As the trial progressed, I had little doubt that we would win on the historical elements. We were able to prove not only that Irving was wrong but that he had access to the documents that proved him wrong. He chose to either ignore or distort these documents. I was, however, concerned that the judge might recognize that Irving was an anti-Semite but fail to connect that to his Holocaust denial. That was one of the reasons why we decided to pay particular attention to Irving's activities in Germany. It was in that setting that his connection between denial and overt anti-Semitism was often most clear.

## Germany: David Irving's "Political Playground"

When Irving visited Germany prior to its unification, he avoided explicit Holocaust denial. He would condemn the bombing of Dresden, decry the "unatoned Holocaust" of the postwar expulsion of Germans from former Reich territories, and question German war guilt, but he would not deny the Holocaust. In the late 1980s, at the time of unification, this began to change. Irving made a series of frequent trips to Germany, often to the former East Germany. He declared that "there had never been a gassing of Jews," that six million murdered Jews was a *"Lebenlüge"* (living lie) by Israel, and that Jews used the Holocaust in order to financially and politically blackmail Germany.[8] According to Professor Hajo Funke, our expert on Irving's German extremism, this change in Irving's public position came at the same time that there emerged in Germany a more violent form of extremism. The purveyors of this new radicalism often engaged in verbal and physical attacks on foreigners and guest workers and depicted ethnic minorities as criminals and parasites. Another change in the political scene at this time was the emergence of an informal alliance between national conservatives and radical extremists.[9]

In his testimony to the court Funke pointed out that Holocaust denial served as an important political tool for this new alliance. It rehabilitated the Third Reich's reputation. This in turn helped make National Socialism seem like a viable political alternative. Above all, it inculcated contempt for Jews, the mythical enemy of all that this alliance stood for. Irving's participation in the rallies and meetings of these groups helped raise their status and helped them depict themselves as something other than violent, fire-bomb-throwing bully-boys. Some German extremists believed Irving could serve to bring "more reserved moderate" elements into the neo-Nazi sphere.[10]

A rally in the Alsatian town of Hagenau was attended by Irving, Zündel, and other deniers. In his speech, Zündel declared that "decent Germans were wallowing in the pigsty [of the] base lie which this Jewish rabble [*Judenpack*] has been spreading." Irving then poked fun at survivors, telling his audience that survivors claimed that the Germans had a "one-man gas chamber" that was camouflaged as a telephone box and carried around through the Polish countryside by two soldiers. They looked for Jews who might have escaped deportation. To his audience's delight, Irving asked: "How did they get the poor soul of a victim to enter this one-man gas chamber voluntarily? Answer: There was probably a telephone bell inside of it and it rang and the soldiers told him: 'I think that's for you.'"[11] When Rampton observed that this story had been met with warm laughter from his audience, Irving insisted that he used the anecdote because it demonstrated how historians selectively use the eyewitness accounts, taking certain ones and ignoring those that are "obviously baloney." Rampton asked Irving, almost rhetorically, why a serious historian would bother with a story that was clearly false.[12]

Rampton, who noted that Irving has used this anecdote on more than one occasion, wondered why Irving's audience always found it so funny. Irving insisted that it was a device he used to keep his audiences attentive and "awake." Rampton had a different perspective. Irving was "mocking the survivors and, indeed, the dead from the Holocaust." When Irving insisted he was not mocking survivors, Rampton reminded Irving of his comment that "ridicule alone is not enough. You have got to be tasteless about it. You have got to say things like more women died on the back seat of Senator Edward Kennedy's car at Chappaquiddick than died in the gas chambers of Auschwitz (applause)."[13] When Rampton asked why his audience applauded, Irving smiled and said because he was a "good speaker." By this point, I was used to hearing the excerpts of Irving's anti-Semitic and racist speeches. But this explanation, offered in front of reporters and a packed gallery of courtroom observers, left me shaking my head in disbelief.

When Funke was in the witness box, Rampton asked him if this kind of rhetoric about *Judenpack* and one-person telephone boxes was "characteristic of the views and attitudes of neo-fascists in Germany?" Funke observed that this was not "soft" anti-Semitism, but "openly rage-based antisemitism. . . . This kind of extreme radical racist, post Holocaust antisemitism is . . . at the core of these groups that I call neo-National Socialists."[14]

Ultimately we won an overwhelming victory. The judge declared Irving a Holocaust-denier who had repeatedly falsified the truth and twisted the evidence. He also, just as I had hoped he would, linked Irving's denial to his anti-Semitism and his racism. Nonetheless, despite my victory, I was deeply troubled by subsequent developments. Holocaust denial proliferated in the Islamic world, particularly in the Middle East. Yassir Arafat's successor, Palestinian leader Mahmoud Abbas (Abu Mazen), who was the chief Palestinian Liberation Organization architect of the Oslo Accords, wrote in his book *The Other Side: The Secret Relationship between Nazism and the Zionist Movement* that the six million figure was "peddled" by the Jews but that the actual number may be even fewer than one million. When he became prime minister of the Palestinian Authority, he was asked to clarify his comments. Rather than repudiating them, he said that he wrote the book when the Palestinians were at war with Israel; "today I would not have made such remarks."[15] Though I was disturbed by his comments, I was more disturbed by the world's willingness to simply ignore this aspect of his background.

But he was not alone in this attitude. Abdul Aziz Rantisi, who served as the "general commander" of Hamas until his assassination by Israel on April 17, 2004, expressed his outrage at the Zionists' success in spreading the propaganda of the "false Holocaust" and claimed that no one has clarified how the "false gas chambers worked." Maintaining a consistent level of historical accuracy, Rantisi decried the fact that David Irving "was sued" because of his Holocaust denial.[16]

A different kind of historical distortion was evident in Europe during the buildup to the Iraq War. The grotesque equation of President George W. Bush and Prime Minister Ariel Sharon with Adolf Hitler—irrespective of how one feels about their policies—constituted a gross whitewash of Nazi crimes. Equally troubling was the use of Nazi motifs to attack Israel's policies. While these metaphysical attacks on Jews may not cause the hardship of physical attacks, they leave Jews terribly dispirited and prompt them to question their place in supposedly enlightened Europe. For me, they were a stark reminder that I might have won a single solitary battle, but this war persists.

# 14

# Anti-Semitism in the United States

*Nathan Glazer*

It would be reasonable, very reasonable, to expect anti-Semitism in the United States to be a major issue for Jews, and perhaps for U.S. society too. All the conditions that could make for anti-Semitism are here. We have a large Jewish population that is disproportionately wealthy, influential, and visible and that is also very different in its values and attitudes and political and social orientation from most of the U.S. population. Americans, we know, are the most religious of the populations of the Western world: Many more people believe in God, believe in the inerrancy of the Bible (in its English translation), are fundamentalist, and attend regular church services than in any other part of the developed Western world. The religion most of them adhere to is Christianity in various forms, and despite the changes in the major Christian religions and denominations in the last few decades—the reforms in the Catholic Church, the shift among many evangelical Christians to strong support of Israel— there is, in the long history of Christianity, a strong built-in animus toward the Jews. This is the country in which every hotel room has a Bible and in which many people, from the president down, regularly read and study the Bible. The part most relevant to them, the New Testament, is a primer of anti-Semitism, and one cannot expect this heritage to be easily overcome by the changes of a few decades.

There are many other reasons why we would not be surprised if anti-Semitism in the United States were stronger than it is. A large part of the population is regularly outraged by the norm-breaking tendencies of its mass media and by the attitudes and outlooks of the highly educated and academically connected. I refer to the war (or if you will, tension) between New York and Los Angeles, on the one hand, and the rest of the country, on the other, between the coasts and the heartland, between the liberal Northeast and the Bible Belt, between the sophisticates of the academy and the rest of the country. The first of these pairs we know is liberal and irreligious, the second conservative and religious. And the first of these pairs, most are well aware, is disproportionately Jewish. It has long been taken for granted in U.S. popular culture that New York City is not "really" part of the United States. One of the striking changes following the events of 9/11 was that in their wake, as a result of this catastrophe, New York City became part of the country. That did not last long. Perhaps that image of New York difference goes back a long way—it has always been commercial rather than, as is the rest of the country, industrial or agricultural, heretical and outlandish rather than conformist. And as the seat of the publishing industry, the major opinion magazines, and the mass media, it celebrated the new rather than the old and established. But certainly one thing that made New York less like the rest of the United States was that for most of the twentieth century, Jews made up a startling proportion of its population—20 to 30 percent—and in the twenty-first, despite reduced numbers, Jews (as individuals, not as an organized group) still dominate its culture, its major economic activities, and much of its politics and still define the city, much as the Irish defined the city for the first half of the twentieth century.

With all these differences between Jews and other Americans, with this striking Jewish prominence in the mass media, the publishing world, among liberal opinion makers so often at odds with other Americans, it would be reasonable to expect more anti-Semitism. But like another great expectation that has been with us for fifty years—the expectation that Jews would become less liberal and more conservative in line with their occupations and their wealth—it has not happened. And I would argue it will not happen. Perhaps this is another form of American exceptionalism.

It is true there has been an increase in anti-Israel sentiment, and more arguably in anti-Semitism, in many other countries that are part of the developed Western world. But the role of anti-Semitism in European countries has been different from its role in the United States. Anti-Semitism has played a much reduced role in politics and in public life generally in the United States. Just recently, Pierre Birnbaum's book on the year 1898 in France has been published in the United States. It describes the wave of anti-Semitism that followed the publication of Emile Zola's attack on the verdict of the Dreyfus trial and his own trial for libel. What we see portrayed in that book is what can only be called a national frenzy of anti-Semitism: daily demonstrations, often led by students but including all elements of the population, all shouting "death to the Jews," attacks on individuals thought to be Jewish, attacks on Jewish stores and establishments. We have had—and we still have in modest measure—all these things in the United States. Read the reports of the Anti-Defamation League. We have inflamed anti-Semitic organizations here—there seem to be hundreds on the Web—and we have arson attempts on synagogues (one successful), swastikas painted on Jewish establishments, attacks on Jews and indeed, over the past ten years, some killings of Jews because they were Jews. In what way are matters different in the United States? I would say they are different because these anti-Semitic incidents occur in this country furtively, generally carried out by disturbed youths. We assume anyone fiercely anti-Semitic and attracted to Nazism in this country is disturbed and deranged rather than in the grip of a widespread and organized ideology.

Anti-Semitism in the United States has never had a large public presence—as it had in France, in Germany, in Austria. There was widespread anti-Semitic behavior, accompanied by anti-Jewish sentiment, among elite groups from the late nineteenth century through the middle of the twentieth century. There was also anti-Semitic sentiment of a different sort among the non-Jewish neighbors of immigrant Jews. But it was not very different from the distaste for unfamiliar others that regularly emerges among immigrant and low-income groups. It did not generally find expression in organized action. I would not consider the attacks on young Jews by the surrounding Irish or Italians or, later, blacks an expression of organized anti-Semitism. Anti-Semitism was a practice in the United States, not a passion or a movement. Now it is hardly even a practice, though there are many entrepreneurs on the Web who try to make it a movement. But they never get very far.

Their output is chilling in the ferocity of their Jew-hatred. *The Turner Diaries* are well-known as a self-published and widely distributed "novel" by one of the most effective and energetic of these entrepreneurs in Jew-hatred, William Pierce. Timothy McVeigh, the bomber of the Oklahoma City Federal Building, gave away or sold copies of *The Turner Diaries*, which seems to have greatly influenced him. The car he was driving had a marked copy in which passages describing the destruction of a federal building and an airliner headed to Tel Aviv were underlined. There are rather worse passages in The Turner Diaries that are quite horrifying, such as one gloating description of "thousands of hanging female corpses" bearing a placard reading, "I defiled my race" —

white women hung from lampposts because they "were married or lived with blacks, with Jews, or other non-white males."[1] The way we interpret our First Amendment—other interpretations are certainly valid—does not permit action against such obscenities. They are easily available. Fortunately, other U.S. peculiarities, such as our easy ability to sue in civil court on all kinds of grounds, has led to large judgments against anti-Semitic groups, judgments that have put some such groups out of business.

Up to now, anti-Semitism has been a minor theme in U.S. history, even if not so minor for U.S. Jews, who had to deal with a period of widespread discrimination in employment and in higher education. But organized anti-Semitism has not developed in any substantial form in the United States. There is the case of the Ku Klux Klan in the 1920s, which was anti-Semitic as well as antiblack, but it fell apart very rapidly. There was the case of Father Charles Coughlin in the 1930s. But we have never had an anti-Semitic party. Perhaps things have changed. History may teach us some things, but one does not count on it to keep on telling us the same thing. Do recent developments suggest that anti-Semitism will become more important in the United States? I think not.

There has been one major change that bears on the question of whether there will be an increase in anti-Semitism. This is the change in the image of Israel and its reverberation on the image of U.S. Jews, who as an organized community are entirely in support of Israel. This is not the place to air one's views on how Israel has been dealing with the problem of the Intifada or the larger problem of reaching a peaceful accommodation with the Arab population of Palestine and the surrounding countries. As we know, it is these policies that have led to a widespread reaction against Israel, and a particularly severe one in academic communities, in the Western countries, a reaction that can very often spill over into anti-Semitism. This has happened in the United States too. This hostile reaction to Israeli policies has probably been as widespread among Jewish as non-Jewish academics, which makes it hard to call it anti-Semitic. If we consider it within the larger question, what does it tell us about the prospects for anti-Semitism in the United States we should consider it in the light of the fact that the presidents of most of the Ivy League colleges and universities have in recent years been Jews. It is hard to characterize higher education in the United States as being a seat of anti-Semitism.

On the level of national and public policy, the U.S. response to the Intifada and the Israeli effort to put it down has not changed the fifty-year record of U.S. support for Israel. This support of Israel by the U.S. Congress and government could well have been the occasion of a widespread anti-Semitism in the United States. U.S. support led to (or could have been interpreted as leading to) a huge increase in the price of oil and shortages of gasoline in the 1970s. It required and continues to require high levels of aid to Israel, far surpassing that to any other country. It has played a large role in creating the fiercely anti-American sentiment among Arabs, which leads to widespread support for anti-American terrorism. Support for Israel by the U.S. government is one of the reasons the anti-Semitic and extremist groups call it the Zionist Occupied Government (ZOG). But most Americans, as we know, support the foreign policy of their government.

So we could find good reasons for popular criticism of Israel and for a measure of anti-Semitism. But it hasn't happened. The issue of the implications and consequences of U.S. support for Israel is little discussed, and Congress simply approves two billion dollars annually in support for Israel without debate. Some congressmen may grumble in private, but U.S. support for Israel is a given. As far as we know, this seems to lead to no reflection for most Americans on the power of American Jews or on the possibility that this power leads our government to take stands harmful to larger U.S. interests. Arabs and Muslim groups protest, but their presence on the U.S. scene is very small compared to that of comparable groups on the European scene, and terrorism puts them, as well as the extremist groups, under general suspicion.

Indeed, if one is concerned about anti-Semitism, one might well worry about this unquestioned support. Shouldn't it be discussed, so that anti-Israel and anti-Jewish sentiment will not fester in the dark, outside of any legitimate realm of discussion? But the larger conclusion should be that it seems it will take a good deal more to fan anti-Israel and anti-Jewish sentiment in the United States than the policies of the present Israeli government and its support by the U.S. government.

The war on terrorism, whatever we may think of it in detail, helps maintain the current benign environment for Jews. The U.S. government has swept up the anti-Israel and anti-Jewish movements of the Arab world and the Middle East under the general rubric of terrorism that must be opposed. We see hints of increasing suspicion at high levels in our government even of our once good friend, Saudi Arabia, to whose inflammatory Islamism and anti-Semitism the U.S. government used to turn a blind eye. Our attitudes on terrorism have even affected our traditional leaning toward Pakistan in its conflict with India. Are not the groups fighting in Kashmir against Indian rule also terrorists? So our ambassador to India dubbed them, to the distress of Pakistan.

One should not underestimate the role of government in affecting public opinion on foreign affairs, particularly in a country like the United States, where there is so little interest in foreign countries. So if the government says France is unfriendly, it becomes overnight an enemy country. If the United States denounces the fighters against Israel as terrorists, they are terrorists for most Americans, not freedom fighters. With this change in how the enemies of Israel are viewed is the associated change in evangelical and fundamentalist Protestantism. Whatever the weird logic that now leads to evangelical support of Israel—a logic that includes the necessary conversion or disappearance of the Jews—in a country where the evangelical orientation maintains a solid position and is particularly influential with Republican presidents and administrations, it contributes to a dampening of anti-Semitism among a part of the population that was once infected with it. Recall the twenties and the heyday of the Ku Klux Klan.

One can see the basis for a wider anti-Semitism in the United States. But that basis—in the form of the prominence, influence, and wealth of the small Jewish community, some 2 percent of the population, and further, its divergence in values and outlook from the majority of the population—has been there for forty or fifty years. During that entire period, while we have seen efforts to create anti-Semitic movements, we have seen no success. If we look at the changes in the current situation, we will see a good deal of anti-Israel sentiment in the academy, among those who viscerally oppose U.S. government foreign policy and among some others too. (The most prominent proponent of this orientation, Noam Chomsky, is himself a Jew and the son of a Hebrew scholar and teacher.) But that policy in favor of Israel is now firmly fixed, and it is hard to see it changing. The mass of the U.S. population depends on government for its views on foreign countries and foreign policies This constellation suggests to me that a substantial increase in anti-Semitism is not likely in the United States.

# 15

# The Globalization of Anti-Semitism

*Daniel Jonah Goldhagen*

Antisemitism is evolving. After a period of remission owing to the horror of the Holocaust, the ancient prejudice has been reactivated, catalyzed by the Arab-Israeli conflict. It has become particularly acute in the context of the Iraq War and its aftermath, with even respectable people among the political and journalistic elites of Western countries suddenly leveling fantastic antisemitic charges.

The wild claims made in 2003, as the Iraq War was winding down, by the longest serving Labour member of Parliament in Britain, Tam Dalyell, are representative of a widespread school of irrational thought. His notions that George W. Bush, Tony Blair, Dick Cheney, Colin Powell, and Donald Rumsfeld, the hard-bitten practitioners of domestic and international realpolitik, are puppets of a "Jewish cabal" and that this cabal has "taken over the government of the United States" can be put forward only by someone in the grip of a fantastic image of Jews and their alleged maleficent power or by someone who, wishing to tap into and inflame popular antisemitic sentiments, cynically seeks political advantage.

Dalyell's adoption of a malignant conspiracy trope that, wittingly or unwittingly, echoes the *Protocols of the Elders of Zion* is symptomatic of the changed nature of today's antisemitism. As Dalyell's comments reflect, antisemitism has entered a new era in which its main focus has shifted from the domestic to the international. Dalyell and his antisemitic outburst are forgettable, but the new antisemitism is a growing menace that needs to be understood and exposed for what it is. Always protean in quality, always changing to take on the idiom of its day, antisemitism in our globalized era has been globalized.

Antisemitism has always had both domestic and international components. During the long era of Christian antisemitism, the transnational institution of the Catholic Church spread the belief that Jews as Christ-killers were a cosmic force for evil. But the principal target of anti-Jewish prejudice was local, the Jews of one's own town, region, and country, who allegedly harmed their Christian neighbors.

In its second era, during the nineteenth and twentieth centuries, antisemitism took on a secular and more racist cast, in which an international conspiracy of Jews worked against humanity. Still, most of the antisemitic fire was aimed locally—by Germans at German Jews, by French at French Jews—for the harm that they allegedly inflicted on their compatriots. The "Jewish problem"—one of the most burning political issues of the day—was overwhelmingly about what Germans, French, Poles and others should do with the Jews within their countries.

Globalized antisemitism is a new constellation of features grafted onto old ones. Varied and complex, it is oriented to the global stage. In most of Europe, and certainly in Western Europe, the domestic "Jewish problem" is all but dead. Only fringe elements in Germany, France, and elsewhere in Europe believe that local Jews are causing great harm—financial, professional, or moral—to their non-Jewish neighbors, and that a radical response in defense of the nation is necessary. Indeed, except among Islamic minorities of different countries, it has almost become taboo to make classical antisemitic charges against one's Jewish fellow citizens. Who but the lunatic fringe says anymore that Jews are fomenting revolution, wreaking financial havoc, exploiting non-Jews, or corrupting the morals of the nation, let alone its blood? Antisemites of most stripes take pains to ensure that their accusations and venom are understood as directed not at their compatriots but at the particular predatory Jews of the globalized twenty-first century.

The focus of the animus against Jews has shifted overwhelmingly to Jews beyond one's borders, to those of other countries—of Israel and the United States—as the alleged central moral and material culprits of the international arena. For many, Zionism has become not only a shorthand for the allegedly illegitimate state of Israel a mythical entity, a destructive agent in the world. And anti-Zionism has become interwoven with anti-Americanism to the point that Russian nationalist politicians can express their fear of U.S. cultural domination by saying that Russia is in danger of being "Zionized."

The center of antisemitism and directions of its transmission are also new. In the previous eras of antisemitism, the demonology about Jews flowed first from the Christian and then from the European, center to the periphery. Today, as is characteristic of economic and cultural movements more generally in this new era, there are many antisemitic centers and multidirectional flows, from Europe to the Middle East and elsewhere and back. Essentially, Europe exported its classical racist and Nazi antisemitism to Arab countries, which applied it to Israel and Jews in general, suffusing it with the real and imagined features of the intense local conflict. Then the Arab countries re-exported the new hybrid demonology back to Europe, got it institutionalized in the United Nations and other governmental and non-governmental international institutions, and have assiduously and successfully worked to spread it to other countries around the world. The 1975 UN General Assembly resolution declaring Zionism—which was a linguistic stand-in for the State of Israel itself—to be racism, and the orgy of antisemitism that was the 2001 UN anti-racism conference in Durban, South Africa, are but two of the most infamous instances among countless others in which the United Nations and other international institutions have been used by Arab countries and others to legitimize and spread the hatred of Israel and Jews. The center for the dissemination of antisemitism worldwide has migrated for the first time outside Christian Europe and is now located in the Islamic world. In Europe, in Germany, France, Great Britain, and elsewhere, today's intense antisemitic expression and agitation uses old tropes once applied to local Jews—charges of sowing disorder, wanting to subjugate others—with new content overwhelmingly directed at Jews outside their countries and their continent.

The imagery characterizing globalized antisemitism is new. Rambo Jew has largely supplanted Shylock in the antisemitic imagination. The sly and stealthy corrupting Jew of the first two eras of antisemitism, now armed with his new military and political power, has become the subjugating, brutalizing, and killing Jew, either doing the dirty work himself, as in Israel, or employing others to do it for him, as the Jews, fantastically, are said to do with the Bush administration and as the East Coast establishment is purported to do with the United States generally.

An emblematic image of globalized antisemitism is that of Donald Rumsfeld wearing a yellow star inscribed with "sheriff," followed by a cudgel

wielding Ariel Sharon with a golden calf beside him. That this scene, expressing the putative globalized nature and predations of the Jews, was created for
an anti-globalization demonstration in Davos in 2003 is no mere coincidence.

Globalized antisemitism has other important and new features, including
its instantaneous, global transmission through the Internet and via television's
biased stories and inflammatory images of Palestinian suffering, which are
incorporated into the antisemitic narrative; its unification of elements of the
European Left and Right, and its semi-concealing cloak of anti-Zionism.
The Internet has enabled Jew-haters of many lands to coalesce for the first time
into a global anti-Semitic community. In innumerable and proliferating Web
sites, they vent and feed their common obsessions, descanting endlessly on the
evil of the Jews, telling ancient tales of putative Jewish malfeasance and
inventing new ones.

Perhaps most distinctive, though, is the unmooring of antisemitism from
its original sources. It is detached from Christianity, even if there are still
powerful Christian sources of antisemitism, which are being renewed by Mel
Gibson's film *The Passion of the Christ*. It is detached from its nineteenth-
century European sources of nation-building, reactions against modernity and
pseudo-scientific notions of race and social Darwinism, even if that era's
demonology is still potent in somewhat transposed form.

Globalized anti-Semitism has become part of the substructure of prejudice
of the world. It is free-floating—located in many countries, subcultures and
nodes—and available in many variations, and to anyone who dislikes international influences, globalization, or the United States. It is propagated the world
over by Arab countries and institutionalized in the United Nations. It is relent-
lessly international in its focus on Israel as the center of the most conflict-rid-
den region today, and on the United States as the world's omnipresent power.
It is self-reinforcing, with its fantastic constructions of Jews and Zionism—
which are divorced from the fair criticisms that can be made of Israel's policies—and by being located totally outside people's countries and experience.
And it is only a few clicks of a mouse away.

After the Holocaust and after the Catholic Church's 1965 declaration at the
Second Vatican Council renouncing its two-thousand-year-old collective guilt
charge against Jews, it seemed that antisemitism had diminished and might
eventually atrophy. It had indeed declined, and in most European countries,
including Germany, the public's conception of their domestic Jews was de-
demonized. In the West, Christian churches have worked hard to develop
among their members a more respectful and positive image of Jews. Many peo-

ple in Europe, North America, and elsewhere today also reject the new antisemitic fantasies.

Yet the reawakening of antisemitism in its new globalized form means that anti-Semitism has succeeded again in metamorphosing and in extending its reach—even to Africa and Asia. It is also having a secondary effect that is beginning to be more discernible; emboldening anti-Semites who are animated by earlier forms of anti-Jewish hatred, especially among Christians who wish to turn back the liberalizing reforms and developments regarding Jews that Christian churches have made in modern times, particularly in the last half century. Gibson's gruesome film, in its attempt to persuade Christians that Jews are guilty for the murder of Jesus, is the most spectacular example of this.

We know that holding some prejudices against a people makes one susceptible to accepting additional accusations against them as true. And we know that when such prejudices are readily available in the public sphere and are being publicly validated by influential figures, it makes the prejudices more plausible to the unprejudiced and more likely to be brought into the open by those who had hitherto harbored them quietly. This is particularly the case when the prejudice, as with globalized anti-Semitism, is intensive and the calumnies are extreme. So far, the new globalized anti-Semitism has not proved to be as dangerous as earlier forms (except in the Middle East), but its disquieting features suggest that it has the potential to spread further, to resuscitate older forms of anti-Jewish prejudice, and to pose danger to Jews around the world. Throughout history, antisemitism has been a volatile, highly inflammable sentiment with a propensity to erupt into violence

The lethal potential of the new antisemitism can already be seen around Europe, especially in its western portions, where sporadic anti-Jewish violence has recently been increasing year by year. During the tranquil decades that followed the Holocaust, it seemed that the antisemitic demons had been laid to rest. Few Jews would have believed the prediction that at the dawn of the twenty-first century, the Jews of democratic Western Europe would live in fear of their physical safety. Yet today in Germany, France, and elsewhere, including countries that have scarcely known antisemitic violence, Jews again feel physically threatened, in some places more than they have ever felt in modern times aside from the Nazi period itself. Antisemites desecrate synagogues and cemeteries. Jewish institutions must be guarded by the police lest they be firebombed. And Jews wearing Jewish garb and symbols in public are subject to being attacked by antisemites, so much so that many Jews avoid outward manifestations of their Jewishness in public. They especially forbid their children from wearing skullcaps and Stars of David, imparting to them the bitter lesson that being a Jew in one's own country is to risk life and limb.

A genuine settlement to the Arab-Israeli conflict would take some of the wind out of this new antisemitism. But antisemitism's deep roots in the ever-more-globalizing consciousness, its proven tenacity and plasticity, and the almost total demonization of Jews that exists in Arab countries, and widely among adherents of Islam elsewhere make its dissipation unlikely. And we already see signs of a potential redemonization of the Jews of various Western countries, not in the classical antisemitic sense of being accused of trying to subjugate and harm their fellow citizens and their own national communities, but as the alleged sinister supporters of the putative, globally predacious Jews abroad. The unprecedented phenomenon of the Left and Right being united in their verbal assault and political agitation against Israel, and by extension against practically the whole of Jewry, has also given rise, not just on the right but for the first time within elements on the left, to the charge that it is the "character" of the Jews that has led to Israel's putative crimes.

There has been a widespread tendency in the West not to acknowledge the magnitude of anti-Semitism and the danger that it poses and to do little of consequence to combat it. The existence of this new, globalized antisemitism, and its real features must no longer be swept under the rug by politicians, the media, and other elites who do not wish to acknowledge that this poisonous hatred of the ages is back, and back in countries whose international standing will be especially blackened in the eyes of the enlightened part of the world if it becomes known that antisemitism and the growing violence it is producing are serious national problems. Statesmen ought to promulgate the character and menace of the rearisen antisemitism in terms as blunt and as unvarnished as those that the president of Austria, Thomas Klestil, employed in a speech commemorating the hundredth anniversary of the death of the founder of modern Zionism Theodor Herzl.

> The hundredth anniversary of Herzl's death lets us see that antisemitism today often disguises itself as anitzionism . . . the poison of intolerance has entered various languages. . . . Daily we have been witnessing that the expressions of the "barbarians' dictionary" have by no means disappeared. Insidiously, words are being spread which derive from the "spirit of resentment" and which promptly produce further resentment.[1]

Such words should be followed not by perfunctory measures but by a vigorous and sustained campaign to combat the barbarians' dictionary and their actions.

# Notes

## 1. Old Demons, New Debates

1. Virginia Woolf, *Carlyle's House and Other Sketches*, ed. David Bradshaw (London: Hesperus, 2003).

## 2. The New Anti-Semitism

1. Adolf Hitler, *Hitler's Second Book: The Unpublished Sequel to "Mein Kampf,"* ed. Gerhard L. Weinberg, trans. Krista Smith (New York: Enigma Books, 2003). For the history of the book's publication, see Weinberg's foreword, ibid., vii–xxviii.
2. Hitler, *Second Book*, 9.
3. Ibid., 47.
4. Ibid., 49, 95–96.
5. Ibid., 53; Götz Aly, *"Final Solution": Nazi Population Policy and the Murder of the European Jews*, trans. Belinda Cooper and Allison Brown (New York: Oxford University Press, 1999).
6. Hitler, *Second Book*, 80.
7. Wilhelm Deist, *The Wehrmacht and German Rearmament* (Toronto: University of Toronto Press, 1981).
8. Hitler, *Second Book*, 116.
9. Norman J.W. Goda, *Tomorrow the World: Hitler, Northwest Africa, and the Path toward America* (College Station: Texas A & M University Press, 1998).
10. Hitler, *Second Book*, 27, 33.
11. Ibid., 105, 109, 114.

12. Ibid., 97–98.

13. Gerald Fleming, *Hitler and the Final Solution* (Berkeley: University of California Press, 1984), 186–89, and insert with original document, 92–93.

14. Hitler, *Second Book*, 229–30.

15. Hitler, *Second Book*, 230–33.

16. Leon Wieseltier,"Hitler Is Dead: Against the Ethnic Panic of American Jews," *New Republic*, May 27, 2002, http://www.tnr.com/doc.mhtml?i=20020527&s=wieseltier052702.

17. Werner Bergmann and Juliane Wetzel, Center for Research on Anti-Semitism, Technische Universität Berlin, "Manifestations of Anti-Semitism in the European Union," first semester 2002, synthesis report, on behalf of the European Monitoring Centre on Racism and Xenophobia (Vienna, March 2003).

18. On January 21, 2004, Jenny Tonge, British MP and the Liberal Democrats' spokeswoman for children, said to a meeting of the Palestinian Solidarity Campaign: "This particular brand of terrorism, the suicide bomber, is truly born out of desperation. Many, many people . . . say it is just another form of terrorism, but I can understand. . . . I think if I had to live in that situation, and I say this advisedly, I might just consider becoming one myself." Nicholas Watt, "Lib Dem MP: Why I would consider being a suicide bomber," Nicholas Watt "Lib Dem MP: Why I would consider becoming a suicide bomber," *Guardian Unlimited*, January 23, 2004.

19. Mark Anderson,"German Intellectuals, Jewish Victims: A Politically Correct Solidarity," *Chronicle of Higher Education* 48, no. 8 (October 19, 2001): B7–B10.

20. Mark M. Anderson, ed., *Hitler's Exiles: Personal Stories of the Flight from Nazi Germany to America* (New York: New Press, 1998).

21. Gerhard Wisnewski, *Operation 9/11: Angriff auf den Globus* (Munich: Knaur, 2003); Thierry Meyssan, *11 septembre 2001: L'efftoyable imposture* (Paris: Edition Carnot, 2002); Andreas von Büllow, *Die CIA und der 11. September: Internationaler Terror und die Rolle der Geheimdienste* (Munich: Piper, 2003); *Haaretz*, October 2, 2003.

22. Dan Diner, *Feindbild Amerika: Über die Beständigkeit eines Ressentiments* (Munich: Propyläen, 2002); Jean-François Revel, *Anti-Americanism*, trans. Diarmid Cammell (San Francisco: Encounter Books, 2003); Philippe Roger, *L'ennemi américain: Généalogie de l'antiaméricanisme français* (Paris: Seuil, 2002); Pierre-André Taguieff, *La nouvelle judéo-phobie* (Paris: Mille et une nuit, 2002); Andrei S. Markovits, *Amerika, dich hasst sich's beser: Antiamerikanismus und Antisemitismus in Europa* (Hamburg: Konkret, 2004).

23. References and discussion in Phyllis Chesler, *The New Anti-Semitism: The Current Crisis and What We Must Do about It* (San Francisco: Jossey-Bass, 2003), 135–36; Gabriel Schoenfeld, *The Return of Anti-Semitism* (San Francisco: Encounter Books, 2004), 89–90.

24. For the debate over this cartoon on the pages of *Independent.co.uk*, January 31, 2003, see "Satire or anti-Semitism: For and against," an editorial that opens with the following statement: "On Monday, 'The Independent' published a savage cartoon of Israel's Prime Minister, Ariel Sharon. It prompted complaints from the Israeli Embassy, Jewish groups, and some of our readers, who were offended by the image. Today, we ask the question: was this cartoon anti-Semitic? and throw the debate open to our Argument channel": http://news.independent.co.uk/world/ middle_east/story.jsp?story=374143. See further: Dave Brown, "Satire or Anti-Semitism? The cartoonist writes": http://news.independent.co.uk/world/middle_east/story.jsp?story=374142; Philip Hensher, "Satire or anti-Semitism? Looking at Goya: 'Exactly

as Goya does, Brown accuses a political leader of sacrificing his own children'":
http://news.independent.co.uk/world/ middle_east/story.jsp?story=374141; Gerald Kaufman,
"Satire or Anti-Semitism? Satire": http://news.independent.co.uk/world/ middle_east/
story.jsp?story=374145. The Independent's cartoonist Dave Brown won the Political Cartoon
of the Year award for this cartoon. See *Independent.co.uk*, "'Independent' cartoonist wins
award": http://news.independent.co.uk/uk/media/story.jsp?story=467627.

25. Ansprache von MdB Martin Hohmann zum Nationalfeiertag, October 3, 2003,
http://www.tagesschau.de/aktuell/meldungen/0,1185,OID2535644_TYP4,00.html.

26. Thomas Haury, "Das Bedürfnis nach Entlastung: Schlechtes Gewissen, nach außen pro-
jiziert," *Frankfurter Rundschau Online*, November 27, 2003 http://www.fr-aktuell.de/
ressorts/nachrichten_und_politik/standpunkte/?cnt=346964.

27. "70% of Germans Are Fed Up with Guilt Feelings About the Holocaust," from news agen-
cies (in Hebrew): *Haaretz*, December 11, 2003: http://www.haaretz.co.il/hasite/
objects/pages/PrintArticle.jhtml?itemNo=371174. The American Jewish Committee conducted a similar poll with similar results. See Toby Axelrod, "Germans have disturbing attitudes
toward Jews, according to a new poll," *JTA Global News Service of the Jewish People*,
December 17, 2004: http://www.jta.org/page_view_story.asp?strwebhead=German+ideas+
of+Jews+%26%238216%3Btroubling%26%238217%3B&intcategoryid=2.

28. New Jersey Solidarity website: "Activists for the Liberation of Palestine: Our Mission,"
http://www.newjerseysolidarity.org/.

29. Joel Landau, "Banners spring up around campus, question free speech," the *Daily Targum*,
October 3, 2003: http://dailytargum.com/main.cfm?include=detail&storyid=389580;
"'Covering' or 'Covering Up' a Palestinian Solidarity Rally?" (no author indicated),
CAMERA: *Committee for Accuracy in Middle East Reporting in America*, July 31, 2003,
http://www.camera.org/index.asp?x_context=22&x_article=516.

30. "An Open Letter From President McCormick on the NJ Solidarity Group Meeting" (no date):
http://www.rutgersclubdc.org/PalestinianControversy.htm.

31. Hannah Arendt, "The Aftermath of Nazi Rule: Report from Germany," *Commentary* (October
1950): 342–53, quote p. 344.

32. Anti-Defamation League, "Anti-Semitism on Display: Marches and Rallies," January 28,
2003: http://www.adl.org/anti_semitism/arab/as_rallies.asp.

33. Quoted in David Rohde, "Radical Islam Gains a Seductive New Voice," *New York Times*,
Week in Review, October 26, 2003.

34. Matthias Küntzel, "Wer Anti-Semitismus sät, wird Dschihad ernten," *Frankfurter Rundschau
online*, November 21, 2003, http://www.fraktuell.de/ressorts/nachrichten_und_politik/
dokumentation/?cnt=343422.

35. Paul Krugman, "Listening to Mahathir," *New York Times*, October 21, 2003.

36. Speech by the Prime Minister of Malaysia, the Hon. Dato Seri Dr. Mahathir Mohamad, at
the Opening of the Tenth Session of the Islamic Summit Conference, Putrajaya, Malaysia,
20 Shaaban 1424H (16 October 2003), 10.00 AM. Available on: http://www.oic
summit2003.org.my/specch_03.php. All further quotations from this speech are from this
source.

37. For analysis and background, see Bernard Lewis, *What Went Wrong? Western Impact and
Middle Eastern Response* (New York: Oxford University Press, 2002), and Lewis, *The
Crisis of Islam: Holy War and Unholy Terror* (New York: The Modern Library, 2003).

38. Matthias Küntzel, *Djihad und Judenhaß: Über den neuen antijüdischen Krieg* (ça ira: Freiburg: 2002). A pre-9/11 perspective appears in Bernard Lewis, *Semites and Anti-Semites: An Inquiry into Conflict and Prejudice* (New York: Norton, 1987). An insider's criticism is Irshad Manji, *The Trouble with Islam: A Muslim's Call for Reform in Her Faith* (New York: St. Martin's Press, 2003).

39. See an article by Pearl's father: Judea Pearl, "The Tide of Madness: The World Must Stand against the Evil That Took My Son's Life," *Wall Street Journal*, February 20, 2003, http://www.opinionjournal.com/editorial/feature.html?id=110003095. See also Mariane Pearl with Sarah Crichton, *A Mighty Heart: The Brave Life and Death of My Husband, Danny Pearl* (New York: Scribner, 2003); Bernard-Henri Lévy, *Who Killed Daniel Pearl?* trans. James X. Mitchell (Hoboken, N.J.: Melville House, 2003).

40. Matthias Küntzel, "Islamic Antisemitism and Its Nazi Roots," *Texte von Matthias Küntzel*: http://www.matthiaskuentzel.de/artikel.php?artikelID=30. Also in *Genocide and Terrorism—Probing the Mind of the Perpetrator*, ed. Dori Laub (forthcoming).

41. Selected Documents Regarding Palestine: Hamas Charter, 1988: http://www.palestine center.org/cpap/documents/charter.html. All further quotations from this charter are from this source.

42. See Omer Bartov, "Nazi State Terror and Contemporary Global Terrorism: Continuities and Differences," in *Jewish History as General History: Festschrift for Dan Diner's Sixtieth Birthday*, ed. Yfaat Weiss and Raphael Gross (forthcoming) for further discussion.

# 5. Israel, Globalization, and Anti-Semitism in Europe

1. Romano Prodi, Speech given at conference of the European Community on anti-Semitism held in Brussels, February 2004.

# 6. Anti-Semitism and the English Intelligentsia

1. See, e.g., Lee M. Friedman, *Robert Grosseteste and the Jews* (Cambridge, Mass.: Harvard University Press, 1934). Grosseteste (1175–1253), the bishop of Lincoln, a scholar of both Hebrew and Greek, wrote at length about the Jews. His views were impeccably orthodox: A curse will rest upon the Jews as long as they persist in blasphemy and unbelief. Rulers who treat them too kindly or favour their usurious practices are themselves guilty of the sin of the Jews. But they may not be killed.

2. Francis James Child, ed., *The English and Scottish Popular Ballads* (Boston: Houghton Mifflin, 1888), vol. 3, 233–54.

3. There are exceptions, of course. During the Readmission controversy, for example, there were anti-Jewish pamphleteers ready to accuse Jews of torturing Christian children and putting them to death. See Bernard Glassman, *Anti-Semitic Stereotypes without Jews: Images of the Jews in England, 1290–1700* (Detroit: Wayne State University Press, 1974), 114, 118–20. In addition, the blood libel has been a staple of twentieth-century anti-Semitic fantasists, in England as well as elsewhere.

4. "A prejudice is a (not necessarily advantageous) mental illumination; a preoccupation is a mental burden." John Lukacs, *At the End of an Age* (New Haven: Yale University Press, 2002), 3.

5. Quoted in Richard Overy, *Interrogations: Inside the Minds of the Nazi Elites* (London: Penguin, 2001), 481.

6. Quoted in Simon Heffer, *Moral Desperado: A Life of Thomas Carlyle* (London: Phoenix, 1995), 263, 379.

7. Quoted in Montagu Frank Modder, *The Jew in the Literature of England* (New York: Schocken, 1960), 171–2.

8. Thomas Carlyle, *Sartor Resartus* (1831). In my edition (London, 1901), the quotations are taken from 29, 60 and 192.

9. David Vital, *A People Apart: The Jews in Europe 1789–1939* (Oxford: Oxford University Press, 1999), 178–9.

10. Bertrand Russell *Autobiography* (London: George Allen & Unwin, 1971), 92. Russell was serving a six-months' sentence for making statements likely to prejudice relations between the United Kingdom and the United States.

11. See Anthony Julius, *T.S. Eliot, Anti-Semitism, and Literary Form* (London: Thames and Hudson, 2003), passim.

12. Avrom Saltman, *The Jewish Question in 1655: Studies in Prynne's "Demurrer"* (Ramat-Gan: Bar–Ilan, 1995), 121.

13. See Thomas W. Perry, *Public Opinion, Propaganda, and Politics in Eighteenth-Century England* (Cambridge, Mass: Harvard University Press, 1962).

14. William Cobbett, *Rural Rides* (London: Penguin, 1967), 119, 342, 345, 395, 402.

15. William Cobbett, *Paper against Gold*. I quote from the 1844 New York edition, 121. See also Mark L. Shoenfeld, "Abraham Goldsmid: Money Magician," in *British Romanticism and the Jews*, ed. Sheila A. Spector, (London: Routledge, 2002),46–53.

16. On Cobbett's *Good Friday*, see Vital, *A People Apart*, (Oxford University Press) 186–87.

17. William Hazlitt, *Cobbett: Prose and Poetry* ed. A.M.D. Hughes (Oxford: 1923), 7. It was, observed G.K. Chesterton, one of Cobbett's principles to have prejudices: *William Cobbett* (London: Oxford University Press, 2000), 64.

18. Richard Shannon, *The Crisis of Imperialism, 1865–1915* (London; Paladin, 1974), 446–47.

19. Or almost no one. It was mentioned with approval in a review of A.N. Wilson's 1984 biography of Belloc that appeared in the Far Right news sheet *New Nation* (Winter 1984, no. 6).

20. Geoffrey G. Field, *Evangelist of Race: The Germanic Vision of Houston Stewart Chamberlain* (New York: Columbia University Press, 1981), 224.

21. Ibid., 359.

22. Belloc, *The Jews*, p vii.

23. Colin Holmes writes of the inauguration in the 1870s of "instances of an anti-Semitism which were to recur at frequent intervals down to the First World War." *Anti-Semitism in British Society, 1876–1939* (New York: Holmes & Meier, 1979), 10.

24. On the press and popular response to one particular incident in this conflict, see David Leitch, "Explosion at the King David Hotel," in *Age of Austerity, 1945–1951*, eds. Michael Sissons and Philip French (London: Penguin, 1964), 58–85.

25. See David Feldman, *Englishmen and Jews: Social Relations and Political Culture, 1840–1914* (New Haven: Yale University Press, 1994), 90–93.

26. See Geoffrey Wheatcroft, *The Randlords* (London: Weidenfeld & Nicolson, 1985), 204–6. The libertarian Edward Carpenter complained at about the same time that British politicians were "being led by the nose by the Jews" (quoted in ibid., 206).

27. Oswald Mosley, quoted by Alastair Hamilton, *The Appeal of Fascism: A Study of Intellectuals and Facism, 1919–1945* (London: Anthony Blonde, 1971), 265.

28. For example: "Hobson's analysis . . . was widely circulated by those opposed to the war. Furthermore, it was not an idiosyncratic view but was a major expression of a well worked contemporary theme." Holmes, *Anti-Semitism in British Society*, 68.

29. "It would be unwise to exaggerate the force of anti-Semitism in Great Britain in this period. The number of people who were seriously swayed by fears of a 'Judaeo-Masonic plot' was a very small percentage of the population." Richard Griffiths, *Fellow Travellers of the Right: British Enthusiasts for Nazi Germany, 1933–1939* (London: Constable, 1980), 65.

30. Cf.: "The degree of unbalance in the participants on both sides of this controversy is extraordinary. Men whose lives and careers were at all other times distinguished by courtesy, goodwill and intellectual integrity seem to have taken leave of their senses. No example is more striking than that of G.K. Chesterton, who was and remained all his life obsessed by the case." Frances Donaldson, *The Marconi Scandal* (London: Rupert Hart-Davis, 1962), 189.

31. R.I. Moore, *The Formation of a Persecuting Society* (Oxford: Blackwell, 1987), 153.

32. "So far was Fascism from enjoying any measure of popularity in England that it seems absurd to ask why it failed. Between the wars England was the scene of events which might well have led to a violent political reaction in other countries—the strikes between 1918 and 1920, the general strike in 1926, the Hunger marches in the thirties: the parliamentary system tottered, but it survived. As far as the majority of the English were concerned, Fascism was a foreign creation for use by foreigners." Hamilton, *The Appeal of Fascism*, 257.

33. "The Testament of an Anti-Semite," an appendix in Moshe Zimmermann, *Wilhelm Marr* (Oxford: Oxford University Press, 1986), 151.

34. Norman Cohn, *Warrant for Genocide* (London: Eyre & Spottiswoode, 1967), 71, 152–53.

35. For a recent survey, see William D. Rubinstein and Hilary L. Rubinstein, *Philosemitism: Admiration and Support in the English-Speaking World for Jews, 1840–1939* (London: Macmillan, 1999).

36. David S. Katz, *Philo-Semitism and the Readmission of the Jews to England, 1603–1655* (Oxford: Oxford University Press, 1982), ch. 1.

37. See, for example, R. Travers Herford, *What the World Owed to the Pharisees* (London: George Allen & Unwin, 1919). See also H. H. Milman, *History of the Jews*, 4th ed. (John Murray, 1866).

38. "It's a shame"; Wilson likes this remark so much he cited it twice: see *Belloc* (London: Penguin, 1986), 230, 261.

39. A. N. Wilson, "The Tragic Reality of Israel," *Evening Standard*, October 22, 2001.

40. A. N. Wilson, "Comment," *Evening Standard*, February 10, 2003.

41. In a letter to the *Independent*, May 1, 2003, Wilson wrote: "Of course I should have checked the source before I wrote the article; and of course I am sorry."

42. A. N. Wilson, "A demo we can't afford to ignore," *Evening Standard*, April 15, 2002.

43. A. N. Wilson, "Three reasons to stay Anglican for all its follies," *Daily Telegraph*, April 10, 2004.

44. Wilson, *Belloc*, 269.

45. A. N. Wilson, *Milton* (Oxford: Oxford University Press, 1987), 252.

46. Wilson, *Belloc*, 262, 383.

47. Tam Dalyell, interview conducted by David Margolick, *Vanity Fair*, June 2003, 227.

48. *Sunday Telegraph*, May 4, 2003.

49. *Herald*, May 5, 2003.

50. *Sunday Telegraph*, May 4, 2003.

51. *Jewish Chronicle*, June 20, 2003.

52. Nicholas Watt, "Dalyell May Face Race Hatred Inquiry," *Guardian*, May 5, 2003.

53. Quoted in Cesarani, "Continuities and Discontinuities in Anti-Zionism in Britain, 1922–2002." www.brandeis.edu/centers/sametparticipants/cesarani.pdf.

54. *Herald*, May 5, 2003.

55. *Scotsman*, May 5, 2003.

56. The text of the adjudication can be read on the PCC's Web site. Paragraph 7 states, "The Code does not cover complaints about alleged discrimination against groups of people." But see, for example, the August 6, 1997 adjudication on Anne Peck's complaint (upholding it): "The columnist's humorous remarks . . . were clearly distressing to the elderly and to those with mental health problems."

57. *Al-Ahram Weekly* online, no. 580, April 4–10, 2002, http://www.ahram.org.eg.

58. Paulin's implication is clear. If a Jew—and a victim of the Holocaust, no less—has made a comparison between Zionists and Nazis, then the comparison is good for all to make. But Klemperer does not compare the Jews to Nazis in the latter's violence, only in what he regards as their regressive, *volkish*, nationalism. There is no reference to Zionism in his later accounts of SS violence.

59. Cf. "There is occasionally a sly smile to be detected when [the Jews] think of how they have tricked the Christians. Indeed the allegorical representation of the Jew is the fox . . . [The Jew] is happy to underline how he has got the better of the Aryan." Edouard Drumont, *La France Juive*, (1886) abridged in McClelland, *The French Right*, (London: Jonathan Cape, 1920), 111.

60. See James Taylor and Warren Shaw, *Dictionary of the Third Reich* (London: Penguin, 1997), 265–71.

61. Tom Paulin, interview, *Guardian*, January 20, 2002.

62. On the participation of children in the two Intifadas, from a pro-Palestinian perspective, see *A Global Report from the Coalition to Stop the Use of Child Soldiers* (London: Coalition to Stop the Use of Child Soldiers, 2001), 287–90.

63. Canto 74 in Ezra Pound, *The Cantos*. For myself, I find "Zionist SS" no less offensive than "yidd."

64. Tom Paulin, "On Being Dealt the Anti-Semitic Card," *Guardian*, January 8, 2003.

65. In a letter published in several national newspapers, Paulin wrote: "My views have been distorted. I have been, and am, a lifelong opponent of anti-Semitism and a consistent supporter of a Palestinian state. I do not support attacks on Israeli civilians under any circumstances. I am in favour of the current efforts to achieve a two-state solution to the conflict between Israel and the Palestinians. The terrible events in the Middle East are a real source of anguish—we are all responsible for what is happening there, and we are responsible, too,

for finding a just and lasting peace." *Daily Mail*, April 19, 2002; *Independent on Sunday*, April 21, 2002.

66. Rappaport, *Jew and Gentile. The Philo-Semitic Aspect* (New York: Philosophical Library, 1980), 13.

# 7. Playground for Jihad?

1. See Farrukh Dhondy, "A Celebration of Terror," *Jerusalem Post*, September 15, 2002.
2. See "Islamist Leaders in London Interviewed," MEMRI, no. 410, August 9, 2002.
3. *Washington Times*, July 8, 2002.
4. "Al-Qa'ida Attack on UK," *Independent*, Sept. 8, 2002.
5. "Islamic Terrorism. Men in Black," *Economist*, Sept. 7, 2002, 93–94.
6. Ali La'idi/Ahmed Salam, *Le Jihad en Europe* (Paris, 2000), 55–57.
7. *Daily Telegraph*, September 11, 2002, viii.
8. *Il Giornale*, Milan, October 14, 2000.
9. MEMRI, no. 73, October 24, 2001, www.terrorism.com/trcctforum 5/000004b5.htm
10. BBC News, October 14, 2000.
11. "London Rally for Fanatics," *Daily Telegraph*, September 11, 2002, 8.
12. Ibid.
13. *London Jewish News*, August 30, 2002.
14. *Daily Telegraph*, February 5, 2003.
15. *Daily Telegraph*, February 5, 2003; *Jerusalem Post*, February 25, 2003.
16. *Azzam Publications*, October 18, 2000.
17. Press release by the International Islamic Front, the Palestine Support Council, the Khilafah Movement, and Al-Muhajiroun, October 7, 2000.
18. Message of October 2, 2000 on Palestine and the Islamic ruling and message to Muslims.
19. Malise Ruthven, *A Fury for God: The Islamist Attack on America* (London: Granta Books, 2002).
20. Robert S. Wistrich, *Muslim Antisemitism: A Clear and Present Danger* (New York: AJC Publications, 2002).
21. The British media line (there are plenty of parallels across Europe) is to blame the suicide bombings on the despair and hopeless misery of the Palestinians in the face of Israeli oppression. See, for example, Sa'id Ghazali, "Suicide Bombers Are the Appalling but Inevitable Result of Decades of Despair," *Independent*, Monday Review, March 25, 2002. Available empirical studies and profiles of Muslim suicide bombers show this assumption to be false. They are usually well educated, highly motivated, religious, and proud of their "martyrdom."
22. *Independent*, June 19, 2002, and *Guardian*, June 19, 2002, predictably defended Mrs. Blair. See Jonathan Freedland, *Mirror*, June 20, 2003, for a more nuanced view; also Trevor Kavanagh, *Sun*, June 20, 2003, who trashed Mrs. Blair's remarks and denounced "the brainwashed suicide zombies [who] want to wipe the State of Israel off the map of the Middle East." See also "Cherie Blair's Suicide Bomb Blunder," *Times*, June 19, 2002, and "What Cherie Really Thinks," *Daily Telegraph*, June 19, 2002, which reminded Mrs. Blair that "hope" rather than "despair" motivated the martyrs. First, the hope they would go to heav-

en if they murdered Jews; second, the hope they would destroy Israel; and third, the hope their families would receive a $25,000 reward from the Iraqi and Saudi governments.

23. Sarah Lyall, "What Drove Two Britons to Bomb a Club in Tel Aviv?" *New York Times International*, May 12, 2003. Also "MI5 Admits: We Let Suicide Bombers Slip through Net," *Daily Telegraph*, May 4, 2003. Sheikh Omar Bakri defended Hanif's action as that of "a freedom fighter who is fighting to liberate his homeland from its occupiers." He did not explain how Palestine could be the "homeland" of an Anglo-Pakistani citizen.

24. Douglas Davis, "UK Muslims Said Planning Attacks," *Jerusalem Post*, October 29, 2003.

25. Martin Bright and Fareena Alam, "Making of a Martyr," *Observer*, May 4, 2003. Also Nick Cohen, "'A Kind, Really Nice Boy.' What drives Western Muslim Adolescents into the Arms of Fundamentalism and Deliberate Death?" *Observer*, May 4, 2003. For the most recent case of a British Muslim suspected of belonging to al Qaeda, see "Terrorist Suspect 'the Bright Star of Our Mosque,'" *Times*, November 29, 2003. The profile of twenty-four-year-old Sajid Badat was remarkably similar to that of Hanif.

26. For a compelling portrait of Omar Sheikh's passage from "perfect Englishman" to Islamist architect of a barbaric murder (in which Pearl's Jewishness played a key role), see Bernard-Henri Lévy, *Qui a tué Daniel Pearl?* (Paris: Bernard Grasset, 2003), 101–210. *Who Killed Daniel Pearl?* trans. James X. Mitchell (Hoboken, NJ : Melville House, 2003).

27. See Dominique Thomas, *Le Londistan. La voix du djihad* (Paris: Éditions Michalon, 2003), 129–46. Also see Alexandre Del Valle, *Le totalitarisme islamiste à l'assaut des démocraties* (Paris: Éditions des Syrtes, 2002), 227–47.

28. Thomas, *Londistan*, 109–28.

29. Ibid., 147–84. Del Valle, *Le totalitarisme islamiste*, 237–39.

30. Thomas, *Londistan*. 185–206.

31. Farrukh Dhondy, "An Islamic Fifth Column," *Wall Street Journal*, December 27, 2001.

32. Abou Qutada al-Filastini, a Palestinian refugee from Jordan, was bin Laden's most important emissary to Europe. For eight years (1993–2001), he lived undisturbed in North London before he was finally arrested by the British authorities. Qutada's charismatic preaching (available on videocassettes) and his jihadist worldview had a great impact on radical British and European Muslims, as well as on the 9/11 hijackers from Germany. For his ideology and pivotal role, see Thomas, *Londistan*, 100–4. Also see Gilles Kepel, *Jihad. The Trail of Political Islam* (Cambridge, Mass: Harvard University Press, 2002) for the general background.

33. BBC News, October 14, 2000.

34. See Del Valle, *Le totalitarisme islamiste*, 243–45. For the rage of young British Muslims over the "Jewish conquerors" in Palestine, see Fuad Nihdi, *Guardian*, May 2, 2003. Nahdi lists "the expansion of illegal Jewish settlements," "colonial-era racism," "apartheid-style zoning laws," Jewish control of Islam holy places, and the plight of the refugees. Typical of this distorted litany is the refusal to acknowledge any Muslim, Arab, or Palestinian faults or responsibility for the perpetuation of the conflict.

35. See Nahdi, in *Guardian*, May 2, 2003.

36. "War Blamed for Anti-Jewish Attacks," BBC News World Edition, May 2, 2003; "UK Jews Ask for More Police Protection," *Jerusalem Post*, May 5, 2002. Also "War against the Jews," *Community Security Trust (CST). Annual Review* (Antisemitism and Jewish Communal Security in Britain in 2002) 4–5. According to reliable reports, as many as four thousand

British Islamist radicals have undergone terrorist training with al-Qaeda over the past decades.

37. "Antisemitic Incidents," *CST Annual Review*, 6–7. The CST defines an anti-Semitic incident as "a malicious attack aimed directly at the Jewish community"—whether physical attacks on Jewish people or property, verbal or written abuse, threats against Jews, or anti-Semitic leaflets and posters. The CST recorded 350 such incidents during 2002, a 13 percent increase on the 2001 total of 310 incidents.

38. *The Community Security Trust (CST). Antisemitic Incidents Report 2002* (London: CST, 2002), 5.

39. Ibid. For example, one woman was called a "filthy Zionist Jew bitch" by a person who was picketing a Marks and Spencer store in London. In Manchester, three Jewish buildings were defaced with "Boycott Israel Apartheid" stickers.

40. Such attacks—there were forty-seven in 2002—have become more violent since the outset of the Palestinian Intifada in September 2000. The danger of Islamic extremists striking at high-profile Jewish institutions or individuals remains serious.

41. CST. *Antisemitic Incidents*, 7. At Queen Mary College in London, following a debate on the boycott, one Jewish student was branded a "Jewish slag" by the demonstrating anti-Israel protestors. Many such incidents, it goes without saying, are not reported.

42. Ibid., 7–8. The CST criticizes the fact that Islamist anti-Semitic literature is almost never prosecuted in Britain, thus encouraging the belief that those who vilify Jews will suffer no consequences. This contrasts with the vigorous prosecution of far-right anti-Semitic literature in the late 1990s. The situation has slowly begun to change since 2001.

43. Ori Golan, "One Day the Black Flag of Islam Will Be Flying over Downing Street," *Jerusalem Post*, June 27, 2003. One factor in this alienation is "Islamophobia," or hateful generalizations about Muslims that stereotype them indiscriminately as terrorists and fanatics. Unfortunately, many Muslims who complain about "Islamophobia" also vehemently deny the existence of Muslim anti-Semitism or simply blame it on Zionism. Few British Muslim leaders have condemned the suicide bombings, and many younger Muslims sympathize with them. This equivocacy as well as the refusal to demonstrate loyalty to British values has greatly aggravated the situation.

44. Jenni Frazer, "Bridges and Breaches: British Muslims. Faith and Rage," *Jewish Chronicle*, May 9, 2003, 32. There are, of course, interfaith forums where dialogue continues at the price of avoiding honest talk about the Israeli/Palestinian conflict. At a grassroots level, Jews and Muslims do live together; and British Muslims are understandably sensitive to being tarred with the terrorist brush. Some younger Muslims also have a sense of fatalism, believing that "Muslim blood is cheap and innocent Muslims everywhere are permissible targets." See Ziauddin Sardar, "Mobilising Islam against Terror," *Observer*, February 16, 2003.

45. See Fuad Nahdi, "Revive Spiritual Cousinhood," *Jewish Chronicle*, May 9, 2003, 33.

46. See the letters column of the *Jewish Chronicle*, May 23, 2003, for critical responses to Nahdi.

47. Fuad Nahdi, "Revive Spiritual Cousinhood.". "Whatever Israel does, it does—in the minds of most young British Muslims—in the name of all Jews."

48. Yasmin Alibhai-Brown, "Why I Try to Understand the Suicide Bombers," *Independent*, July 7, 2003, repeats this charge. See also Linda Grant's insightful article on how the Arab world is exporting an old hatred to the West, published in *Guardian*, December 18, 2001, 2–5.

49. Mitchell Symons, "Fears That Force Jews to Stand Up and Shout," *Daily Express*, November 28, 2003.

50. "Minister's Remarks Spur Concern," *Jewish Chronicle*, November 28, 2003.

51. Ibid. Initially, the MCB was silent about the al Qaeda bombings of two synagogues in Istanbul in November 2003.

52. Ibid. Richard Stone, chairman of the Jewish Council for Racial Equality, even called McShane's words "unacceptable."

53. "Race Chief Says Antisemitism Up," *Jewish Chronicle*, October 3, 2003.

54. "Our Dulled Nerve," *Guardian*, November 18, 2003. The leader pointed to rising attacks in France, Belgium, and Germany as well as the deliberate targeting of Jewish civilians in Morocco, Tunisia, and Turkey.

55. Ibid.

56. The editorial also welcomed the fact that the police were being more proactive in pursuing Islamists who spread virulent anti-Semitic literature.

# 8. The Retreat of the Strong State and the New Anti-Semitic Mobilization in France

1. *Le Monde*, December 4, 2001.

2. Press office of the French presidency.

3. *Libération* and *Le Monde*, November 18, 2003.

4. Press office of the prime minister.

5. *Le Monde*, January 10, 2003.

6. Annual report of the National Consultative Commission on Human Rights (La Documentation Française, 2003). In a separate text accompanying these statistics, Nonna Mayer pointed out that "over the past two years, France has experienced an exceptionally serious resurgence of anti-Semitic violence." In the 2001 annual report of the same commission, Nonna Mayer and Guy Michelat noted that "the rise in overt anti-Semitism is apparent in all segments of the population, including men and women, young and old, workers and managers, left and right."

7. Annual report of the National Consultative Commission on Human Rights (La Documentation Française, 2004).

8. See *L'Arche*, January-February 2002.

9. Emannuel Brenner et al., *Les territoires perdus de la République* (Paris: Mille et une nuits, 2002).

10. *Le Monde*, November 20, 2003.

11. *Les Antifeujs. Le livre bilan des violences antisémites en France* (Paris: Calmann-Lévy, 2002). See also Pierre-André Taguieff, *La nouvelle judéophobie* (Paris: Mille et une nuits, 2002).

12. *Information juive*, June 2002.

13. "Shouts of 'Death to the Jews !' Heard in Strasbourg," *Le Monde*, November 7, 2000.

14. *Libération*, April 2, 2003.

15. *Le Monde*, April 12, 2002.

16. *Le Monde*, December 23, 2003, and January 20, 2004. See also Emmanuel Brenner, "France, prends garde de perdre ton âme." in *Fracture sociale et antisémitisme dans la République* (Paris: Mille et une nuits, 2004), 124 ff.

17. Pierre Birnbaum, *The Jews of the Republic* (Stanford: Stanford University Press, 1995).

18. Hannah Arendt, *The Human Condition* (Chicago: University of Chicago Press, 1958).

19. *Le Monde*, September 20, 2003.

20. *Libération*, April 24, 2003. See also the special section of the magazine *Le Point* (October 20, 2000) entitled "Jews of France. The Sorrow and the Anger," a title obviously chosen to evoke the film about Vichy, *The Sorrow and the Pity*.

21. *Le Figaro*, April 8, 2002. *Le Monde*, April 9, 2002.

22. Pierre Birnbaum, *Jewish Destinies*, trans. Arthur Goldhammer (New York: Hill and Wang, 2000), ch. 12.

23. *Libération*, April 8, 2002.

24. *Information juive*, May 2002.

25. See *Tribune juive*, June 6, 2002. See also Erik Cohen's survey of French Jews and French Jewish values and identities in *L'Arche*, December 2002.

26. *Le Monde*, December 10, 2003.

27. For a comparison of the situation of Jews in the United States and Israel along these lines, see the introduction to E. Ben-Rafaël, *Qu'est-ce qu'être Juif? Suivi de 50 Sages répondent à Ben Gurion* (Paris: Balland, 2001).

28. On the origins of this vertical alliance, which was first established through relationships with kings and princes, see Yosef H. Yerushalmi, "Servants of Kings and Not Servants of Servants: Some Aspects of the Political History of the Jews" (unpublished in English). "Serviteurs de Rois et non serviteur des serviteurs," *Raisons politiques*, Aug-Oct 2000.

29. Pierre Birnbaum, *Sur la corde raide* (Paris: Flammarion, 2002), and *Géographie de l'espoir. L'exil, les Lumières, le déassimilation* (Paris : Gallimard, 2004).

30. See Jean-François Chanet, *L'ecole républicaine et les petites patries* (Paris: Aubier, 1996) ; Anne-Marie Thiesse, *La Création des identités nationales* (Paris: Editions du Seuil, 1999).

31. See Charles Taylor, "The Politics of Recognition," *Multiculturalisms and the Politics of Recognition* (Princeton: Princeton University Press, 1994), 51; Will Kymlicka, "Penser le multiculturalisme. Entretien avec Will Kymlicka," *Mouvements*, no. 7, January-February 2000), 121–22.

32. Pierre Birnbaum, "La France dans la théorie politique contemporaine," in *La constellation des appartenances*, ed. Alain Dieckoff (Paris: Presses des Sciences Politiques, 2004).

33. Paula Hyman, *The Jews of Modern France* (Berkeley: University of California Press, 1998), 218.

34. See Pierre Birnbaum, *The Anti-Semitic Moment: A Tour of France in 1898* (New York: Hill and Wang, 2003).

35. Such a correlation was demonstrated in Pierre Birnbaum, *Antisemitism in France: A Political History from Leon Blum to the Present* (Oxford: Blackwell, 1992). In a recent work, William Brustein criticized this model, which he says cannot explain significant variations in the intensity of anti-Semitism in states of similar type. See his *Roots of Anti-Semitism in Europe before the Holocaust* (Cambridge: Cambridge University Press, 2003), 39–40. In contrast, I am trying to show that it is precisely the decline of the strong state that allows other types

of anti-Semitism to express themselves with greater intensity by way of less-state-centered forms of mobilization.

36.  Quoted in *L'Arche*, October-November 2001, 14–15. See also *L'Arche*, May 2003.
37.  Vincent Geisser, *Ethnicité républicaine* (Paris: Presses de Sciences Politiques, 1997).
38.  Sylvie Strudel, *Votes juifs* (Paris: Presses de Sciences Politiques, 1996).
39.  Until recently, most reputable work showed that French of North African descent were keen to integrate and preferred to confine religion to the private sphere. See Rémy Leveau and Gilles Kepel, eds., *Les Musulmans dans la société française* (Paris: Presses de Sciences Politiques, 1988); Jocelyne Cesari, *Etre musulman en France* (Paris : Hachette, 1977); Hervé Vieillard-Baron, *Les banlieues françaises ou le ghetto impossible* (Paris: Editions de l'Aube, 1994); Michèle Tribalat, *De l'immigration à l'assimilation* (Paris: La Découverte, 1996).
40.  Elie Barnavi, *Le Monde*, August 8, 2001.
41.  I borrow this image from Michael Walzer, *What It Means to Be an American* (New York: Marsilio Publishers, 1992), 5.

# 9. Esau Can Change, but Will We Notice?

1.  Jan Gross, *Neighbors: The Destruction of the Jewish Community in Jedwabne, Poland*. (Princeton University Press, 2001).
2.  *Rzeczpospolita*, Nov. 18, 1999.
3.  *Gazeta Wyborcza*, Oct. 23, 1990.
4.  *Biuletyn Neutrum*, Jan. 1996.
5.  During a debate in 1981, at the then government-controlled Jewish Historical Institute in Warsaw, when I asked the director why he did not publish the Jedwabne documents, he answered: "I cannot. The reaction of the Polish anti-Semites would be devastating."
6.  *Polityka*, #14, 2001.
7.  *Gazeta Wyborcza*, July 11, 2001.
8.  *Nasz Dziennik*, May 15, 2001.

# 10. Telling the Past Anew: Recent Polish Debates on Anti-Semitism

1.  Antisemitism and Xenophobia Today/AXT, http://www.axt.org.uk/index.htm.
2.  Ireneusz Krzemiński, ed., *Czy Polacy są antysemitami?* (Warsaw: Oficyna Naukowa, 1996), 14–16.
3.  Jan Tomasz Gross, *Sasiedzi: Historia Zaglady zydowskiego miasteczka*. (Sejny: Pogranicze, 2000)
4.  Jan Gross, *Neighbors: The Destruction of the Jewish Community in Jedwabne, Poland*. (Princeton University Press, 2001), 134.
5.  Quoted in Antony Polonsky and Joanna B. Michlic, eds., *The Neighbors Respond: The Controversy over the Jedwabne Massacre in Poland* (Princeton: Princeton University Press, 2004), 94–95.

6.  Ibid., 107
7.  Quoted in ibid., 147.
8.  Quoted in ibid., 228.
9.  Quoted in ibid., 90–91.
10. Ibid., 434–439.
11. Krzeminski, *Czy Polacy,* 20.
12. Gross, *Neighbors,* 169.
13. Pierre-André Taguieff, *La nouvelle judéophobie* (Paris: Mille et une nuits, 2001).
14. Ruth Wisse, *If I Am Not for Myself: The Liberal Betrayal of the Jews* (New York: Free Press, 1992).
15. Ibid., 47.

# 11. Anti-Semitism in the Spanish-Speaking World

1.  Jorge Luis Borges, *Prólogos.* Torres Agüero, ed. (Buenos Aires, 1975) 77–8.
2.  Gonzalo Álvarez Chillida, *El Antisemitismo en España, La Imágen del Judio (1812–2002).* (Marcial Pons Historia Estudios, 2002).
3.  Maria Moliner, *Diccionario de uso del español* (Madrid: Gredos, 1990).
4.  Benito Pérez Galdós, *La segunda casaca,* 1883.
5.  Quoted in Álvarez Chillida, p. 363. Millán Astray, Franco's Chief of Propaganda said this in September 1936.
6.  Julio Caro Baroja, *Los Judíos en el España Moderna y Contemporánea* (Madrid: Istmo, 1986)

# 12. Anti-Semitism and the Vatican Today

1.  The text of "We Remember" can be found at http://www.vatican.va/roman_curia/pontifical_councils/chrstuni/documents/rc_pc_chrstuni_doc_16031998_shoah_en.html, from which all quotations are taken.
2.  *Der Stürmer* devoted many articles to Jewish ritual murder beginning in 1934, and in May 1939, it dedicated an entire issue (no. 20) to the topic.
3.  The story of Leo XIII and the Vatican's strong support of Karl Lueger, based on documents from the Vatican archives, can be found in David I. Kertzer, *The Popes Against the Jews* (New York: Knopf, 2001), 187–95.
4.  Kertzer, *The Popes Against the Jews.* Some of the polemics generated by publication of *The Popes Against the Jews* can be found via www.davidkertzer.com.
5.  *The Anchor* 45, no. 13 (March 30, 2001): 1.
6.  The listed principles are translated from the section Il Rapporto con la Santa Sede at http://www.laciviltacattolica.it/Storia/Storia.htm.
7.  *Civiltà Cattolica,* 1880, IV, 108–9.
8.  "La morale giudaica," *Civiltà Cattolica,* 1893, I, 145–53.
9.  Beilis was charged with the ritual murder of a Christian boy in Kiev. The two pieces denouncing the not guilty verdict in the Mendel Beilis case were written by Paolo Silva and

published as "Raggiri ebraici e documenti papali: a proposito d'un recente processo," *Civiltà Cattolica* 1914, II, 196–215, 330–44.

10. Giovanni Sale, "Antigiudaismo o antisemitismo? Le accuse contro la Chiesa e la *Civiltà Cattolica*," *Civiltà Cattolica* 2 (2002): quaderno 3647.

11. Giovanni Sale, "La Chiesa cattolica e gli ebrei: Antigiudaismo sì, antisemitismo mai," *Jesus* (June 2002).

12. Enrico Rosa, "Il pericolo giudaico e gli Amici d'Israele," *Civiltà Cattolica* 1928 II: 340.

13. From the 1922 II issue of the journal, 112–21.

14. David I. Kertzer, "La Chiesa e la trappola del 'sano antisemitismo,'" *Corriere della Sera*, February 26, 2002; Giovanni Sale, "Altro che 'leggenda nera', i gesuiti non furono mai antisemiti," *Corriere della Sera*, February 28, 2002.

15. Adolf Hitler, *Mein Kampf*, vol. 2, ch. 9.

16. Charles E. Couglin, *"Am I an Anti-Semite? Nine Addresses on Various "isms" Answering the Question . . . Broadcast over a National Network, Nov. 6, 1938–Jan. 1, 1939* (Detroit: Condon, 1939).

17. Leonard Schapiro, "The Role of the Jews in the Russian Revolutionary Movement," *Slavonic and East European Review* 40 (1961–62): 164. This, incidentally, raises another issue, of what it meant to characterize such Marxist revolutionaries as "Jews." Any attempt to characterize Adolf Hitler as a "Catholic" meets howls of protest from those around the Vatican, on the grounds that although he was born a Catholic to a Catholic family and baptized, he did not follow Catholic creed or practice Catholic ritual.

18. Cardinal Edward Idris Cassidy, speech in Reno, Nevada, November 9, 1998. Text found at www.unr.edu/chgps/cn/sp99/06.htm. The cardinal does go on to say, however: "It is our firm conviction that there is no intrinsic link between the anti-Judaism of the Christian Church and the anti-Semitism of National Socialism." According to some experts, the first draft of "We Remember" did go much further in acknowledging the Church's role in the rise of modern anti-Semitism, but pressure was exerted in the Vatican to ensure that this admission was excised from the final draft.

19. "Judaism and the Vatican: Part II," *Seattle Catholic*, February 12, 2002, www.seattlecatholic.com/article_20020212_Judaism_and_the_Vatican_html.

# 13. Holocaust Denial

1. The law under which Zündel was convicted was eventually declared unconstitutional by the Canadian Supreme Court. Second Zündel Trial, *Her Majesty the Queen v. Ernst Zündel*, District Court of Ontario, 1988, 45–46, 88, 186.

2. *David Irving v. Penguin, UK and Deborah Lipstadt* (hereafter *IvP&DL*) Day 1 (January 11, 2000), 99–101. Transcripts of trial can be found at www.hdot.org.

3. *IvP&DL*, Day 29 (March 2, 2000), 16, 22–27.

4. *IvP&DL*, Day 7 (January 20, 2000), 185–89, 192

5. *IvP&DL*, Day 14 (February 2, 2000), 88–96.

6. Ibid., 90–96.

7. *IvP&DL*, Day 15 (February 3, 2000), 10–15.

8. Hajo Funke, *David Irving, Holocaust Denial, and His Connections to Right-Wing Extremists and Neo-Nazis in Germany*, expert opinion, *Irving v. Penguin and Deborah Lipstadt,* 3.2.10, 3.2.27–30, 3.3.6, pp. 23, 30–31, 34 [hereafter *Funke Report*]. The report can be found in the Evidence section at www.hdot.org.

9. *Funke Report*, 3.1, 5.9, 8.3, pp. 19–20, 101–4, 135.

10. *Funke Report*, 5.7, 8.7, pp. 93–101, 136.

11. *IvP&DL*, Day 28 (March 1, 2000), 190–91.

12. *IvP&DL*, Day 29 (March 2, 2000), 14–15.

13. *IvP&DL*, Day 29 (March 2, 2000), 16, 22–27.

14. *IvP&DL*, Day 28 (March 1, 2000), 194.

15. "Palestinian Leader: Number of Jewish Victims in the Holocaust Might be Even Less Than a Million," MEMRI Inquiry and Analysis Series, No. 95, May 30, 2002, pp. 1–5.

16. "Hamas Leader Rantisi: The False Holocaust," MEMRI Special Dispatch, August 27, 2003, p. 1.

# 14. Anti-Semitism in the United States

1. Quoted in Carol M. Swain, *The New White Nationalism in America* (Cambridge University Press), 37.

# 15. The Globalization of Anti-Semitism

1. "Rede von Bundespräsident Dr. Thomas Klestil anlässlich der Eröffnung des 5. Internationalen Theodor Herzl Symposiums am Montag, dem 13. Juni 2004 im Wiener Rathaus," http://www.hofburg.at/klestil/de/praesidenten/klestil/reden2004/inla/herzl_symposium_2004.htm.

# Contributors

**Jaroslaw Anders** is an internationally known essayist and journalist.

**Omer Bartov,** Birkelund Professor of European History at Brown University, is the author of several books on German and Holocaust history, including *Germany's War and the Holocaust* and *Mirrors of Destruction.*

**Pierre Birnbaum,** professor of political science at the University of Paris I (Pantheon Sorbonne) and senior member of the Institut d'Etudes Politiques, is the leading authority on the political history of Jews in France. His most recent book to appear in English is *The Anti-Semitic Moment: A Tour of France in 1898.*

**Konstanty Gebert** is a columnist and international reporter for *Gazeta Wyborcza*, Poland's foremost daily newspaper.

**Nathan Glazer** is professor emeritus at Harvard and author of many influential books on ethnicity in the United States, including *We Are All Multiculturalists Now* and (with Daniel P. Moynihan) *Beyond the Melting Pot.*

**Daniel Jonah Goldhagen**, of Harvard University's Minda de Gunzburg Center for European Studies, is the author of *Hitler's Willing Executioners: Ordinary Germans and the Holocaust,* for which he won Germany's triennial Democracy

Prize, and *A Moral Reckoning: The Role of the Catholic Church in the Holocaust and Its Unfulfilled Duty of Repair*. He is writing a book on genocide in our time.

**Hillel Halkin**, author, translator and columnist for the *Jerusalem Post* and *New York Sun*, writes widely on Zionism and Israel. He is the author of *Across the Sabbath River: In Search of a Lost Tribe of Israel*.

**Anthony Julius**, author of a number of books, including *T.S. Eliot, Anti-Semitism, and Literary Form*, is a practicing British lawyer.

**David I. Kertzer** is the Paul Dupee University Professor at Brown University and author, most recently, of *The Kidnapping of Edgardo Mortara, The Popes against the Jews,* and *Prisoner of the Vatican*.

**Enrique Krauze**, Mexican historian, essayist, and journalist, is a well-known expert on anti-Semitism in the Hispanic world. Among his books is *Mexico: Biography of Power*.

**Mark Lilla** is professor in the Committee of Social Thought at the University of Chicago. A well-known essayist, he is the author of influential books on European intellectuals and political philosophy, including *The Reckless Mind: Intellectuals in Politics*.

**Deborah Lipstadt**, professor of Modern Jewish and Holocaust Studies at Emory University, is the author of a number of books on the Holocaust, including *Denying the Holocaust* and *The Irving Judgment*.

**Fiamma Nirenstein** is an Italian journalist based in Israel and a frequent guest on Italian television. Her most recent book is *Betrayal: How the West Abandoned the Jews*.

**Leon Wieseltier** has been the literary editor of the *New Republic* since 1983 and is the author of, among other books, *Kaddish*.

**Robert S. Wistrich**, professor of Jewish History at the Hebrew University, directs the Sassoon International Center for the Study of Antisemitism. Among his books are *Hitler and the Holocaust* and *Anti-Semitism*.

# Acknowledgments

This book grew out of a conference organized by the YIVO Institute for Jewish Research, and held in New York in May 2003. It was a remarkable gathering, put together by an impressive organizing committee consisting of Leon Wieseltier, Martin Peretz, Leon Botstein, Bruce Slovin, Max Gitter, Joseph Greenberger, and Arnold Richards. The success of the conference was also a product of the outstanding work of Karen Kennerly, who directed it, and Carl Rheins, the executive director of YIVO. The ambitious international conference was made possible by support from many foundations and individuals, only some of which can be mentioned here. These include the David Berg Foundation, the Open Society Institute, the Joseph Alexander Foundation, the Morris and Alma Shapiro Fund, the Nash Family Foundation, Nelson Peltz, Bruce and Francesca Slovin, Joseph and Beate Becker, Joseph Flom, David Polen, Martin and Anna Peretz, Charles J. Rose, and Richard and Joan Scheuer.

Most of all, I would like to thank the fourteen authors who agreed to join me in preparing the chapters for this volume. In many cases, this involved a tremendous amount of work beyond that which went into the preparation of the presentations for the conference.

Thanks as well to the *New Republic* for permission to publish Mark Lilla's presentation to the YIVO conference, which was previously published in the June 23, 2003 issue of the *New Republic* and for permission to publish Omer Bartov's chapter, which is a substantially revised version of the essay "Did

Hitlerism Die with Hitler?" published in the *New Republic* in its February 2, 2004 issue.

I would also like to thank Carl Rheins, who, sharing the belief of the YIVO Board of Directors that it was important for these pieces to reach a broad public, worked hard to make this book a reality. Thanks are also due to Arthur Goldhammer for his elegant translation of Pierre Birnbaum's chapter, and my graduate research assistant, Vika Zafrin, for all of her work on this manuscript. Thanks, finally, to Miriam Holmes for sharing our belief in this book.

# Index

# F

# G

# H